Flute, Accordion or Clarinet?

of related interest

Music Therapy in Schools
Working with Children of All Ages in Mainstream and Special Education
Edited by Jo Tomlinson, Philippa Derrington and Amelia Oldfield
Foreword by Dr. Frankie Williams
ISBN 978 1 84905 000 5
eISBN 978 0 85700 474 1

Creating Change for Complex Children and their Families
A Multi-Disciplinary Approach to Multi-Family Work
Jo Holmes, Amelia Oldfield and Marion Polichroniadis
Foreword by Professor Ian Goodyer
ISBN 978 1 84310 965 5
eISBN 978 0 85700 440 6

Music Therapy with Children and their Families
Edited by Amelia Oldfield and Claire Flower
Foreword by Vince Hesketh
ISBN 978 1 84310 581 7
eISBN 978 1 84642 801 2

Interactive Music Therapy in Child and Family Psychiatry
Clinical Practice, Research and Teaching
Amelia Oldfield
Foreword by Dr. Joanne Holmes
ISBN 978 1 84310 444 5
eISBN 978 1 84642 548 6

Pied Piper
Musical Activities to Develop Basic Skills
John Bean and Amelia Oldfield
ISBN 978 1 85302 994 3

Flute, Accordion or Clarinet?

Using the Characteristics of Our Instruments in Music Therapy

Edited by Amelia Oldfield,
Jo Tomlinson and Dawn Loombe

Foreword by Sarah Rodgers

Jessica Kingsley *Publishers*
London and Philadelphia

First published in 2015
by Jessica Kingsley Publishers
73 Collier Street
London N1 9BE, UK
and
400 Market Street, Suite 400
Philadelphia, PA 19106, USA

www.jkp.com

Library of Congress Cataloging in Publication Data
A CIP catalog record for this book is available from the Library of Congress

British Library Cataloguing in Publication Data
A CIP catalogue record for this book is available from the British Library

ISBN 978 1 84905 398 3
eISBN 978 0 85700 766 7

Printed and bound in Great Britain

Contents

Foreword

David played the harp and Saul was refreshed; a simple and true statement of the power of music.

Music has accompanied every human journey since the historical record began – not surprising, perhaps, in the light of the planet's deep and connected natural sounds and rhythm.

In this book, music therapists tell us about their personal journeys with their first instruments and how they have been able to use these instruments in clinical music therapy to accompany clients on their journeys.

Although I am not a music therapist, the power of music came home to me in a profound way when I lived for two years in Sierra Leone, working for VSO (Voluntary Service Overseas). As a very new graduate, I was responsible for training music teachers. My work took me 'up country' to native schools in the African bush where, notwithstanding the very English-based curriculum, I was privileged to experience the depth of meaning brought to people's lives through their engagement with the indigenous music. Here, music meant communication, conversation, approval, achievement, recognition, rite of passage, as well as work, community, relaxation and entertainment.

That music could be so intrinsic and specific a part of life – fundamental, essential, connecting and completing – opened my eyes, ears and mind to a relationship that already had my heart! My musical experience began with my father who played saxophone and piano in dance bands and my own formal training started on the piano at the age of five. Bassoon, flute, guitar and cello followed and, later, all were eclipsed by composing and conducting. Music was central to my childhood, making its claim on me through family, friends, education and recreation – all adding pathways on the map of my adult musical life.

In the same way, almost all the music therapists writing in this book trace their passion for their first instrument and for music in general to childhood or to family experiences.

My career in music has led me through many fascinating encounters, not least of which was a commission for the City of London Sinfonia for a cross-cultural work I composed and conducted called *Saigyo*, named for the Japanese warrior poet on whose work I drew for inspiration. The scope of this commission embraced working with many different kinds of musicians in many different circumstances, from the Japanese *shakuhachi* player whose instrument featured in the new composition, to the school children who developed projects around the new piece and the community groups with whom I worked to produce a pre-concert performance in Peterborough cathedral.

A special needs group, an adult recorder ensemble and a samba band met under my guidance, not only to work together but also to perform as an integrated creative entity. This unusual combination immediately threw into sharp relief very different approaches to music and contrasting but complementary aspects of musical experience, from emotional directness, to intellectual exploration to sheer physical immersion.

As we work-shopped our ideas, the participants played not only as their existing groups but also cross-fertilised in subgroups of threes. There were challenges of communication, of technical ability, of aspiration, and of interaction. Those whose musical repertoire was usually more complex found themselves seeking simplicity and those whose experience was more simple were drawn to greater complexity. Those whose musical interest was focused on rhythm experienced the joy of sonority and those who were more accustomed to restricted practices broke out into extremes of dynamic, range and emotion.

This was a wonderful, touching and highly instructive experience. Music was the differentiating element and it became the combining force. Similarly, chapters in this book show that while each instrument has its own characteristics, ultimately, it is through the music-making itself that interactions can develop and changes can occur.

Music is nothing more or less than a disturbance of the air – the very air around us without which we would not exist. Music inhabits this world of vibration by pipe, by string, by skin, by block, and this in turn is what resonates with the human being.

This I believe is one of those unsung secrets, one of those truths that we as musicians all know and yet somehow do not often articulate and it is the reason why this publication is so important. To hear from musician practitioners their experiences of opening up the love, knowledge and intimacy of their first instrument to those they are there to help, is a joy.

For me as a composer, my music must touch an emotional chord, provoke an emotional response, leave an emotional resonance. The essays in this book make a valuable contribution to the understanding of how we invite and make that emotional connection with music. I wholeheartedly recommend that *Flute, Accordion or Clarinet? Using the Characteristics of Our Instruments in Music Therapy* is disseminated beyond the realm of music therapy and is read by as many musicians as possible.

Sarah Rodgers,
Composer and conductor

Acknowledgements

The authors would like to thank:

- The children, adults and families who have taken part in music therapy sessions and have agreed to be included in this book.

- The children, adults and families who have contributed to the book through writing, commenting on the work or allowing photographs to be printed.

- The multi-disciplinary teams and the colleagues who have supported the music therapy clinical work.

- The music therapy students who have been on placement with the authors and have provided practical help and inspiration for the writing.

The editors would like to thank:

- The authors, without whom the book could not exist. With over 50 contributors it has been a lengthy process with many prolonged exchanges of emails. Thank you for your patience and endurance. Your excitement and enthusiasm about your instruments shines through and has helped us to keep going.

- Alan Turry for helping us find instrumental music therapists in the USA and Italy, and for consistently providing support, help and humour when it was most needed.

- Alex Street for helping out with the unexpectedly lengthy process of including note ranges for each of the chapters.

- Sarah Rodgers for writing such an original, thought-provoking and moving foreword at very short notice.

- Phyllis Champion for once again coming to our rescue with her insightful, thorough and always thoughtful editing.

Amelia, Jo and Dawn have thoroughly enjoyed working together. The editing process has been much enhanced by Jo's delicious wine and cheese.

Amelia is grateful to her colleagues at the Croft Child and Family Unit and at Anglia Ruskin University for their support and patience. She would also like to thank her now grown-up children and her husband, David, for their enduring help and love.

Jo would like to thank her parents for their support and encouragement in all her musical endeavours, her children Charlie and Natasha for their patience and understanding, and her husband, Hugh, for being wonderfully supportive.

Dawn would like to thank her husband David for his love and support – and for his patience as she burned the midnight oil.

Dawn, Amelia and Jo would also like to thank David Loombe for his patience, artistic flair and diplomacy in organising all three of us and our instruments to create our cover photograph.

Introduction

Amelia Oldfield

In 1978 and 1979, when I was looking into the possibility of training as a music therapist, I was fortunate enough to observe some clinical work with a music therapist who was a first-study oboist. She was working with a ten-year-old girl with severe learning disabilities and autism. She played her oboe and the girl was transfixed by the beautiful sound of the instrument, following the therapist around the room and showing great interest in the instrument and the player. This was remarkable because the girl was usually very passive, disengaged and oblivious to people around her. I knew then that I wanted to learn to improvise and play the clarinet in this way and share my passion and love for the sound of my instrument with others, using my playing to attempt to engage or help in some way.

In 1979, I applied to do a one-year postgraduate music therapy training course in the UK. At that time there were only two possible places to train in the UK, the Guildhall School of Music and Drama and the Nordoff-Robbins course. When I was lucky enough to be offered places on both courses, I tried to find out as much as I could about them both, but in the end the decision was easy. If I went to the Nordoff-Robbins course, I would be exclusively focusing on the use of the piano, whereas on the Guildhall course I would be able to develop the use of the clarinet in my clinical work, as well as the piano. As an enthusiastic and dedicated clarinettist, the Guildhall had to be the place for me.

During my training I was never actually taught clinical improvisation skills on the clarinet, although I remember classes where I struggled to improve my keyboard improvisation. However, the head of the course, Juliette Alvin, was a professional cellist and often described case studies where she played the cello. On my placements with music therapists who had all been trained by Juliette, I observed two music therapists who played the violin. Students on the course were encouraged to present case material from their placements where they used their first-study instruments. This was enough to give me the confidence to continue using my clarinet in my clinical practice. However, I was surprised by how few of my colleagues at that time continued to regularly use their first-study orchestral instruments in their work.

In 2015, 35 years later, there are now eight music therapy training courses in the UK. All music therapy students remain proficient musicians, but they will be experts on different instruments. The courses vary in their approaches; the majority emphasise keyboard skills, some will teach guitar accompanying techniques and most encourage students to develop the use of their voice. In recent years there has been a greater emphasis on encouraging music therapy students to develop clinical improvisation skills on their first-study instrument, whether this is a violin, a trumpet or a double bass, for example, or a less well-known instrument such as steel pans, the hang or the Chinese erhu. As a result most music therapy students will now continue to play their first-study instrument and use it at least some of the time in their clinical practice.

As a lecturer on the Anglia Ruskin MA music therapy training course in Cambridge, I teach single-line improvisation, encouraging students to discover their own specific strengths and weaknesses when improvising on their single-line instrument, and exploring with them how each different instrument may be used in a wide range of clinical settings. In recent years many students have become quite passionate about using their own instrument in their work and have chosen, in their second year, to write their MA dissertation specifically about the particular use of that instrument in music therapy. Recent MAs have described the use of the accordion (Loombe 2009), the use of the violin (Roe 2011), the use of the harp (Lo 2011), the use of steel pans (Glynn 2011), the use of the erhu (Tsui 2011) and the use of the hang (Fever 2012).

Given that all the music therapy training courses in the UK have for some years now been actively encouraging students to develop their clinical improvisation skills on all the instruments they are proficient at, it is surprising how little literature there is on the use of orchestral instruments in music therapy clinical work. One of the few people who did write about this was Juliette Alvin, who set up the music therapy training course at the Guildhall School of Music and Drama in 1968. She mentions the use of her cello in several case studies (Alvin 1966).

More recently, Salkeld writes about using her clarinet (2008, p.151) and Haire and Oldfield (2009) refer to the use of the violin. However, very few authors actually reflect on the use of their instrument in music therapy, rather than mentioning the instrument in passing as part of a case study. McTier (2012) gives several examples of how he played the double bass when working with young people with autistic spectrum disorder. He writes that 'the double bass seems to provide a rhythmic and harmonic framework... which is subtly transparent and hence not overbearing'. In my book *Interactive Music Therapy, a Positive Approach*, I explore the different ways in which I use the clarinet in my work (Oldfield 2006, pp.33–35). In her MA thesis Loombe (2009) examines the literature of two other accordion-playing music therapists, Bright (1993) and Powell (2004), who have written in some detail about how they use the instrument in their clinical work.

These examples in the literature are relatively rare. In the recent collection of 34 case studies edited by Meadows (2011) there is no mention of orchestral instruments. Many case studies describe various uses of the voice and a number talk about using the piano. The guitar is also used, but mainly as an accompaniment to the voice, although Carpente (2011) does mention using the guitar to improvise. Drums and other percussion instruments are often mentioned, and there is a description by Fouche and Torrance (2011) of a marimba group, which is led by a community musician rather than a music therapist. Erkkilä (2011, p.207) describes a case where he taught an adolescent girl some easy bass lines to songs on the bass guitar. However, the bass guitar was mainly played by the client, although the therapist must have had some knowledge of and ability on the instrument in order to facilitate the work. It is interesting that the only two cases that mention the use of instruments other than the piano, the guitar and general percussion, or the voice, are cases where the clients learnt to play the instruments rather than the therapist using the instrument to interact or communicate with the clients in some way. One explanation could be that some of these authors may play and use single-line instruments in their work, but don't happen to use the instrument in the case they are writing about in this book. In Chapter 5, for example, I describe a case in child and family psychiatry where I used the piano, my voice, the guitar and percussion, but not my first study, the clarinet (Oldfield 2011). So perhaps instruments such as the piano and the voice are used more frequently in our work and this is one reason the other instruments are not so frequently mentioned.

Elsewhere in the literature, many music therapists describe case studies where they use the piano, percussion, or the voice sometimes supported by guitar playing (Bunt and Hoskyns 2002; Darnley-Smith and Patey 2003; Nordoff and Robbins 1971, 2007; Oldfield and Flower 2008; Tomlinson, Derrington and Oldfield 2012). Orchestral instruments, however, are only rarely referred to.

So, there is a gap between the teaching on UK music therapy training courses that accept and train students whose first-study instrument could be any orchestral instrument, the clinical practice where a wide range of instruments are being used, and the existing literature regarding these instruments in music therapy. This book attempts to bridge that gap.

Clients will have a different experience if they are faced with a violin, a tuba or a concert harp, for example. Some music therapists may use their instrument in all sessions, others may only use it with specific clients, or at specific times. Improvisation will be slightly different on each instrument, depending on the tessitura, tone colour and harmonic possibilities. In this book the three editors seek to address these issues by asking practising music therapists to write about their experience of using their first instrument in music therapy sessions. Authors reflect on their own relationship with their instrument, their own love of the instrument, the different ways they use it and what they see as the advantages and disadvantages of that instrument in music therapy. Authors have chosen to write in different ways and some chapters have emphasised some aspects more than others. The editors have chosen to maintain this diversity rather than attempt to standardise the structure of each chapter. Nevertheless, each of the chapters starts with an overview of the instrument itself (which varies in length and detail), includes a number of case vignettes and concludes with a section outlining the characteristics of the instrument in clinical music therapy practice. All the authors have obtained permission from clients to write about the work and publish photographs. Names and details have been changed to maintain confidentiality.

Over 50 music therapists have written for this book. Nearly all the contributors have written about their first instrument, although a few, such as Tomlinson (flute) and Derrington (trumpet), write about instruments they do not consider to be the one they are most expert at, and a few music therapists are equally proficient on several instruments. Most of the authors are from the UK but there are also authors from the USA, Italy, Slovenia, Cyprus and Norway. When looking for contributions the editors found it relatively easy to locate music therapists using popular instruments such as the violin, the flute and the clarinet. It was harder to find double bass players and brass players and the editors were not able to find French horn playing music therapists, although, in the concluding chapter, when I write about training music therapy students, I have included a letter that one of the students wrote to her French horn. I am very grateful to Caroline Swinburne for allowing me to publish this letter and pleased to report that she has now been practising as a music therapist for over a year, and regularly uses her French horn in her work.

The editors decided to include all orchestral instruments as well as harp and guitar. We also included the accordion because this instrument is used by a number of music therapists but has not been written about very much in the past. However, we did not include percussion, keyboard or voice as these instruments have been written about more extensively in the music therapy literature. The same could be said about the guitar, but we felt that most of the literature mentions the use of the guitar as an accompanying instrument rather than as a melodic instrument, so it was worth including a chapter exploring the use of the guitar in its own right. Because of the problems of space it was decided not to include the steel pans, the hang, or instruments from other countries such as the Indonesian Gamelan, the Chinese harp or the erhu. Perhaps a future book could be devoted to the use of these instruments in music therapy.

Since the emphasis in this book is on the use of the music therapist's own instrument in clinical settings, the work described here is all improvisational music therapy where live music is created by the therapist to engage, support or aid the client in some way. The use of recordings of different instruments in music therapy, or of other receptive music therapy methods, has not been documented in this book. Again this might be a topic for a future publication.

In each of the chapters, the editors have tried to ensure that case studies in different clinical areas have been included, such as work with children and adolescents, adults with learning disabilities, adult psychiatry and work with the elderly.

The use of the voice, the piano and percussion has been explored and written about in the music therapy literature. However, no previous book has examined how therapists use other specific instruments. This book will be of interest to music therapists, student music therapists, music therapy educators and anyone interested in music therapy, including healthcare professionals, teachers and parents. More generally, it will be relevant to those who are intrigued by the unique qualities of particular musical instruments.

References

Alvin, J. (1966) *Music Therapy*. London, UK: Stainer and Bell.

Bright, R. (1993) 'Cultural Aspects of Music in Therapy.' In M. Heal and T. Wigram (eds) *Music Therapy in Health and Education*. London, UK: Jessica Kingsley Publishers.

Bunt, L., and Hoskyns, S. (2002) *The Handbook of Music Therapy*. Hove, UK: Brunner-Routledge.

Carpente, J. (2011) 'Addressing Core Features of Autism: Integrating Nordoff-Robbins Music Therapy within the Developmental Individual Difference.' In T. Meadows (ed.) *Developments in Music Therapy Practice: Case Examples*. Gilsum, NH: Barcelona Publishers.

Darnley-Smith, R. and Patey, H. (2003) *Music Therapy*. London, UK: Sage.

Erkkilä, J. (2011) 'Punker, Bass Girls and Dingo-man: Perspectives on Adolescents' Music Therapy.' In T. Meadows (ed.) *Developments in Music Therapy Practice: Case Examples*. Gilsum, NH: Barcelona Publishers.

Fever, J. (2012) *The Use of the Hang in Music Therapy*. Unpublished MA thesis, Anglia Ruskin University.

Fouche, S. and Torrance, K. (2011) 'Crossing the Divide: Exploring Identities within Communities Fragmented by Gang Violence.' In T. Meadows (ed.) *Developments in Music Therapy Practice: Case Examples.* Gilsum, NH: Barcelona Publishers.

Glynn, J. (2011) *An Exploration of the Steel-pan in Music Therapy.* Unpublished MA thesis, Anglia Ruskin University.

Haire, N. and Oldfield, A. (2009) 'Adding humour to the music therapist's tool-kit: Reflections on its role in child psychiatry.' *British Journal of Music Therapy 23*, 1, 27–34.

Lo, F.S.Y. (2011) *The Use of the Harp in Music Therapy.* Unpublished MA thesis, Anglia Ruskin University.

Loombe, D. (2009) *The Use of Piano Accordion in Music Therapy: A Qualitative Study and Critical Analysis of My Own Case Work.* Unpublished MA thesis, Anglia Ruskin University.

McTier, I. (2012) 'Music Therapy in a Special School for Children with Autistic Spectrum Disorder, Focusing Particularly on the Use of the Double Bass.' In J. Tomlinson, P. Derrington and A. Oldfield (eds) *Music Therapy in Schools: Working with Children of All Ages in Mainstream and Special Education.* London, UK: Jessica Kingsley Publishers.

Meadows, T. (ed.) (2011) *Developments in Music Therapy Practice: Case Examples.* Gilsum, NH: Barcelona Publishers.

Nordoff, P. and Robbins, C. (1971) *Therapy in Music for Handicapped Children.* London, UK: Victor Gollancz.

Nordoff, P. and Robbins, C. (2007) *Creative Music Therapy: A Guide to Fostering Clinical Musicianship* (2nd edition). Gilsum, NH: Barcelona Publishers.

Oldfield, A. (2006) *Interactive Music Therapy, A Positive Approach: Music Therapy at a Child Development Centre.* London, UK: Jessica Kingsley Publishers.

Oldfield, A. (2011) 'Exploring Issues of Control through Interactive Improvised Music Making.' In T. Meadows (ed.) *Developments in Music Therapy Practice: Case Examples.* Gilsum, NH: Barcelona Publishers.

Oldfield, A. and Flower, C. (eds) (2008) *Music Therapy with Children and Their Families.* London, UK: Jessica Kingsley Publishers.

Powell, H. (2004) 'A Dream Wedding: From Community Music to Music Therapy with a Community.' In M. Pavlicevic and G. Ansdell (eds) *Community Music Therapy.* London, UK: Jessica Kingsley Publishers.

Roe, N. (2011) *An Exploration of the Use of the Therapist's First Instrument: The Experience of Interaction and Emotion in Music Therapy Focussing upon the Violin.* Unpublished MA thesis, Anglia Ruskin University.

Salkeld, C. (2008) 'Music Therapy after Adoption: The Role of Family Therapy in Developing Secure Attachments in Adopted Children.' In A. Oldfield and C. Flower (eds) *Music Therapy with Children and Their Families.* London, UK: Jessica Kingsley Publishers.

Tomlinson, J., Derrington, P. and Oldfield, A. (2012) *Music Therapy in Schools: Working with Children of all Ages in Mainstream and Special Education.* London, UK: Jessica Kingsley Publishers.

Tsui, L. (2011) *The Use of Erhu in Music Therapy.* Unpublished MA thesis, Anglia Ruskin University.

CHAPTER 1

The Clarinet

Contributors: Henry Dunn, Amelia Oldfield (introduction and case vignette), Catrin Piears-Banton and Colette Salkeld

Introduction

Compared with other orchestral instruments, the clarinet is a relative newcomer. It was invented near the beginning of the 18th century and appeared increasingly often in orchestras throughout that century. As a result clarinettists do not have original parts to play in earlier music, although there are many successful transcriptions or arrangements where clarinets might play viola, oboe, French horn, trumpet and sometimes even violin or flute parts if these are not too high. The range of the modern Bb clarinet is from D below middle C, to G two-and-a-half octaves above middle C (or higher depending on the player). It can sound smooth and mellow in the lower range, and more clear and piercing higher up. Composers who have written for the clarinet include Mozart, Brahms, Poulenc, Gershwin, Copland and Finzi. In addition to concertos and orchestral parts, the clarinet features in a wide range of chamber music, as well in wind band music, and clarinet choirs, which include bass and contrabass clarinets, alto clarinets and small high-pitched Eb clarinets. The instrument is also prominent in jazz, folk music and traditional Klezmer music.

The clarinet has a mouthpiece with a single reed, which has to be moist for the instrument to play effectively. When using the clarinet in music therapy, this can be a disadvantage if the music therapist wants to pick up the instrument to respond quickly to a client, as the reed might have dried out. It is possible to use plastic reeds to overcome this problem, but this changes the quality of the sound.

Most clarinet playing music therapists use mainly B♭ instruments in their clinical work, although occasionally bass clarinets make an appearance because of their particularly appealing sound in the lower register. Henry Dunn mentions his interest in jazz improvisation in his contribution.

The clarinet is a transposing instrument where, for example, on the B♭ instrument a written C sounds a tone lower: B♭. In addition, unlike the flute or the oboe, the fingering is different in each octave. To deal with these problems orchestral and chamber music clarinet parts are often written for both B♭ and A clarinets, and most classical players will have a pair of instruments and can quickly swap from one to the other. However, since most music therapists only bring B♭ clarinets to sessions, when improvising they have to get used to transposing as well as overcoming the technical difficulties of using different fingerings in different octaves. It is also possible to get clarinets in C, but these are comparatively rare.

Figure 1.1 Clarinet range (B♭, A and E♭)

The clarinet is a popular instrument and is played by many music therapists, so it has not been difficult to find contributors for this chapter. Both Salkeld (2008) and Oldfield (2006a and 2006b) have written before about how they have used the clarinet in their clinical music therapy practice. Salkeld matches her client's energetic and loud music on the buffalo drum by playing a bright melody in C major on the clarinet and marching around the room with him. After this he appeared more confident, not needing to hide any more (Salkeld 2008, p.151). Oldfield writes about many different uses of the clarinet when working with children and families at a child development centre (Oldfield 2006a) and when working in child and family psychiatry (Oldfield 2006b). She lists a number of reasons why she feels the clarinet is invaluable in her work (Oldfield 2006a, pp.34–35), and many of these overlap with the 'Clarinet characteristics in music therapy practice' described at the end of this chapter. When describing her improvisation on the clarinet during music therapy sessions she writes:

> On the clarinet, I often play in A minor, which in reality is G minor as the clarinet is a transposing instrument in B♭. This is because the reed horns that I have are pitched at G and C, and as I often offer these reed horns to children and parents while I am playing the clarinet, I have become accustomed to improvising in this key. Quite often, I might be moving around the room while I play, so my phrases might be quite long and flowing with no predictable rhythms to accommodate the child's unpredictable movements. At other times I use quite jazzy styles and rhythms as the clarinet is well suited to this style. (Oldfield 2006a, p.33)

Forging connections with the clarinet

Catrin Piears-Banton

I was inspired to learn the clarinet after seeing Emma Johnson win Young Musician of the Year in 1984. I met her at a concert the following year when I had already started lessons, and we have been in touch ever since. Emma's clarinet playing spoke volumes to me, she showed confidence and communicated such emotion in her playing; there was something about the sound of the rich tones of the clarinet that I wanted to experience. As a shy and tentative young girl, Emma's gentle demeanour and quietly spoken words of support gave me, as a shy and tentative young girl, hope that I too could express a world of difference in my clarinet playing.

As a music therapist, playing the clarinet in my clinical work gives me access to a variety of characteristic sounds across a wide pitch range: from the rounded, smooth resonance of the chalumeau register to the soaring, vibrant higher notes. This type of music can communicate humour, joy, drama, pain, sympathy, melancholia, as if I am truly speaking the emotion through my breath. My facial expression may stay similarly pursed as I play but the sounds produced can speak more than words and penetrate deeply within the shared musical experience.

Case vignette: Ben

Ben, a six-year-old child on the autistic spectrum, was referred to music therapy for help with his frustration at not being understood and to support him with difficulties in turn-taking and sharing.

Figure 1.2 Clarinet hide-and-seek
(photo by Dr. Alan Robson FRPS)

From our first few sessions, I noticed that Ben responded vocally when I played my clarinet. Ben was most comfortable using his voice and he would experiment with a range of different sounds, as if exploring his capacity for vocal expression. My use of the clarinet could acknowledge something of his vocalisations without being too imitative.

Ben sometimes came and touched the bell of the clarinet for a moment as I played, feeling the vibrations with his hand. At first, Ben would often move far away from me, sitting or standing with his back to me as he vocalised. It was my use of the clarinet that enabled us to play together and forge something of a connection. Ben's vocal sounds were playful and rhythmic and he gained confidence in his own sounds when he hid behind some long curtains in the music therapy room.

Our vocal and clarinet interactions and exchanges evolved into a musical game of hide-and-seek with Ben hiding behind the curtains as I crept nearer and nearer to him, the sound of my clarinet giving him a clue as to how close I was getting. I also sometimes played the mouthpiece alone – a loud and vibrant sound that Ben found comical.

Being able to move around the room freely whilst playing the clarinet supported the development of this shared music-making and helped Ben to explore and tolerate shared interaction. Ben's confidence in relating to and trusting others increased, and our hide-and-seek turn-taking game came out from behind the curtains as Ben gained a curiosity and confidence in exploring the other instruments in the room. Eventually Ben invited me to play the bongos with him, demonstrating something of how far things had come from the opposite sides of the room and behind the curtains.

Case vignette: Michael

I began working with Michael, 45, when he was referred to the adult community mental health service for support with his increasingly isolated lifestyle. Michael was diagnosed with post-traumatic stress disorder, depression and anxiety. Music therapy aimed to help Michael build confidence to feel safe with others and re-engage with the community.

Having taught himself the keyboard, Michael had spent the best part of several years playing for long hours at home on his own. Though committed to music therapy, Michael struggled to relate to me in our sessions: his instrument of choice was a large electronic keyboard set at full volume and mostly set to textured synthesised sounds. Michael was confident performing to me in his own particular musical style of busy patterns at varying tempos, and he played continuously with no obvious pulse; alternatively he would play songs that he had composed. Michael's music was difficult to engage with, and he seemed to maintain a musical wall of defence around himself.

Most instruments I played to meet Michael in his music were rendered powerless and ineffective as he sped up and slowed down or stopped suddenly, only to then start a different sequence of chordal structures. I chose to introduce my clarinet in our sessions, and this was accepted by Michael, but a competitive dynamic arose. I knew I needed somehow to play in parallel to Michael's music, to gain his interest and trust not by acknowledging his patterns – which seemed to feel like hijacking to Michael – but by being a non-threatening 'other'. This was achieved by providing contrapuntal motifs at the ends of phrases as Michael performed his songs, or inserting a few trills, or long-held notes over his busy keyboard playing.

Gradually, over a few weeks, Michael seemed to expect me to play my clarinet in this way, and began to leave longer gaps between his phrases for me to play; he sometimes even imitated my clarinet motifs in his music. Over time the improvisations took on a symphonic, soundtrack feel to them; there was less anxiety and he was able to listen and accept my music as complementary to his own, rather than threatening. Michael was then able to acknowledge the shift in the music verbally and to relate some of his musical defences to his fear of society.

From the beginning, Michael had been dismissive of the percussion instruments in music therapy and it took my use of a sufficiently complex instrument in the form of the clarinet to make a connection with him. The challenge with Michael had been for him to hear and accept me. If I played the piano, it was heard as an attack on his skill and sound perhaps, and was probably too close emotionally in some way. The clarinet was my instrument; separate and distinct from Michael's keyboard, yet as meaningful to me as his keyboard was to him. We could be two people conversing, but through our own chosen, personal instrument that we both had our own way of playing. Michael played patterns and songs dear to him, and I improvised around his structure. Eventually he could improvise, share and acknowledge something of the experience with me.

Case vignette: Group

I currently use my clarinet regularly in a group for people with severe to profound and multiple learning disabilities. The group's music is often very much centred around people's personal vocal and body sounds. I find that by blowing air through the clarinet, rather than sounding notes, I can acknowledge breathy sounds from all group members that so often become a very important part of sessions for this group. I can also offer something with a unique tone that has become my non-verbal voice in the group.

When I am assessing clients or when I sense an uncertain quality to the dynamic in the therapy room, I know that I can pick up my clarinet and explore the situation with confidence. Alongside the personal and emotional connection I have with playing the clarinet, I can rely on the tone of the instrument to match, acknowledge and support the client in their playing, particularly when they play chordal instruments – piano, keyboard, guitar even – in such a way that they become increasingly absorbed in their playing, filling the room with a dense texture of sound. Playing the clarinet can state my presence subtly or not so, depending on the need, and can challenge or tenderly coax a response as appropriate. I consider the clarinet an instrument for many eventualities that is a more flexible alternative to my voice, yet as personal, unique and communicative.

The clarinet in a family's loss

Colette Salkeld

I have been playing the clarinet since the age of eight, and prior to training as a music therapist I worked as a professional clarinettist for a number of years. I have always felt the clarinet was an extension of myself, a means of personal expression, a way of conveying meaning beyond words. Since working as a music therapist I have found that the clarinet seems to allow me the freedom to respond empathically and to be physically closer to the clients, particularly in group work.

Case vignette: Artem

Artem was a five-year-old boy from Ukraine who was in the terminal phase of cancer. I was asked to see him during my first week in a new music therapy post and was told that he had only a matter of weeks to live. I was aware of the work of Nigel Hartley at St. Christopher's Hospice and the importance of supporting the whole family at this stage in a child's life, and because the work was in Artem's room my intuitive response was to take my clarinet.

Session 1: Lullabies and dreams
When I first met Artem he was lying in his hospital bed, in a private room, with his father sitting beside him. Because of the nature of his cancer, Artem had lost the ability to use his limbs and also his voice.

His only means of communication was his eyes. To say 'yes' he would look up, and to say 'no' he would look down. I was aware that I was coming in to this family's life at a very sensitive time and I did not want to appear as an uninvited guest. Artem's play specialist, who had worked with him for a number of months and had made the referral for music therapy, introduced me and stayed for the first session. In this way she provided the link, as someone whom they could trust.

To begin with, I sat beside Artem and sang hello to him, and following this Artem's father supported him in strumming on the guitar. Artem communicated that he enjoyed this and during this time I improvised vocally, to support his playing. The play specialist then said that Artem had wanted to become a soldier and loved marching music. It was at this point that I used my clarinet for the first time and, supported by his father, Artem beat his hand on the drum. Again, Artem said that he liked this. It was interesting as I found myself standing and marching as I improvised on the clarinet, almost as though we were in a marching band, soldiers together. In this way the music seemed to reflect Artem's dreams, his wishes. Shortly after this Artem began to yawn and to close his eyes, and I improvised a lullaby on the clarinet as he drifted off to sleep.

Session 2: Storytelling

When I arrived for the next session Artem lay in his bed and this time his mother sat on one side, his father on the other and a family friend was also sitting in the room. Through the interpreter I was told that Artem wished to play the guitar and the drum once again. He then wanted me to play the clarinet. As I improvised, Artem's mother stroked his head, holding his hand and as he gazed into her eyes she told him a story. I will never know what the story was, but it struck me that her words and phrases seemed to reflect the musical phrases of the clarinet and the highs and lows of the melodic line seemed to be mirrored in the intonation of her voice. It was also remarkable that we ended the 'story' together. I have often wondered since that day about how it was possible for two people from entirely different cultures, speaking different languages, to connect so closely on a first meeting except through the language of music.

Following this improvisation, I asked through the interpreter if the family might like to sing a song in their native tongue. Artem's father asked if he could play my guitar and tentatively he began plucking a melody line. It was at this point that the room began to glow, rather like candles being lit on a dark night as first Artem's mother and then each member of the family and the interpreter joined in, singing with the guitar. As they sang, I wove a harmony on the clarinet, connecting and empathising without words. Once again, Artem and his mother gazed into each other's eyes and she stroked his head. It was very moving, an acknowledgement of Artem's cultural heritage and a brief piece of Ukraine in London.

Session 3: Goodbye

My third session with Artem and his family was to be the last time that I saw him. When I entered the room he seemed pale and lethargic. The room was full of family members, with his mother, father, two other adults and another child sitting around the bed. I asked Artem's mother if she wished me to call the interpreter and she said strongly, 'But music is universal, you can talk to me and I understand.' I wondered if she wanted to keep this session between the family and myself. Maybe the interpreter would feel like an intrusion. Her comment also reminded me of the previous session when she and I had connected so strongly in the storytelling.

After I had sung hello to Artem, his father took the guitar and once again Artem's mother began to sing a Ukrainian song. Just as in the previous session I took my clarinet and wove a harmony to support their music. This time I felt that I was supporting the family in their loss, the music enabling them to share together in their grief in a culturally appropriate way. As she sang, Artem's mother became very tearful, choking on her words. Following the song she allowed me to comfort her and to acknowledge the pain of her loss. Following this exchange she asked me if I could play the Beatles song 'Yesterday'. As we sang and played this symbolic song she gave an ironic laugh as the tears flowed. I then sang goodbye to Artem to end the session.

I was not aware at this point that this would be the final time I would see him and his family. I feel immensely privileged to have had the opportunity to meet Artem and his family at such a precious time. I believe that the choice of the clarinet enabled me to draw near to them and support them in their loss, especially when my relationship with them was so brief. Shortly after this session Artem and his family returned home where he ended his days in a hospice.

Finding a different voice

Henry Dunn

I first fell in love with the clarinet as a young boy, at the age of about eight or nine. Some family friends were having a musical evening at their home, and I heard someone playing the clarinet. I immediately decided that I had to learn, and fortunately my parents supported me in that aim. I worked my way through the graded exams, but wasn't able to improvise, despite my love of jazz. That changed as an adult, and I discovered that I could improvise and create my own music, expressing myself through the voice of the clarinet. I now find that my playing in jazz informs and improves my playing in therapy, and vice versa, although the purposes are very different – the former to entertain, the latter to express emotion, no matter how unpleasant it may sound.

This ability to improvise developed on a working party at a beautiful Christian community in North Devon when I was about 20 years old – we were gathered round a piano, playing songs, and I suddenly found myself playing notes on the clarinet without really knowing where they were coming from. For this reason improvisation also has a strong spiritual element for me, reaching a very deep, unconscious part of myself. This in turn is reflected in the psychoanalytically informed approach I have to music therapy, which seeks to find the unconscious dynamics behind people's musical expression. I find myself drawn to depth, musically, spiritually and psychologically.

When I was 30 I embarked on my music therapy training and found that the piano and the clarinet were equally valuable in my work. I find the piano helps most in providing structure and containment, but it feels, to me at least, quite a masculine instrument. The clarinet gives me access to a more tender, fluid, feminine voice, with a greater pitch range than my rather low singing voice. This can be particularly useful when working with people whose mother was absent or abusive. They can experience a maternal voice that is caring and responsive, expressing unconditional positive regard (Rogers 1957).

Although I use the piano a lot of the time, finding it very expressive and valuable, I sometimes observe a tendency to use it defensively, with it creating a physical barrier between the client and myself. It can also be connected with my expertise on the piano compared to that of the client, who might feel intimidated and unable to use the piano to express themselves. The clarinet, although also requiring expertise, doesn't seem to have that effect, as it mirrors the voice closely and reveals a vulnerability in the therapist that the piano might not. If I become emotional in our shared music, this will affect my breath, which will affect my playing. My tone may crack or seem a bit wobbly, reflecting the way I feel. This is in response to the client's emotion and can happen without conscious thought, in the moment. I feel that the clarinet is my voice in a way that the piano never could be, and that this vulnerability on my part gives the client permission to also become vulnerable. It is this sense of joint openness that can be so powerful in music therapy and is perhaps harder to achieve with verbal therapies.

The clarinet is also very portable. I can move around with it and not be fixed to the spot as I am on the piano. I can sit on the floor and play, or I can chase round the room playing it. It is also useful in environments where there is no piano or keyboard.

Case vignette: Julie

Julie, a woman in her 50s, was referred to me owing to her anxiety and her bipolar disorder. Not long into our work she was given a diagnosis of breast cancer, which spread to her spine. She loved to hear the clarinet, either played by me or in recordings that we listened to in order to aid relaxation. She particularly liked listening to Mozart's Clarinet Concerto.

During our improvisations she played a variety of percussion instruments and requested that I play the clarinet. Sometimes she would stop for a while and just listen to me play. I found that I could respond very quickly on the clarinet to any changes of mood, tempo and volume, and it was easier to sit facing towards her than it would have been at the piano. Playing the clarinet seems to give a greater intimacy – it is more an extension of me than the piano, as it is my breath that is making the music, with less of a mechanical gap between the player and the resulting sound than on the piano. I could then non-verbally express care and compassion in a way that felt more powerful and warm than words alone.

Julie had been estranged from her mother for several years and did not want any contact with her. It occurred to me that the maternal sound of the clarinet was providing some kind of substitute for this. It also enabled me, as a male therapist, to provide an element of maternal function that would not otherwise be accessible to me.

I often use the clarinet to mirror vocalisations of clients who are non-verbal. The communicative vocalisations are reflected back in a more musical form, moving from mirroring to affect attunement (Stern 1985). I am taking the client's emotional communication and transforming it in a way that is still recognisable but also distinctly mine. This sense of shared meaning, balanced by an awareness of the other, can be a crucial development in therapy. For clients with autism, this type of exchange can help to develop the ability to relate to another as a distinct and separate person who attends to, and responds empathically to, their emotional communication. In addition, the expressive qualities of the clarinet can encourage clients to move from a monotone voice to one with more variation in pitch and expressiveness. It can encourage non-verbal dialogue that is playful and creative, and that is able to convey a wide range of emotions.

I have also used the clarinet with children who have suffered trauma to the brain or were born with an underdeveloped brain. For example, I worked with a young boy who had nearly drowned, suffering hypoxia. He was left in a virtually comatose state. I played my clarinet to fit with his breathing and eye movement, and there was some small sense of reciprocation in the way his breathing and eye movement changed with my playing. I also worked with a six-month-old baby whose brain scan had not shown any activity. When I played the clarinet she seemed to come alive, her eyes showing life, a hint of a smile on her face. There seems to be a quality about the clarinet that is able to awaken even the most unreachable clients. Maybe this is connected with the maternal sound, maybe there is something about the vibrations it causes. With children who are deaf, or deaf and blind, I frequently play the instrument close to their body so that they can feel the vibration. This often seems to have a calming effect and can relax the muscles. Many people that I work with find the sound relaxing, sometimes falling asleep – the opposite of the awakening effect mentioned earlier.

In short, I would not want to be without my clarinet in music therapy sessions. The only time I would not use it is if the client showed an active dislike of the sound or if I felt there was a risk that a client might want to damage it, but this is not something that happens too often. The clarinet is my musical voice in therapy, so to deprive myself of it would be pointless and counter-therapeutic.

I used to dream of the perfect clarinet sound…
Amelia Oldfield

As a child I learnt to play the piano first. Then as a teenager I wanted to play an orchestral instrument so I could play with other musicians. I spent hours listening to orchestral recordings as well as to the *Young Person's Guide to the Orchestra* by Benjamin Britten, and quite quickly decided that I liked the sound of the clarinet best of all. As I was living in Austria at the time, I started learning the clarinet in Vienna, but luckily my teacher realised I would not be staying there for very long and started me off on the commonly used Boehm fingering system, rather than on the simple system clarinets that were still being used uniquely in Austria at that time. After a couple of years I moved to France, where I continued to have lessons, first at the Conservatoire in Montpellier, then at the Conservatoire in Aix-en-Provence from two clarinettists who happened to be brothers. Four years later I moved to Canada and had lessons at the music department at McGill University. By this time I had seriously fallen in love with the clarinet and it had become my first rather than my second instrument.

When I moved to the Guildhall School of Music and Drama to do my music therapy training I did not like the very different English clarinet sound my new teacher was suggesting to me. One day, as I was wandering down the corridor, I heard the most beautiful clarinet sound coming out of one of the practice rooms. I immediately knew this was what I was striving for and walked in to find the renowned Israeli clarinettist Yona Ettlinger. He agreed to teach me, and I continued having lessons with him, and then with his wife Naomi, for several years after I started working as a music therapist. I particularly remember the fortnightly Saturday master classes at the Guildhall, which usually led to dreams about the ultimate, perfect clarinet sound on Saturday nights.

I have always enjoyed using the clarinet in my music therapy clinical work. I love playing it, revel in producing as good a sound as possible, and feel I can convey emotion through my playing more effectively than through any other instrument. I have continued to play in various chamber groups and orchestras throughout my 34 years of music therapy practice. This keeps my own music and my passion for the clarinet alive, and provides me with inspiration for improvisations in my clinical practice. Conversely I have found that my regular use of improvisation in my music therapy practice has improved my tone and confidence when playing chamber music. I find I need to play, on average, about three evenings a week to maintain the control and flexibility of my embouchure in my clinical practice. If for some reason I don't play my clarinet for a couple of weeks, I often notice that I start getting grumpy and irritable; somehow, I need to play to feel whole and complete.

Case vignette: Tim

Three-year-old Tim, who has a diagnosis of autistic spectrum disorder, gets up from the piano, which we have been playing together, and wanders to the other side of the room. He has no speech, but glances at the clarinet on top of the piano and then at me. I know exactly what he is communicating to me: 'Come on, do what you usually do, pick up your clarinet and walk around the room with me.' As soon as I start playing the clarinet he grins broadly. We march around the room together and I improvise a tune to match our walking pace. Then he lies down on the floor and kicks his legs in the air. I play a version of 'Row, row, row your boat' while his mother holds his legs and sways from side to side. Occasionally I stop playing to join in with the singing, but incorporate low trills on the clarinet to add excitement when the 'crocodile' appears. We repeat several variations of the song and on the third time, when we leave a gap before the dramatic 'scream' at the end of the song, he makes a tentative vocal sound, looking quite surprised that he has done this. His mother looks at me and grins; we are both delighted that Tim is starting to use his voice.

In later sessions Tim masters the technique of producing a sound by blowing the recorder or a reed horn. This enables us to have clarinet and horn dialogues and further encourages Tim to use his voice.

For Tim the clarinet is associated with a moment in the music therapy session when he moves around the room and I take his lead and follow him while playing at the same time. This is particularly useful for Tim, who finds it hard to remain seated or focused on any one activity for very long. He has always been interested in the clarinet, making good eye contact and smiling whenever I start playing. Tim's mother is proud of her son's particular interest in this slightly unusual instrument. It is also useful for me to be able to alternate playing and singing because it means I can use words in the songs, but then continue the tune on the clarinet to maintain the musical line and Tim's interest. Tim recognises the sounds of the words and can occasionally be prompted to vocalise himself, but he needs the clarinet sound accompanied by my movements to maintain his interest.

Case vignette: Ella

Figure 1.3 Listening to that special sound

Ella is also three years old. She has profound and multiple learning disabilities, is very restricted in her movements, has severe epilepsy and is partially sighted. She does not sleep well, so both she and her mother are often quite tired. She can sometimes move her arms and hands a little to strum the guitar, or to scratch or tap a drum. She will also occasionally vocalise. For Ella the high point of the session is usually when her mother holds up some wind-chimes for her and I play the clarinet. Like Tim, she will nearly always smile when I start playing, and will sometimes get very excited, kicking her legs and moving her hands towards the chimes. At other times she plays more quietly and both she and her mother look sleepy. I try to match her mood while improvising, keeping the melodic line flowing and 'open', playing in pentatonic or modal keys. I know that high notes, squeaks and glissandi often make her smile, while lower, legato phrases help her to relax. In addition, the fact that I can bend the pitch of the notes to match her vocalisations is often useful. Ella's mother is also affected by the clarinet. Like Tim's mother, she takes pride in Ella's interest in this instrument and is always pleased when Ella becomes engaged and interactive.

Case vignette: Group

In my weekly group of five children with a variety of emotional difficulties (Asperger's syndrome, eating disorders, Tourette's syndrome, attention deficit disorder) the children eye my clarinet case with suspicion. I have just suggested that there might be a rabbit in the case… but after some discussion allow them to convince me it must be a musical instrument. We establish that it is a clarinet and I ask them to guess how many pieces it consists of. One little boy who is six and has been to the group before shouts out 'seven' and is delighted when I put the instrument together and show he is right. I play a short tune, the children listen and I then suggest that they shut their eyes and guess how many notes I have just played by putting their hands in the air and showing a number.

Later in the group, my music therapy student who is a violinist gets out her violin and we form two teams, half the group play the xylophone when they hear the violin, the other half play the metallophone when they hear the clarinet. At first we take it in turns to play to make it easier for the children, but then we overlap and intermingle so they really have to listen.

Here I use the children's interest in a slightly unusual instrument packed in a box to gain their interest and enthusiasm. The fact that it is a single-line instrument makes it easy for the children to distinguish and listen to how many notes I am playing. It is then possible for them to listen both to the violin and the clarinet and play as a group.

Clarinet characteristics in music therapy practice

An attraction to the particular sound of the clarinet

It was generally felt that many clients were attracted to the sound of the instrument and would either specifically request it, or show pleasure when it was played. One clarinettist wondered whether the clarinet sound was a maternal sound, or whether it caused special types of vibrations. For some clients it was particularly important that the clarinet was a 'proper' instrument rather than an educational school percussion instrument.

Eliciting vocalisations

All of the clarinettists felt that the tone quality of the clarinet is similar to the voice. The clarinet was successfully used to encourage clients to vocalise and then to have non-verbal dialogue with the client using both the clarinet and the voice. The instrument was also used to mirror intonation and match the speaking voice. In addition it was mentioned that the expressive qualities of the clarinet could help clients with monotone voices to introduce more variation in their spoken voices.

Mobility

All four clarinettists mentioned the fact that playing the clarinet in music therapy sessions allowed them to be mobile, either to walk around the room with the client, or to be by their bedside or on the floor. This is also mentioned in the existing literature (Salkeld 2008, p.151 and Oldfield 2006a, p.34).

The therapist's own instrument

All the clarinettists felt it was important to play their own instrument and that some clients particularly valued the fact that the clarinet was the therapist's personal instrument.

Playfulness

Three clarinettists mentioned using the clarinet to be playful with their clients, running around the room, playing 'peek-a-boo', or accompanying movements in a humorous way. One clarinettist mentioned engaging a group of children by getting them to guess what was in the clarinet case and how many pieces it was divided up into.

A physical link between the therapist and the client

It was mentioned several times that the clarinet can be played directly opposite the client, which can be an advantage when attempting to interact or communicate. Clients would sometimes touch the bell of the clarinet to feel the vibrations, and the instrument could provide a physical link between the client and the therapist.

Combining the clarinet with other wind instruments such as reed horns

Clarinet playing can provide an incentive for clients to master the technique of blowing, and then create an opportunity for turn-taking and exchange. It helps that wind players have to stop playing at times to take a breath, and these pauses can then be used to dramatic effect. This is clear from the case material in this chapter, as well as from the previous literature by Oldfield (2006a).

Associating the clarinet with specific events

The clarinet was often specifically chosen by clients and in some cases associated with clear events, such as an activity involving walking around the room. Clients and relatives took pride in this definite choice. In one case the clarinettist was able to link into the child's past interest in becoming a soldier by marching around the room playing the clarinet. In another case the client had a particular preference for a famous piece of clarinet music, which the therapist was able to explore in the session.

Accompanying breathing or breathy sounds

This was mentioned as a special feature of the clarinet, enabling the clarinettist to follow the client's breathing and use a combination of breathy clarinet tones and vocalisations to play with clients with very limited abilities.

Eliciting responses through special effects

Playing with the mouthpiece on its own, glissandi, bending notes and squeaks were all mentioned as ways to surprise, engage or be humorous.

Characteristic tone colour of the clarinet

The fact that the clarinet has a very distinct sound allows music therapists to accompany chaotic synthesiser music or weave a melodic line under a sung melody. One music therapist wondered whether the distinct clarinet sound made it easier for children with a weak sense of self to distinguish between themselves and the therapist. The specific clarinet sound was also used as a contrast to the violin sound in a music therapy group to encourage children to listen, and follow either one or the other.

References

Oldfield, A. (2006a) *Interactive Music Therapy, A Positive Approach to Melody*. London, UK: Jessica Kingsley Publishers.

Oldfield, A. (2006b) *Interactive Music Therapy in Child and Family Psychiatry – Clinical Practice, Research and Teaching*. London, UK: Jessica Kingsley Publishers

Rogers, C. (1957) 'The Necessary and Sufficient Conditions of Therapeutic Personality Change.' *Journal of Consulting Psychology 21*, 2, 95–103.

Salkeld, C. (2008) 'Music Therapy after Adoption: The Role of Family Therapy in Developing Secure Attachments in Adopted Children.' In A. Oldfield and C. Flower (eds) *Music Therapy with Children and Their Families*. London, UK: Jessica Kingsley Publishers.

Stern, D. (1985) *The Interpersonal World of the Infant*. New York, NY: Basic Books.

CHAPTER 2

The Piano Accordion

Contributors: Susan Greenhalgh, Dawn Loombe
(introduction and case vignettes – these case vignettes
also include case material by Harriet Powell,
Bert Santilly and Michael Ward-Bergeman)

Introduction

Accordions and their close relatives, the harmonica, melodeon, concertina and bandoneon are all descendants of the Chinese sheng – an ancient mouth-blown free-reed instrument consisting essentially of vertical pipes and dating from around 2700 BC.

Early accordions first appeared in Europe in the 1820s and in the USA slightly later in the 19th century, though there are conflicting accounts as to exactly where, when and by whom the original accordions were built. The first accordions to arrive in Britain were actually melodeons (button accordions, each button producing two different notes on the push and pull of the bellows) and were used by music hall performers, Scottish folk musicians and later by English Morris dance musicians.

Accordions with piano keyboards were developed in 1852 by Parisian Jacques Bouton and by the beginning of the 20th century the accordion's bass keyboard had been developed sufficiently to provide accompaniments in all keys. These relatively new piano accordions gained popularity in the UK from the late 1920s, when they began to be imported from Italy and introduced into dance bands to produce more authentic-sounding tangos. Pianist George Scott-Wood imported a piano accordion from Italy in 1927 and

became Britain's first professional accordion player. The 1920s and
'30s also saw the rapid expansion of cinema, with accompanying
organ entertainment – usually on a Wurlitzer or Compton organ
– and 'the arrival of the piano accordion in Britain's music stores
in large quantities from 1927 onwards…allowed the possibility of
owning and playing what was virtually a small-scale theatre organ
capable of playing all the popular songs and tunes of the time'
(Howard 2005, p.16).

However, from the mid-1950s the accordion's popularity began
to slump and it quickly became a very unfashionable instrument.
Rock and roll music had introduced the guitar to popular culture,
and the guitar was 'cool', relatively inexpensive (especially compared
to the accordion), accessible and easy to play; learning to strum
a few simple chords allowed the playing of many pop songs of
the day. Young people were keen to emulate admired guitar heroes
and a different kind of pop music emerged. At the same time, there
was a general decline in the popularity of variety shows, and the
accordion became very passé, generally an object of ridicule in the
world of music.

In recent years, though, the accordion has seen a rebirth of interest,
with an increasing prevalence in pop and rock music, television
themes, advertisements and film scores, as well as becoming a more
accepted instrument in the classical world. In addition, the interest
in World music has provided new and eclectic styles of accordion
music, which have brought new audiences to the accordion.[1]
The resurgence of ballroom and Latin dancing, particularly from
television series such as *Strictly Come Dancing*, has raised awareness of
traditional dance styles and also the use of the accordion for tangos,
waltzes and polkas.

In the classical world, works have been written for the accordion
by Tchaikovsky, Prokofiev and Shostakovich, and the music of Bach
and Scarlatti along with many others has been transcribed for the
modern accordion. Increasingly, composers are writing classical
music for the accordion and including accordion parts in orchestral
scores and group compositions.

---

1   See for example, Accordions Worldwide at www.accordionlinks.com.

For the purposes of this chapter, accordion refers to the piano accordion. The accordion is defined as a hand-held free-reed aerophone, in which the sound is produced by tempered steel reeds that vibrate when air is forced through them by a set of bellows. On one side of the bellows there are rows of buttons or a keyboard on which the melody is played, while on the other side there are buttons for the bass notes and chords (Wade-Matthews and Thompson 2002).

The accordion is held close to the player's chest, supported by means of straps. The accordionist's right hand plays a piano keyboard, usually (but not always) the melody. The left hand plays a series of buttons producing single bass notes, chords or a combination of single notes and chords, usually a bass accompaniment.

Most people are aware that there are rock, classical, Western, jazz and folk-style guitars but few realise that there are at least as many types of accordions. Just like the guitar, accordions are built for different styles of music and have a variety of temperaments or tuning schemes.

Accordions are usually classified by the number of bass buttons they have, ranging in size from small, simple 8- or 12-bass instruments to complex accordions of 120 basses or more.

Figure 2.1 The piano accordion

In addition, most accordions have switches or couplers that allow the use of different combinations of reeds (rather like the stops on an organ), and these can give the player great scope in pitch range and quality of sound. The larger models, although superior in sound quality, can be heavy and unwieldy, while a smaller instrument might not give a satisfying enough sound, or enough musical scope for the therapist.

Accordions are also classified according to their timbre:

- **Musette** accordions have a characteristic shrill timbre, which is produced by a particular tuning of the three middle-voiced reeds of the instrument. The two outer reeds are tuned slightly off-key (one slightly sharp and one slightly flat of the perfect pitch reed) to produce this typical accordion sound, favoured by players of traditional French, Scottish and Irish music.

- **Dry-tuned** or **straight-tuned** accordions have the reeds tuned to produce a purer, more harmonious sound required for modern music, and particularly tango and other Latin styles. It is also used for playing classical music.

- **Chambered** or **Cassotto** tuning gives the particular mellow accordion sound preferred by jazz accordionists. This is achieved by engineering the reed blocks into chambers, which add tonal warmth. This is very distinctive and a development that has contributed greatly to the maturing of the accordion as a classical musical instrument. However, accordions with tone chambers are much more expensive to buy and are also much heavier instruments.

These different mechanisms allow the accordionist great musical scope in terms of pitch and quality of sound (by means of the reeds and couplers) and also dynamic control, touch, phrasing and musical expression (by means of effective use of the bellows).

The accordion has always been close to my heart

Dawn Loombe

The piano accordion is my principal instrument and provides my identity as a musician. It is therefore the instrument with which I am most likely to communicate effectively. I am passionate about the accordion, having played since I was ten years old. My school friend had pestered her parents to buy her a small accordion, having seen an accordionist playing Irish jigs and reels. I was already learning the piano and violin and I became intrigued by her fascinating instrument, which seemed to me to be alive and so different. After trying her small piano accordion, I too was hooked. My father bought me a small second-hand instrument and I began taking lessons. I also played bass accordion and then first accordion in the Norwich Accordion Orchestra in the 1970s and 1980s. My friend and I grew up together playing accordion and we still get together to play now. I have been performing as a solo accordionist and community musician in various bands and ensembles for around 40 years.

There is something special about the way the accordion becomes part of me and moves with me as I wear it and the way that the bellows can be used to express exactly what I want to say with a piece of music; it is literally always close to my heart.

I am often asked to play musette accordion pieces for French-themed events, traditional Neapolitan tunes for Italian weddings, with ceilidh bands for Scottish or English traditional dancing, at outdoor carnivals and village festivals, in local pubs and folk clubs, European folk and classical music with a multi-instrumental trio, Klezmer tunes (together with clarinet and violin), Piazzola tangos, German drinking songs with an 'oom-pah' band, polkas, Russian folk songs, Cajun, Tex-Mex, jazz standards, or to accompany singers. Many of these styles of accordion music and particular techniques I have learned have – at different times and in many diverse ways – found their way into the music I play with clients in music therapy sessions and influenced my work as a music therapist.

Of course, I do use a variety of instruments in my clinical work and I make choices depending on the needs and likes of the clients with whom I work. However, I have found that there are some unique aspects of the accordion that can be particularly useful in music therapy, and since training at Anglia Ruskin University in 2003 I have been thinking about these features. My MA dissertation (Loombe 2009) explored the use of the accordion in music therapy through my own casework in various settings, as well as a literature review and interviews with other accordionists also using their instruments in music therapy.

Figure 2.2 Music therapy with the accordion at the Child Development Centre, Addenbrooke's Hospital, Cambridge

As other music therapists have found, I have a therapy instrument, which I use in sessions rather than risking the use of my more precious performance accordion. However, there is always a compromise, and it can be a challenge to find an accordion with good-quality reeds and a satisfying sound that is small enough and suitable for music therapy use, yet not too expensive or heavy.

Another challenge when using the accordion in music therapy results from the wearing of the instrument on my body: it can sometimes be difficult to remove quickly and safely. The bellows straps need to be fastened top and bottom, to prevent the bellows opening as I take it off, and there is usually a backstrap to unclip before putting down the accordion safely. For this reason, I never use my accordion where I might be physically compromised in a session, where either the instrument or I might be at risk or where a client has challenging behaviour (for example where I need to be physically ready to respond to prevent a child from harm).

My music therapy accordion is a medium-sized, straight-tuned accordion (without the shrill musette sound that typifies French or Scottish accordion music). This is mainly because it is my preferred accordion tuning and also because I find that it is the single reed sound that most resonates with people; the accordion sound that allows me to respond immediately and most effectively. I rarely use the tremolo reeds (unless I want to produce a particularly strident sound for dynamic effect), as I find the single-reed couplers much more responsive and useful for a variety of musical styles.

Accordionist Santilly (2009) uses a 120-bass accordion that has both straight-tuning and musette-tuning, giving him a diversity of accordion timbres within one instrument in all aspects of his work as both teacher and performer. Santilly has found the purer single-reed sounds to be more useful in his school work than the tremolo or musette couplers, particularly in working with children with autistic spectrum disorder. We have both noticed that many children find the accordion's musette sound particularly painful, such that they recoil, sometimes putting their fingers in their ears. This is most noticeable with the three-voice musette tuning, because this has two different sets of vibrato, meaning that the points of coincidence for the sound are very complex; this can be too uncomfortable for those with very sensitive hearing, for whom the harmonic beats can be very prominent. Santilly also switches out the accordion's musette reeds to use just the straight tuning, which can be more sympathetic to sensitive ears. Michael Ward-Bergeman (2009) also noted how the pure single-reed tone resonated in his therapeutic work, commenting that this resembles a basic sine wave – the simple building block of all sound. He said that he uses the dynamic range of his accordion to 'try to tune in to frequencies people are resonating with'.

Use of the accordion in music therapy

There has been little mention of the use of the accordion in music therapy literature. Limited reference to the use of the accordion – mainly as a useful portable and harmonic instrument – have been made by Bang (2006), Gaertner (1999) and Aldridge (2000 and 2005), among others. However, two authors in particular – Harriet Powell and Ruth Bright – have explored the use of the accordion in music therapy in more depth and their findings are examined here.

Harriet Powell (2004a) begins with a humorous look at the accordion, acknowledging its iniquitous image using Gary Larson's famous cartoon. In his Far Side sketch, described by Powell, Larson depicts St. Peter handing a harp to an angelic figure at the gates of Heaven, saying 'Welcome to Heaven. Here's your harp'. Whilst at the fires of Hell, accordions are being handed out with the message 'Welcome to Hell. Here's your accordion'. Powell acknowledges this particular image of the accordion before explaining how useful this instrument has been in her own music therapy work. Prior to training as a music therapist, Powell studied piano and organ and worked in community theatre and music workshops, where she found the accordion a useful instrument with all ages. When she began training as a music therapist her supervisors did not discourage her use of the accordion, but there was never any time spent on how to use it effectively. Despite this, Powell has continued to play her accordion successfully for many years in her clinical work with older people with dementia. She also uses it in her Nordoff-Robbins work with children and adults with learning disabilities.

Powell (2004a, p.21) lists the accordion's advantages, particularly: its portability; its ability to be played in close proximity to her clients; the way that she can provide a left-hand accompaniment whilst dancing and singing with a client; and the accordion's ability to sustain and hold. She says the accordion is a versatile and useful instrument in music therapy and that she feels it becomes a part of her, allowing the freedom 'to be with the person physically and musically'.

In one of her case studies, Powell describes the particular importance of the accordion for Peter, a 70-year-old man in the early stages of dementia, in a group session:

> When I played the accordion he began to cry and said that his brother used to play. He proceeded to sing 'Alexander's Ragtime Band' which he remembered his brother playing. Then I offered him the keyboard of the accordion to have a

go. He played a few notes tentatively and as I provided the rhythmic and harmonic structure on the buttons with my left hand he became bolder. He played with vitality, melody and increasing virtuosity with glissandi up and down the keyboard to the cheers of encouragement and appreciation from the rest of the group. He still had tears in his eyes with a broad smile on his face. (Powell 2004a, pp.20–21)

With James, a frail and elderly ex-miner suffering from confusion, memory loss and depression, Powell (2004b) explained how their musical relationship became more interactive over time, with James playing harmonica and Powell playing her accordion. These sessions helped James to free himself from isolation, rediscover his musical skills and regain a sense of identity. Powell's use of accordion seemed to have resonated with James, who had played accordion and harmonica in his youth; indeed she mentions that there were times when he corrected her accordion technique (2004b, p.174). It is also relevant that the accordion and harmonica are related free-reed instruments, which provided another link between the two players. Bright (2007) believes that it is essential for all music therapists to play a portable instrument. She specifically mentions the accordion as being ideal for work in dementia and writes:

I myself play a piano accordion, sitting at the same level as the individual, making direct eye contact and playing appropriate music for each in turn. (I got an accordion originally for work in a children's ward of a big hospital and the two situations are not dissimilar – each child wanted different music, played to him or her personally). (Bright 2008, p.3)

Bright (1997) also describes a particular piece of work in hospital with a stroke patient, where she was working 'to change the cycle of fear and pain'. A physiotherapist was working simultaneously with this particular patient, facilitating passive movements of the woman's arm to prevent her shoulder from becoming frozen and painful. As the woman saw the physiotherapist lift the arm she screamed in pain, but when Bright played accordion music to her on the other side, 'the arm could be lifted…without any awareness of pain' (Bright 1997, p.142). It could be argued that the strength and self-contained harmonic completeness of the accordion were particularly effective here at engaging the attention of the patient and distracting her from the pain.

In another case, Bright (2006, p.4) describes a piece of group work involving an elderly man who had recently undergone an above-knee amputation. When group members were asked to choose favourite pieces of music, this man chose a romantic waltz, which was important to him from his courtship. As Bright played his music on her accordion the man wept, saying 'I can't dance any more!' The music represented both movement and dance, areas of significant loss to this man who had recently lost a leg. Bright goes on to explain how the dance music then provided a focus for grief-work over the life changes endured by this man.

Bright considers how to choose the best instrument in palliative care (Bright 2002, p.73). She suggests that the therapist should choose an instrument on the basis of her own preference and skill but also crucially, taking into account the preference of the client and suitability of the instrument for the patient's capabilities. Bright describes several specific instruments that she finds useful in this work, and again she values the accordion, explaining that it:

> Is useful because it gives a clear melody that is easily heard even by those with partial deafness, who can touch the instrument, feeling vibrations to support what is heard; player and listener are in eye contact and in close proximity, and the instrument brings back varied memories. I have been told of church services and bush dances, the accordion being used for both. (Bright 2002, p.73)

Case vignette: The dancer

Dawn Loombe

In a case described by Harriet Powell (2009), she met an elderly lady with dementia sitting on a chair in the corridor of the care home. The lady soon became engaged with Powell's accordion music and stood up to dance. Powell found that holding the lady's left hand with her own right hand was not quite supportive enough, so she guided the lady's right hand to hold on to the accordion bellows. Powell and the lady were dancing face-to-face in this way for several minutes, with the accordion between them. Importantly, the lady's keyworker then arrived and took the lady's hands to dance and sing with her, freeing Powell to play more in support of their dancing. The lady was very engaged with both the accordion music and her keyworker and they danced together for a while. Powell explained how significant this was, as the lady and her keyworker had needed to work on developing their relationship and this gave them an opportunity to connect. The accordion was a key feature in providing this breakthrough. Powell commented that in her opinion, no other instrument is as good as the accordion is, in dancing with older people.

Case vignette: Eva's hymn

Dawn Loombe

In a long-standing piece of work in a residential home for people with dementia, I worked with a group of four elderly residents (all aged over 85 years) with severe dementia, in a small private room. All of the group members were in wheelchairs and were very frail. They had few remaining verbal skills and could often be very confused and agitated. Usually, at least one member of the group would be unable to come to music therapy because they were too unwell; and if they did come, they would often fall asleep in their wheelchairs and could remain asleep for the whole session. This group was no longer able to take part in the home's organised activities, owing to the advancement of their dementia. The staff valued this music therapy group, as it provided important opportunities for these patients to interact, to engage in holding and playing instruments, and to sing or join in with musical activities.

The accordion was of great value in this setting; familiar tunes from the war era, or hymns and organ pieces often elicited responses and it was possible to get very close to individuals to capture the brief moments when they were able to participate. As well as sharing percussion instruments, the keyboard of the accordion could also be offered to an individual to play a solo; the piano keys being relatively easy to press down, offering less resistance than actual piano keys and the therapist remaining in control of the bellows and the left-hand accompaniment.

In one very memorable session with this group, 95-year-old Eva began to sing the hymn 'Now the Day Is Over'. As she did this, she moved her fingers in the air in front of her, as if playing the piano. I quickly moved close to her, to allow her fingers to touch the accordion keys. Eva found the middle C on the accordion keyboard with her right thumb and her other fingers followed. I soon realised that she had learned this hymn on the piano, or perhaps the organ, as she suddenly became more animated and said 'How does it go?', fumbling for the notes. Gently I began to sing the hymn with her. Hesitantly, Eva found the starting note and began to sing, with increasing confidence as she picked out the melody:

> Now the day is over,
> Night is drawing nigh,
> Shadows of the evening
> Steal across the sky
> Jesus, give the weary
> Calm and sweet repose;
> With thy tend'rest blessing
> May our eyelids close.

We played and sang the hymn again together and this time I provided an organ-like, chordal bass accompaniment on the accordion with my left hand. When Eva had finished, she looked up at me, smiling in a brief, shared moment of connection. It was then that the poignancy of the lyrics suddenly dawned on me. All of the other group members were now fast asleep and seemingly oblivious to our playing.

The accordion's portability, its ability to be shared in this way and also its organ-like sound were all important aspects of this particular piece of work. The interaction could not have happened in the same way with a piano, as even if there had been space for one, it would have been too remote to engage Eva. A guitar, violin or clarinet could not have provided the same complete organ-like sound to accompany this hymn; and these instruments are not able to be shared in this way. Even a portable keyboard would not have provided the same element of intimacy and sense of connection.

Case vignette: Brenda's fears

Dawn Loombe

I worked with Brenda, a lady with cerebral palsy, in a residential home. Brenda is non-verbal, in her late 40s and, although she seemed cognitively able, was physically very restricted in her movements and used a wheelchair. She was referred to our music therapy group, as she loved music and had shown a particular liking for both the harmonica and the accordion. Although Brenda was physically unable to hold a harmonica, when her helper held it up in front of Brenda's mouth, she was able to move towards it, blow into it and make a pleasing sound to accompany the group's playing. Brenda had a large collection of accordion CDs in her eclectic mix of recorded music and often became animated when listening.

However, she had never seen anyone play an accordion, and when presented with the actual instrument as I put it on my body, she unexpectedly became very upset. Her carers and I were initially quite shocked at this but we worked through it, explaining how the accordion works, helping Brenda to understand how it is played, giving her time to feel it and warning her when I was about to pick it up to play, so that she would not be too startled. I wondered about the reasons for this with my supervisor, and in a later session when I explained to Brenda and the group how much I enjoy playing the accordion and that wearing it 'doesn't hurt me' she suddenly became totally relaxed and began again to enjoy my playing of her favourite accordion tunes.

The staff at the care home and I wondered whether Brenda viewed the instrument as a piece of medical equipment worn on the body, in a similar way to some of the medical paraphernalia she had witnessed in her life. I continued to work with this group for some months and there seemed to be no issues with the accordion after that; in fact, Brenda really loved joining in with our playing of authentic accordion jigs and reels.

This case made me consider exactly how and when I introduce the accordion to different client groups and to acknowledge others' preconceptions and expectations of the accordion and the music traditionally associated with it.

I have also found the accordion extremely useful in my work with children who have a diagnosis of autistic spectrum disorder, for whom the accordions buttons, keys, couplers and bellows seem to have a particular attraction. Alvin (Alvin and Warwick 1978) wrote about the autistic child's interest in geometric shapes, which is reflected in his behaviour towards certain musical instruments, for example running his finger round the tambour, following the parallel lines of strings on the violin or autoharp, and building constructions of drums or chime bars. This first perceptual contact with the instrument is an important non-verbal, physical communication.

With the use of the accordion, it is significant that the therapist is wearing the accordion and operating the bellows, meaning that the child has to interact with the player, as well as the accordion. This promotes good eye contact, as both face each other with the accordion between them. Also, this eye contact does not need to be too intense for the child, as he can briefly look at the therapist and then back at the instrument. It is possible to readily explore basic concepts, such as on–off, stop–go, fast–slow and up–down, whilst playing together. It is also sometimes useful to be silent, and this can easily be effected by keeping the bellows closed. This stopping in silence can encourage the child to interact with the therapist to restart the activity. While the therapist has general control of the instrument and can play to musically support, she can also offer a child some aspects of the playing, or control of her playing, allowing the accordion playing to be shared. This can develop into interactive improvised music, using the accordion sounds and vocalisations.

The ability of the child to physically feel the instrument change shape and move has also been an important aspect of Bert Santilly's work with children (2009). He talks passionately about the accordion being a 'visually arresting instrument', and both Santilly (2009) and Michael Ward-Bergeman (2009) highlight the important characteristic of 'what you see is what you hear'; that is, when you hear a long accordion note, you also see it visually and simultaneously as the accordion bellows expand or contract.

Case vignette: Robert and the sensory aspects of the accordion

Dawn Loombe

Four-year-old Robert, who has a diagnosis of autistic spectrum disorder, received weekly music therapy sessions at the Child Development Centre in Cambridge and attended with his father for 11 months. Robert was extremely interested in the accordion from his very first session. At first, he would touch each part of the instrument, feeling the different textures of the bellows, the hard outer casing, the buttons, keys and switches. He marvelled as the bellows opened and closed (as I used only the air valve button) to produce a faint hissing sound, which I imitated vocally and he copied. Robert would press down an accordion key or button and I would respond by singing the note he played. He would then look up at me briefly before trying a different note and immediately looking back at me for a reaction, visibly pleased when I also sang this note.

He repeated this cause-and-effect game many times, sometimes running away excitedly before running back to play another accordion note for me to sing. Sometimes I waited a second or two before offering a vocal response, and he would watch my lips intently, waiting for me to sing, often bursting into a fit of giggles when I again vocally reflected his sound. This was a favourite game in sessions and Robert enjoyed this element of control.

In later sessions, Robert began to vocalise more freely with me, and his verbal language developed sufficiently for him to be able to request specific instruments or favourite games. Robert enjoyed watching the accordion bellows changing shape, following their patterns with his hands. He also noticed the colours: when the bellows opened, shouting 'Red!' as this colour was gradually revealed by the opening bellows – and this colour would disappear again as the accordion bellows closed.

Robert's parents were pleased with his responses in music therapy and often mentioned an absence of what they called 'stimming' (his repetitive and isolated self-stimulatory behaviours) and more interactive, playful communication in our music therapy sessions. His father commented that the accordion is visually interesting, has many different surfaces to touch, a variety of sounds to explore, and buttons and keys to press. He thought that what particularly attracted Robert to the accordion was its complexity. Robert also brought his own small toy accordion to sessions and we regularly improvised accordion duets together, which seemed to be very satisfying for him.

*Figure 2.3 Dawn and a visually-impaired little boy
dance and play their accordions together in his music
therapy sessions at the Child Development Centre*

Case vignette: Kieran initiating interaction

Dawn Loombe

Five-year-old Kieran, who has profound autistic spectrum disorder,
was also immediately extremely attracted to the accordion. For him,
the most interesting aspect seemed to be the way the bellows moved
in and out. I picked up on his interest by keeping the bellows tightly
closed and building anticipation by singing slowly 'I... 2... 3... OPEN!'
before playing a long drawn out G7 chord as the bellows opened
wide. Then 'STOP!', briefly waiting with bellows open before singing
'I... 2... 3... CLOSED!', playing a loud C chord until the bellows were
completely closed. Kieran responded extremely well to this; laughing
excitedly and vocalising. He soon realised that he could sing the phrase
'I... 2... 3... OPEN!' to make this happen himself and began to initiate
this game, singing and watching for my reaction. He would hold the
bellows, feeling the vibration and supporting them to open and close
with me. Kieran rarely talked and generally found interaction difficult,
so for him, this was a first step towards positive communication.

The game then expanded gradually to singing some of his favourite songs together with an accordion accompaniment. Kieran seemed very aware that the bellows changed direction when breaths were taken. He also began to conduct my accordion playing, shouting 'LOUD!' or whispering 'Quiet…sssshhh' and ensuring that I responded appropriately. Modifying the volume is easy to do on the accordion, using the bellows, and this can also be visually exciting. I continued to work on sharing this element of control and increasing Kieran's awareness of turn-taking and this was important in encouraging his social interaction both in and out of sessions.

Figure 2.4 Kieran interacting with the accordion

One of the characteristics of the accordion is the extent to which the player can vary the volume of a note whilst sustaining it. An accordion note (or indeed a chord) can begin very quietly and increase in volume, either suddenly or gradually. In fact a note or chord can have a series of peaks. Conversely a note can begin loud and then quieten, suddenly or very gradually. This makes the accordion sound more, as Santilly (2009) proposed, 'animal-like; more like a voice'. Some wind or stringed instruments can do this in a limited way but the accordion is the only polyphonic instrument that can do this; the accordionist has the choice of varying the volume either with a single note or with several – and also has the option of using his own voice at the same time. The accordion can appear alive because it moves and breathes with its player and can recreate natural sounds in a manner that is unique among musical instruments.

In some settings it might be useful simply to use the accordion bellows to breathe, perhaps to reflect a quiet feeling in the room, or to match a client's breathing. This can be done by simply operating the air valve button to use the bellows (without sounding notes by pressing keys or buttons). Both Bert Santilly (2009) and Michael Ward-Bergeman (2009) have explained how they had also used their accordions to reflect breathing in this way. Ward-Bergeman said that for him, the most important feature of the accordion is its ability to 'breathe and to connect with life. The accordion's bellows are like a giant lung and can communicate something we all have in common – breathing'.

Case vignette: Breathing together in music therapy

Dawn Loombe

Whilst training as a music therapist, one of my first placements was at a day centre, working with a group of six teenagers with profound and multiple disabilities. All of the group members were in wheelchairs and all were non-verbal, although most had the ability to vocalise. Some were visually impaired and one was hearing impaired. All had complex needs and all except one of the group were unable to hold any of the instruments or beaters.

This group had not had music therapy before, and it was apparent from my first appointment that this centre receives very few visitors, other than the health professionals working with the young people. The music therapy sessions were therefore eagerly awaited. Much was expected of the music therapy, and the staff prepared for the sessions diligently, ensuring that each member of the group had finished eating, had their requisite personal care and medication and that their wheelchairs were all positioned in a perfect semicircle, awaiting my arrival. On the day of the first session, I felt an incredible pressure to do something amazing with this group. I was a student on my first placement and I was extremely nervous.

The staff sat at the sides of the room, having put the box of percussion instruments in the centre. My chair was waiting for me, facing the semicircle of young people. Everyone was quiet. What should I do? What could they do? I looked around; in fact everyone looked slightly wary. I took a deep breath and started to sing a simple welcome song, just using my voice. There were a few slight movements but no sound. Then I realised that there was a faint sound – the sound of breathing. I could hear several different breathing patterns and a barely perceptible murmuring. I picked up my accordion and without really thinking about it, I used only the air valve to open and close the accordion bellows to breathe with them. I said what I could hear in the room and reflected the different breathing patterns of each person with the accordion bellows. I moved around the group, slowly weaving in and out of the chairs with my accordion, noting their individual sounds. Some of them moved their head towards me and there was definite recognition of what was happening. The sounds were slow and gentle. Gradually, there was more murmuring and some other vocalising, and I began to play some soft breathy sounds, using a single reed sound and a single-line right-hand melody. When I stopped, there were some different vocalisations and a few smiles from the group, which seemed to reflect humour and anticipation.

Focusing on what we could all do – breathe – was a useful opening to working with this profoundly disabled group of young people. We did this to begin each of our subsequent sessions and it seemed to help to reduce any feelings of anxiety and prepare for music therapy. The use of our breathing patterns and vocal sounds became the main musical theme of this group. Some of the group also responded to the sensory aspects of the accordion; feeling the vibrations through the instrument and touching the different surfaces or playing notes.

Using the accordion percussively

The accordion can be a very tactile instrument, as shown in the case vignettes of Robert and Kieran above. It can also be used percussively. There are many different surfaces to tap, producing different rhythmic effects. The bellows can be played with the fingertips like a guiro, to produce a rasping sound. The bass buttons can be gently tapped to produce various clicking sounds. Although the accordion is not unique in this – the guitar, harp or piano, for example, can also be played percussively – the accordion does have many different types of surfaces to play in this manner. Both Bert Santilly (2009) and Michael Ward-Bergeman (2009) make use of the accordion percussively. I have also used these rhythmic effects successfully to engage children in music therapy.

The Bellows Shake is a musical effect used by accordionists, whereby the player uses his left hand to vibrate the bellows whilst they are only very slightly open, by small rapid rocking movements to and fro with the bass end. This can be particularly useful to imitate train sounds or for sudden dramatic effect. I have used the bellows train sounds particularly in my sessions with one young boy, with autistic spectrum disorder, for whom the theme of trains was both important and interesting. This accordion effect, along with my vocalising, seemed to motivate and help him to feel secure enough in sessions to begin to participate in musical interactions and eventually to move on to other themes and musical ideas.

My first encounter with the accordion

Susan Greenhalgh

I grew up in the Dockland area of Liverpool, and as a young child I was frequently taken by my mother, father and sisters to evangelical open-air meetings held in the streets where I lived. It was here that I clearly remember the piano accordion being played and it being (as well as the preacher!) the star of the show. The piano accordionist would robustly, energetically and with colossal volume, lead the singing of the hymns and without a doubt required no electronic amplification. These visits to the open-air meetings are indeed happy memories for me.

I trained as a music therapist some years ago and my principal instrument is the piano. I also use the violin, guitar and a variety of other instruments in my therapy work, which is mainly based in schools and mental health settings.

A few years ago and in total contrast to the musical quality (and volume) of the accordionist at the evangelical meetings of my childhood, I was to discover the beautiful and more sensitive aspect of the accordion when I heard a colleague play some lovely French tunes. This became my inspiration to start playing the accordion, and subsequently I began using it in school assemblies, in bands I belong to, and eventually in my mental health groups and individual casework. Although a relatively new instrument for me, the amalgamation of my own positive emotional experiences with the piano accordion was what led me to being able to use it in my work. The following case vignette demonstrates how an instrument that provided me as a music therapist with new, positive and happy experiences could also be shared with my clients to generate interest and emotional well-being for them.

Case vignette: Joshua explores dismantling and putting back together before finding the accordion and ultimately, himself

Susan Greenhalgh

I worked with Joshua in his school. At the time of referral to music therapy he was 14 years old. He had recently been taken into care and separated from his three younger siblings, who were still living with their mother. Joshua had become extremely withdrawn, his behaviour was disruptive in the classroom and he was often isolated in school. He found it difficult to concentrate on any given task and was finding it unbearable to remain in any school lessons. It was felt that he might benefit from music therapy intervention, where he might learn to trust another adult and begin to express some of his feelings of loss and anger within a safe and contained space.

Joshua began attending music therapy on a weekly basis. Initially he found it difficult to come into the therapy room and he would often stay outside the door for at least ten minutes. As time went on, he seemed to feel a little more confident, and slowly he began to explore some of the instruments in the room. It became immensely apparent that Joshua was interested in how the instruments worked. He began to dismantle the hi-hat and to question and investigate how the violin and guitar strings are attached and how the sounds are created. He also began to delight in plugging in the electric violin and guitar and seeing how loud he could set the volume. He was developing the ability to ask me questions about the instruments in the room. However, it was still difficult for him to stay focused on an instrument for more than a couple of minutes without becoming anxious and looking sad.

During these first three months of therapy it was brought to my attention that the one school lesson that Joshua would occasionally find motivating was design and technology, where he would be able to learn how to dismantle objects to see how they worked and learn how to put them back together again. His fascination with both the tactile and constructional element of objects had also become very apparent in his music therapy sessions. In addition, I had noted his attraction to varying gradations of dynamics. However, although these seemed to be the two things that did motivate and engage him, it was still very obvious that he struggled to stay focused, even on something he liked. Joshua had still not found something in the room that would capture his interest long enough to enable him to feel settled.

It was at this point that, after much consideration, I decided to introduce the piano accordion into Joshua's session. This would be something very different from the instruments in the room already. Would the aesthetic quality of the accordion, its tactile and varying dynamic elements, capture his attention? Would the instrument enable him to feel safer and be the means of developing an increased sense of trust with the therapist?

It was Joshua's 13th music therapy session. He entered the room, immediately spotted the accordion sitting proudly on the floor and smiled at me as I had never seen him do before, an expression I will not forget. It was joyous to see how just the mere sight of the accordion had captured his immediate attention.

Joshua immediately lifted the accordion off the floor and began to try to work out how to produce the sound. He asked how to put on the straps and could not get it on quickly enough. He became totally absorbed in experimenting with the keys and the buttons and soon learnt that the bellows were the heart and soul of the instrument and its main means of expression.

Over the coming months in therapy Joshua began to express some of his intense sadness in the course of his accordion playing; he played long bass drone sounds and I would support him musically with similar sounds on the lower register notes of the piano. When we were engaged in this type of sustained playing, Joshua would become so absorbed and calm that he was able to start verbally to articulate some of his sad and lonely feelings in between our improvisations. Joshua began to sustain his concentration for longer periods during his accordion playing, and what became very apparent was that his anxiety began to decrease during our shared musical improvisation.

His music was still reflecting his intense feelings of being lost and sad, but very quickly he began to discover how to express some of his more positive feelings on the accordion. He had initially been unable to feel positive about anything in his life, but occasionally he was demonstrating a small spark of happiness through his accordion playing.

For the subsequent two months in therapy, Joshua continued to use the piano accordion as his stabilising object in our sessions. Initially, it was the only instrument he chose to play, until eventually he became strong enough to start using some of the other instruments too.

Joshua attended music therapy for three years. The piano accordion had become the turning point in music therapy that had enabled him to take huge steps forward and start to feel better about himself. He started attending some of his school lessons again, gradually stopped blaming himself for what had happened to him and began to like himself again. He started to make friends with his peers and he became less isolated and more able to cope with some of his difficult feelings.

Social and cultural aspects of the accordion

Dawn Loombe

The unique timbre of the accordion and its history has some cultural connotations in many countries and communities and can have particular resonance with certain social groups. The relevance of accordion music in a variety of communities could be considered socially and culturally important music, described as 'community music therapy' (Ansdell 2002; Pavlicevic and Ansdell 2004; Ruud 2004).

Harriet Powell (2009) has described her use of the piano accordion in multi-cultural groups in Hackney, encompassing older people from Italy, Poland and Latvia and from diverse social and cultural backgrounds. Powell has also noted that the accordion often evokes memories of happy social occasions:

> Many would not have been able to afford a piano in their home and might have an accordion instead. It was a familiar sound in pubs and at parties and people I work with often relate memories of accordions being played on trips to the seaside or in large community gatherings. (Powell 2004a)

The accordion is useful in playing Jewish Klezmer music and also in providing an easy, effective accompaniment to Middle-Eastern as well as Eastern European music. Santilly (2009) described the use of different scales on the accordion to produce an Asian or Middle-Eastern effect, which has been important in his work.

With relevance to music therapy work, older people who are now in their 70s, 80s and 90s will undoubtedly remember the piano accordion in its heyday. In my work with groups of people with dementia, the accordion has often proved a valuable reminiscence object as group members recall their dance band days and beloved family members who used to play the accordion for social functions. They consistently tell stories of a treasured old accordion in an attic somewhere.

Accordion characteristics in music therapy practice

Portability and adaptability to different therapeutic environments

The ability to play in close proximity to clients in different situations was specifically noted by all of the accordionists. All stressed its suitability for use in hospitals, schools and residential homes, or outside, where they could play wherever the person was, rather than where the instrument was situated. The importance of the client being able to both see and hear the accordion from wherever they were was described by all the therapists, who mentioned that playing accordion allowed interaction visually and through facial expression, which is of course particularly important with those who had lost the ability to communicate verbally. Bert Santilly (2009) explained how he has played his accordion in a special school whilst lying on his back on a mattress beside a child having physiotherapy.

Dawn Loombe found her accordion useful in a children's nursery, where space was limited. It has also been valuable in circle games involving movement, where the accordionist could dance and physically be a part of the group, rather than remotely playing the piano. In dementia groups, the accordionist can walk around the room playing, which seems to hold the group together, whilst also being able to move to support an individual who is singing or playing a solo.

Use of the accordion bellows to breathe

The accordion is unique in its bellows arrangement. All of the therapists noted the likeness of the accordion bellows to human lungs and to breathing. The accordion's air valve can be used effectively to produce breathing and sighing sounds without using the reeds.

The accordion's ability to be shared

Harriet Powell and Dawn Loombe both described sharing the playing of an accordion in their work. The therapist wears and retains overall control of the instrument, whilst allowing the melody to be played by a client on its keyboard.

The changing aspect of the accordion

The accordion is unique in the way that it changes shape as it is played. Different colours are revealed as the bellows open and close. Also, when a long note or chord is played on the accordion, the bellows expand or contract accordingly, meaning that it is represented visually as well as audibly.

Percussive effects

The accordion has many different surfaces to tap, producing a variety of rhythmic effects – its hard casing to use as a drum, buttons couplers and keys to tap or click, and bellows to use as a guiro.

Vibration

Santilly (2009) and Claus Bang (2006) both mentioned the importance of the accordion in their work with deaf and hearing-impaired children, where the children could touch or hold the outer casing of the instrument as the therapist played, enabling them to feel the music.

The attraction of mechanical aspects – buttons, keys, couplers and bellows

As noted in the case vignettes of Dawn Loombe and Susan Greenhalgh, children have been particularly interested in the mechanics of the accordion; especially children with autistic spectrum disorder, who seem drawn to its geometric shapes, buttons and couplers and the way it is constructed.

The dynamic range of the accordion

The use of the accordion couplers allows the player a wide pitch range and also a range of timbres. The use of the bellows for dynamics and musical expression was also mentioned, allowing the player to vary the volume of a single note or a chord whilst sustaining it, or even to have a series of peaks. (Also, the accordionist can sing at the same time as playing the instrument.)

A complete harmonic instrument

Bert Santilly (2009) called the accordion 'an orchestra in a box'. It is capable of providing a full, strong, harmonic accompaniment. All of the accordionists remarked on the fact that the accordion provides the therapist with a variety of musical options: a single-line melody with or without a chordal accompaniment, as well as being polyphonic.

Social and cultural aspects

The accordion is a popular instrument in many cultures and social groups and has associations with certain styles of music, which might have particular relevance with clients in music therapy. Also, the accordion can be a useful reminiscence object with older people in music therapy. The increased use of the accordion in TV and film soundtracks and in pop culture was also mentioned as relevant.

References

Aldridge, D. (ed.) (2000) *Music Therapy in Dementia Care.* London, UK: Jessica Kingsley Publishers.

Aldridge, D. (ed.) (2005) *Music Therapy and Neurological Rehabilitation* London, UK: Jessica Kingsley Publishers.

Alvin, J. and Warwick, A. (1978) *Music Therapy for the Autistic Child* (2nd edition, reprinted 1994). Oxford, UK: Oxford University Press.

Ansdell, G. (2002) 'Community music therapy and the winds of change.' *Voices: A World Forum for Music Therapy 2*, 2. Retrieved 5 April 2009 from https://voices.no/index.php/voices/article/view/83/65.

Bang, C. (2006) *A World of Sound and Music.* Retrieved 11 April 2014 from www.clausbang.com.

Bright, R. (1997) *Wholeness in Later Life.* London, UK: Jessica Kingsley Publishers.

Bright, R. (2002) *Supportive Eclectic Music Therapy for Grief and Loss.* St. Louis, MO: MMB.

Bright, R. (2006) 'Significant music in externalising grief in coping with change: The supportive role of the music therapist.' *Australian Journal of Music Therapy 17*, 64–72.

Bright, R. (2007) *Thoughts on Music Therapy.* Retrieved 11 April 2012 from www.fightdementia.org.au/common/files/NAT/20050500_Nat_CON_BrightMusicTherapy.pdf.

Bright, R. (2008) 'Editorial.' *Creative Expression, Communication and Dementia Newsletter, 2* (March), p.3. Retrieved 24 August 2014 from http://cecd-society.org/assets-australia/Hilary_Newsletter_mar_08.pdf.

Gaertner, M. (1999) 'The Sound of Music in the Dimming, Anguished World of Alzheimer's Disease.' In T. Wigram and J. De Backer (eds) *Clinical Applications of Music Therapy in Psychiatry.* London, UK: Jessica Kingsley Publishers.

Howard, R. (2005) *An A to Z of the Accordion and Related Instruments, Volume 2.* Stockport: Robaccord Publications.

Loombe, D. (2009) *The Use of Piano Accordion in Music Therapy: A Qualitative Study and Critical Analysis of My Own Case Work.* Unpublished MA thesis, Anglia Ruskin University, Cambridge.

Pavlicevic, M. and Ansdell, G. (eds) (2004) *Community Music Therapy.* London, UK: Jessica Kingsley Publishers.

Powell, H. (2004a) 'Light on my feet – the Accordion.' *Musicing: The Newsletter of Nordoff-Robbins Music Therapists*, December 2004. Retrieved 11 April 2014 from http://steinhardt.nyu.edu/music.olde/file_uploads/Musicing_2004.pdf.

Powell, H. (2004b) 'A Dream Wedding: From Community Music to Music Therapy with a Community.' In M. Pavlicevic and G. Ansdell (eds) *Community Music Therapy.* London, UK: Jessica Kingsley Publishers.

Powell, H. (2009) Personal communication, February 25, 2009.

Ruud, E. (2004) 'Foreword.' In M. Pavlicevic, and G. Ansdell (eds) *Community Music Therapy* London, UK: Jessica Kingsley Publishers.

Santilly, B. (2009) Personal communication, February 17, 2009.

Wade-Matthews, M. and Thompson, W. (2002) *The Encyclopedia of Music: Instruments of the Orchestra and the Great Composers.* New York, NY: Anness Publishing.

Ward-Bergeman, M. (2009) Personal communication, February 17, 2009.

CHAPTER 3

The Flute

*Contributors: Caroline Anderson, Veronica Austin
(introduction and case vignettes), Emily Corke,
Mary-Clare Fearn (within Veronica Austin's
contribution), Esther Mitchell and Jo Tomlinson*

Introduction

The flute is the oldest of all instruments that produce pitched sounds, and its evocative tones have been associated with healing and lifting the spirits from before the Middle Ages. The scientific journal *ScienceDaily* reported the discovery of what is thought to be the oldest flute, made from bird bones and mammoth ivory with two holes in it, and approximately 40,000 years old (University of Oxford 2012). Although no one can be sure of the precise function of these flutes it is generally thought they would have been used for rituals, ceremonies, pleasure and perhaps, even then, for healing.

When taking into account the history of the flute worldwide, we find there are many versions of primitive flutes and their flute families remaining in the sounds, music and traditions of different world cultures and healing practices today. It is worth considering that some of the ideas raised in the use of the orchestral flute in music therapy are applicable to the use of these other types of flute, such as the Irish tin whistle, the panpipes of Ecuador and Peru, the Japanese *shakuhachi*, the Indian *bansuri* flutes, the Indonesian *suling*, the Chinese bamboo flute or the wooden dual-chamber North American flute (one side plays a drone and the other pitched notes). There is much to inform and draw on from these world flutes for the benefit of music therapists. In order to appreciate the modern orchestral flute it is useful to understand a little of its history.

The primitive flutes of hollowed-out bone or horn and later clay, bamboo or wood of the medieval and Renaissance periods were a one-piece design with up to six holes and a mouthpiece. They were either played straight down, using a block to direct the air at the edge of the mouth hole (like the recorder), or played to one side (transverse), requiring the player to direct the air across the mouthpiece. Fingers covered and uncovered the holes to create different pitches. Intervals of the pentatonic scale and later diatonic scale of one and then two octaves evolved.

The quality of timbre, expansion of pitch range and capacity for the flute to convey expression developed over time as flautists increased their skills, composers wrote more complex music, and technology advanced. The second half of the 17th century saw a revolution in flute making (Wilson 2013) with the new flexibility of the three-piece transverse flute (mouthpiece, centre and foot piece) of the Baroque era, with its three-octave range, brighter tone and ability to effect more dynamic contrast. The one-keyed flute was developed into the six-keyed flute in the latter half of the 17th century and the tone became more even. Mozart's *Flute and Harp Concerto* of 1778 was intended for such a flute. Throughout the 19th century the flute continued to undergo more changes, evolving to the modern Boehm system metal flute predominantly in use today.

Figure 3.1 Range of the modern concert flute

The wider implementation of instrumental lessons in schools, as well as the internationally acclaimed flute virtuoso James Galway (b.1939) did much to popularise the flute in the 1970s and 1980s. Galway's flute version of John Denver's 'Annie's Song' in 1978 reached number three in the UK pop charts, and a surge of new young flautists followed. He became a household name and is still successful today as a cross-over artist, bringing classical, folk and popular music to different generations of flute players and a diverse range of music lovers. New careers in flute playing have expanded to provide opportunities for flautists to work as therapists, performers, teachers, composers, recording artists and flute specialists in manufacture and industry. Among music therapists the flute is the orchestral instrumental most frequently used.

Of course invention has not stopped, and since the advent of the 21st century, developments of the quarter-tone flute by Robert Dick and Eva Kingma[1] have been established in a new kind of flute called the Kingma System flute. With the help of additional keywork, players no longer have to use alternative fingerings for correcting intonation, playing trills or effecting extended or contemporary techniques, as they are sometimes called (Clarke 2012; Dick 1986). Players at all levels are now becoming acquainted with extended techniques. Clarke (2012) described this development: 'They are becoming a natural *augmentation* of core technique both with respect to the requirements of new repertoire and learning approaches.'

Many techniques are still possible on the ordinary concert flute, though the open-holed flute with a low B footjoint is favoured. Techniques include the development of new tonal colours and sonorities as well as note bending, jet whistles, harmonics, flutter tonguing, percussive articulations (mouthsounds), multiphonics and quarter tones.

Music therapists will be able to expand their range of available responses to their clients by employing some of these additional methods on their flute. In imitating sounds of the early flutes using non-standard fingerings, therapists might connect with clients by creating more primitive or other-worldly sounds. Special effects with multiphonics and jet whistles may bring surprise and novelty. Singing into the flute and percussive articulation lend themselves to popular or avant-garde styles, where it might be important for the therapist to sound contemporary or even cool! While critics have called these ideas gimmicky and a generation of flute playing therapists may feel challenged by learning new ways of playing, our clients may motivate us to explore these options. When feeling, imagination and technique come together, the therapist is best equipped to use the flute to its full potential.

---

1   See www.kingmaflutes.com for more information.

The flute in music therapy literature

Music therapist Juliette Alvin (1966) wrote about Greek mythology where the flute was 'Athena's gift' from the gods, and went on to describe the attitudes of the Greek philosophers towards the flute and healing. Alvin quotes Aristotle's opinion that the flute is not an instrument that has a good moral effect – Aristotle considered it 'too exciting' and his belief was that it should consequently be employed only on occasion when the object of the music is the purging of the emotions rather than the improvement of the mind.

From a practical perspective Alvin also discusses the positive impact of blowing into flutes for people with malformation of the mouth, and the possibility of developing muscle strength through playing (Alvin 1966).

Music therapists Sweeney-Brown and Wilkinson have written about their work with children in hospices, using the flute to calm, soothe or stimulate children who were approaching the end of life. Wilkinson (2005) observed the range of responses to the flute from a group of children: some listening quietly whilst another vocalised in imitation of the flute sound. Even when children were too unwell to engage with active playing, the sound of the flute provided reassurance and allowed the child to feel that they were not alone. This in turn supports the families of the children and created positive memories during times of severe stress (Sweeney-Brown 2005).

Tomlinson (2012) described the use of the flute in music therapy work with young children in special schools, and the way in which the flute could be used as imitator of the child's musical contribution. 'Shaky' playing on the egg shaker was reflected back by the therapist playing trills on the flute and making similar physical movements to those of the child. The element of humour lightened the intensity of this exchange, engaging the child and creating much less resistance to shared interaction. In a similar way rhythmical imitation on the flute provided a musical framework for the child, encouraging him to sustain interaction and distracting from obsessive or repetitive behaviours. Tomlinson stated that this type of imitative play using the flute can be used 'to reinforce existing behaviour, or at other times it can be used to promote change…imitation and reflection used within a therapeutic context can be powerful and valuable tools' (2012, p.115).

Keeping connections through flute playing

Veronica Austin

I was born into a musical family and was drawn to carry on the flute-playing tradition. I loved the sound of the flute and was surrounded by some of the finest flute-playing sounds in England in my formative years. My father, a musician and businessman, and then Richard Taylor took me on as my teachers and mentors. My relationship with the flute is embedded with family memories and relationships, as my sisters, brother and I regularly went to concerts and also played together as a wind quartet. For the past 15 years I have continued to play in a wind quartet but with music therapists, all of us wanting and needing to stay connected to our instruments and finding it musically and socially fulfilling.

On a practical level, the modern orchestral flute is easy to carry around and can be relatively inexpensive to buy. It is easy to care for and to learn as a beginner because it does not involve a reed and the complications that can bring. For anyone who has made a start on the recorder, fingerings can be easily transferred to the flute, and frequently you can enjoy playing the melodic line. The playing posture required allows the music therapist to face the client, and the small size of the instrument means movement around the room is possible. But perhaps it is the particular sound that is first and foremost the flute's enduring attraction; it is a versatile instrument capable of a wide range of timbres over a three-octave pitch range. The lower octave can be rich, smoky or mellow, while in the higher registers the sound of the flute can be piercing, with bird-like trills and rapidly moving notes. It is possible to play extremely quietly on the flute, and allow the sound to fade away to a whisper of breath, or play around with breathing sounds.

I have noticed that music therapists using their flutes effectively in therapy tend to be at ease with their instrument, as if their instrument is simply an extension of themselves. I experienced a revived connection and confidence with my flute after a period of more intensive flute practice and inspiring flute lessons. In the following clinical example with a group of early-years children in a local authority Sure Start Centre, the flute offered a profound connection with all the children.

Case vignette: Early-years group

A group of four very different four-year-old children, two girls and two boys, were in their sixth music therapy session. They had been referred for music therapy for a variety of reasons, some having difficulties making relationships and one having challenging behaviour. After directing the first five sessions in a mixture of structured and semi-structured activities, I wanted to open up the group play with more free improvisation. The group began exploring percussion sounds as separate individuals, and one child broke off to start dancing. This child was moving in breakdance movements, and in the absence of a keyboard I took up my flute and with this single line using the Dorian mode and an off-beat jazzy kind of rhythm I accompanied him and the other children as they began to join in. The flute sustained a group dance in a most joyous way, which also proved a turning point in the therapy.

In the example above, the flute practice and lesson in the weeks before had helped renew my connection to the flute, which I then transferred to the group in a strong accompaniment. Using the flute here also enabled me to move about with the group and give my own occasional dance-like movements in response too.

Keeping a connection to one's instrument promotes artistry in music therapy. Artistry sets apart the ordinary player/therapist from the one who is maintaining and honing their skills with workmanship and imagination. For the flute, these involve technical mastery of the fundamentals of flute playing, a rich clear and focused tone, evenness of tone over the range of the instrument, warmth of expression, articulation and dynamic contrasts, control over breathing and vibrato, and the ability to project the sound and rhythms into the clinical space. More advanced or experienced players may have a greater 'sound palette' (Clarke 2012) at their disposal, a repertoire of well-known tunes to produce at any given moment in any style or key, and be able to communicate an idea, feeling or thought with conviction. The artiste will add a quality to their sound, the way it is conceived, produced and projected, with nuance and variation in attack, articulation and timing. The artiste has their own authentic style of playing and interpretation that comes from within. However, there is a note of caution from music therapists Sobey and Woodcock (1999, p.138) for the therapist who 'has brought into the session too much of his own musical and cultural world'; in their case example 'the client in a purely musical sense was left with no other options than to join this world, go actively against it or to remain passive and silent'. Therapists aware of their tendencies through supervision and listening back to recordings learn to continuously monitor the connection their music is having with their client and how best to employ their music for therapeutic benefit. As music therapist Pavlicevic (1997, p.121) writes: 'The significance of clinical improvisation is that it is an interpersonal event, rather than only being a musically interactive one.'

The flute as object

The flute, and sometimes its case as well, may be seen as an object in itself carrying significance in the therapy space. When the flautist makes the decision to take their flute into therapy work they do so with care. It is necessary to consider whether the situation can be made safe and practical. Many therapists will have a second, cheaper flute to take into therapy work in order to preserve their other more precious instrument. A therapist can also think through the ways in which the client might potentially respond to this flute in the room today. Will they embrace it, be ambivalent or reject the flute? If they do have any of these responses, we might interpret the feelings as being about us. We might even actually feel rejected or embraced by their attitude as we consider the object we have taken into the room as an extension of ourselves. With some clients, wondering out loud with them about their responses might be possible, and if not, the therapist can still reflect on them.

The gifted cellist and pioneer music therapist Juliette Alvin taught that in her method of music therapy the instrument and the music took the transference feelings from the client (Bruscia 1987), thereby providing psychological safeguarding for the client and therapist. Object-relations thinking also allows us to consider that the therapist, the environment or their instrument may be construed or unconsciously used as a recipient of transference and projections by the client. This can provide information for the therapist and clues to the client's predicament or feelings.

A young girl on meeting a therapist for the first time had a panic attack on seeing the flute and needed another adult to calm her and the flute to be removed. Because the work was happening in a hospital setting and the young child had had a tracheotomy, the therapist could conjecture that the flute could have been perceived as a medical instrument that might cause her physical pain, or a blowing instrument needing the mouth, causing her psychological pain. Finally, the flute may also be considered as a transitional object (Winnicott 1971) that simultaneously separates and brings together therapist and client, belonging 'to the border between the child's early fusion with mother and his dawning realisation of separateness' (Gomez 1997, p.93).

A wind instrument – connecting with breath and blowing

In flute playing, the breath can be readily seen, heard and emphasised. The fact that this aspect can be brought to the fore in a very natural and appealing way is a significant role for the flute in therapy. Young children with speech and language difficulties and developmentally delayed babies can benefit from attention being drawn to the movement of the mouth and breath. The connections with the body and arousing mental and physical awareness can also be developmentally advantageous. There is stimulation in the feel of the air and children are also captivated by the sound and sight of the flute. I have seen children automatically put beaters to their mouths and hold them sideways in imitation of the therapist, or pucker their lips in a way that mirrors the therapist's embouchure. To illustrate some of these ways of using the flute here are two examples of clinical work from music therapist Mary-Clare Fearn, whose main instrument is the piano but here finds her flute a very valuable tool as part of the therapeutic process.

Case vignette: Nicholas

When I commenced work with Nicholas, he was eight years old and had learning disabilities with associated emotional and behavioural problems. He was very controlling, often saying 'Shut-up!' or 'Be quiet!' if I started playing the piano. However, Nicholas did allow me to play the flute and this led to him using the melodica. It was clear that he was motivated to choose the melodica because of his desire to blow into an instrument. Nicholas accepted the boundary that he could not play the therapist's flute and took ownership of the melodica. He has since used it many times in the past three years, gradually experimenting with different scales, chords and intervals. Each time, his music is beautiful, sonorous and moving. Nicholas has a troubled home life but is very loving and keen to learn; unfortunately his keenness is often hindered by his emotional state. He can get very angry but his music, particularly the flute and melodica duets, seem to tap into the gentle side of his character, which he allows to come to the fore in these moments. Nicholas always makes clear endings using a diminuendo, giving the feeling of a sigh.

Case vignette: Anna

Anna is a profoundly disabled girl who I began to work with in music therapy sessions when she was three years old and this work continued for four years. Anna engaged in music and movement therapy work with an adult facilitating her movements. She was blind and could not move unaided but clearly wanted to get close to the source of the music. Frequent early sessions with Anna's head resting on the therapist's crossed legs and moving her flute close to the young girl's face produced delight when she felt the breath and, with adult facilitation, touched the flute as I played. This felt extremely close. My mirroring of the rhythm of Anna's breathing added greater security to our relationship. The flute being 'breathy' seemed to make the perfect link and helped her to realise that she was dictating the improvisations.

In both of the case studies above, the flute was a far more appropriate instrument of choice than the piano. It was not so intimidating for the children and the sound appealed to them. In addition to this, the flute facilitated the children's self-expression and I was able to get physically closer, which created a more personal feel to the music-making and enabled a relationship to develop.

The flute as an extension of the voice

The flute can be thought about and used as an extension of the therapist and his or her voice. First, it is possible quickly to take away the flute in the middle of a melody and sing the rest with your voice in a seamless way, providing a continuous melodic line whilst also simultaneously enabling your client to become actively engaged. The following case example used this technique.

Case vignette: Simon

One-year-old Simon was seen for music therapy in a hospital ward and was recovering from an operation to counteract the damage to his lungs from continuous vomiting. He watched transfixed as I put my flute to my mouth and started to play a few notes mid-register. I stopped and then played a few more notes moving up and down scales in a melodic way, watching Simon intensely for signs of response. At first he seemed startled, but then his face softened and he began to move his body to and fro from his steady base in his Bumble chair. He looked up and smiled and I then sang the next phrase. After this, I blew the flute and sang again to Simon's movements. He increased his movement and engagement with me in this joint activity and when I next blew and then waited, Simon made his own vocal sound in the space. A series of flute and vocal exchanges then took place to both his and his mother's delight.

In this case, the waiting was as important as the notes. Also, I paid extra attention to Simon's tempo and timing, wondering whether I had perhaps played too quickly before. Simon almost fooled the doctors by his incredibly sunny disposition, despite vomiting and being in hospital. By looking at his X-rays the doctors discovered that his lungs were badly affected. In a similar way, by slowing down the musical interaction I began to notice Simon's breathing and aimed for more control and ease for him, by paying attention to his internal movement as well as his external movements.

A second function of the flute acting as an extension of the voice is that it can accompany a vocal line when the client is singing. The combination of the flute and the voice creates an opportunity for a shared experience with the therapist. If the therapist joins in through singing, this will often mean the client drops out and stops singing. By accompanying with the flute we can do the same thing, but we are also different and separate.

The instrument that reached where others could not

Esther Mitchell

At the age of nine, I discovered a small black and silver box in the dining room. It looked remarkably like something I had seen at the doctor's. Was someone ill? Guiltily, unseen, I opened the lid. Within, however, was not the stethoscope I expected but, in three enticing pieces, my first flute.

Although I studied technique and tone for 14 years through the joy of lessons and chamber music and the struggles of exams and performances, it was not until I came to train as a music therapist that I really connected with my flute. It was through improvisation that it really became a part of me, an extension of my voice through which I could express my emotional state and also increasingly, reflect back that of another.

I have used my flute within clinical work with a wide variety of client groups and have often wondered why it can apparently entice individuals into interaction where other instruments have seemed to fail. My conclusion is that this is due to its similarity with the human voice. My voice is naturally low, and the flute provides me with the higher pitches I lack. With it I can meet a range of vocal sounds produced by those I work with, which test my voice beyond its limits.

I work for Thomas's Fund, a registered charity that provides music therapy in the home for children and young people with life-limiting conditions and/or disabilities, who, owing to their medical condition, are too unwell to attend school for prolonged periods. Our work is short-term, with clients being offered on average 14 sessions, including assessment. Those referred, from babies up to the age of 19, vary greatly in their physical and mental state. Some clients live a few minutes' walk away from where I park my car or up several flights of stairs. So our instruments need to be compact, and I have come to respect the choice my parents made – that I should learn the flute, not the harp – as I swing its bag over my shoulder or open the case in the confines of a small cubicle, never ceasing to delight in the wonder on a child's face as I put the shiny pieces together.

Case vignette: Ben

Ben, aged 20 months, grinned broadly as I began to sing hello to him, softly strumming the guitar. The child, who had been on the move constantly, rolling over and over across the room at our initial meeting, barely aware of me, was sitting attentively on the floor in his living room. His mother sat next to Ben and he was giving me steady eye contact. I inched a little closer and began to sing again. Ben's face dropped and he began to sob, then to shake with fear. He could not be consoled or distracted whether I sang, played or moved away, leaving instruments near him, which his parents explored with him. After 15 minutes, we ended the session, Ben calming as I packed away and left. Sessions two and three continued in a similar manner with his parents becoming understandably uncertain about music therapy in general. I decided therefore to work without instruments; I would use my voice and props such as puppets and scarves and I hoped would slowly gain his confidence.

Ben has Rubenstein Taybi syndrome, a chromosomal disorder that affects his mental development, his sight and hearing, his digestion, his joints and his growth. Much of Ben's first traumatic year of life was spent in hospital, and it was hoped that music therapy could support him in the development of his very delayed communication, social and physical skills. Ben made virtually no vocal sounds and gave very little eye contact.

Ben was used to noise from the television, which was on much of the time, and he enjoyed shared play, yet appeared unable to cope with musical interaction. However, I noticed that as I worked with only my voice, he gradually began to let me in. Our sessions were filled with action songs, which were new to his mother, whose first language is not English. She was keen to learn and Ben appeared increasingly motivated, pausing in his relentless activity of rolling to sit for increasing periods and engage. In session six, feeling as if I were treading on egg shells, I tentatively reintroduced instruments. Within weeks Ben moved from tolerating first the tambourine, to exploring and mastering an understanding with delight that his play on the egg shakers could impact on how his mother and I played too.

In session ten I introduced the flute. Ben was exploring the wind-chimes for the first time and seemed quite captivated. As I started to play my flute, mirroring his phrases, he immediately stopped playing, sat forward and watched me intently, giving me a level of attention that I had not felt before. Ben's mother moved the wind-chimes and turned to watch his face. I continued, tentatively moving higher up in the register to meet his sounds; Ben's face dropped and he began to sob. I immediately stopped playing, fearing I had taken him back to square one. I wondered if the sound was hurting his ears, or whether this was something much deeper; perhaps too emotionally intense?

Spurred on by his initial response to the flute, I began to use it weekly, introducing it within our interaction with a variety of instruments. Ben would stop what he was doing as I began to play and, now crawling, would approach me as if drawn by some magnetic connection. Our interaction would at that point become more focused, and I noticed from the video that his mother would sit totally still. Ben was now able to turn-take for brief periods, giving more consistent eye contact and enjoying a variety of action songs; he had apparently begun to anticipate phrase endings within our shared play. He was increasingly vocal in and outside sessions, using his voice now as a medium for self-expression, rather than intentional communication, through closed 'hmmmmm' sounds.

In our final individual session Ben, his mother and I shared the gathering drum. Ben played with steady beats, yet I felt he was not really interested in communicating. I lifted my flute to play... he sat up, leant forward across the drum and beamed, tilting his head to one side, his eyes suddenly full of life. As I played, responding to his movements through my own, he began to use the drum to turn-take with my sounds. Ben's mother commented on how much he was listening. Later, adding in the egg shakers, the music became more upbeat, with his mother and me mirroring his play. Ben suddenly began to vocalise, mirroring the pitches and shape of my melodic flute phrase for the first time. Each time he responded to my sounds he launched himself at the drum, trying to kneel up and support his own weight. Our shared dance went on and on, pausing briefly as he toppled over, then back to reinitiate the interaction through a repeated vocal phrase, a big smile and pleading eye contact.

It can be difficult to work within the parameters of short-term music therapy with those who would benefit from something more long term and I was very fortunate to soon see Ben again, now in a small group situation. He continued to develop his confidence, his awareness, his communication and his social and physical skills. Having spent a long time in hospital, then much of his time at home, he was now enjoying being a part of various groups in the community. This was reflected in his interest in the other children in the group, his eagerness to explore the large room each week and his confidence to be the first to reach out to try the instruments, even the guitar, which he could now at last accept. Interaction during the session was naturally more structured and I did not feel the same intensity within interaction as we had had in our individual therapy. However, each time I introduced the flute, he would immediately approach and sit directly in front of me, whether it meant sitting on top of instruments or another child! In our penultimate session, Ben approached me and placed his hands on my legs as we sat together on the floor, and each time I stopped playing he would push the flute back up towards my lips. I laughed, asking and signing 'Do you want more?' Ben nodded, smiled and vocalised an affirmative.

From our very tentative beginnings to the end of our time together, Ben had undoubtedly become motivated by the percussive and melodic instruments I offered him each week. Through shared play and turn-taking exchanges, he had shown clear development towards his therapeutic aims and would most likely have done so without the presence of the flute. It was, however, through the use of the flute that I felt Ben and I really met in the music emotionally. It touched him on such a level that his whole being became alive. In that moment we had a shared understanding, our relationship was taken to a deeper level and it was from that level that interaction flowed unconsciously. This intimacy did, I believe, support Ben's development further, taking us a step beyond where we would have been without the flute.

The calming effect of the flute

Emily Corke

At school, my earliest musical memory is being part of the recorder ensemble, which developed my interest in woodwind instruments. The novelty of breathing into something but making a sound other than one's voice led me to begin learning the flute, and I discovered its many further qualities. In keeping one's breath steady one can create musical phrases and melodies with a pleasing soft tone. Its sound is soothing, yet crisp. I was attracted to its delicate and intricate nature, the shiny, striking metal out of which it was made. I went on to play the flute for eight years at school, and was particularly grateful for orchestral opportunities not afforded me through my two other 'instruments' of piano and voice. The flute was my gateway to relational music, corporate musical discovery, mutual support and performance. I neglected the flute upon leaving school, but when

I started my training as a music therapist I remembered the flute's communicative possibilities in creating powerful music with others.

I now use my flute in nearly every session, and I delight in seeing my clients drawn to it in the same way that I am. The flute includes a different dynamic in three main ways. First, it is the only instrument that I play but the clients do not, allowing them to enjoy merely listening to and absorbing the sound. Being able to simply listen to the soothing sound allows my clients to feel less pressured to 'do', and therefore, counter-intuitively, they seem more at ease to respond. Second, it is seen as a special, delicate instrument, attracting clients to listen intently and gaining their attention for prolonged times. Finally, its portability allows me to move around with it easily and remain free to both play and physically mirror my clients' responses.

Figure 3.2 The engaging effect of the flute

Case vignette: James

James, a 13-year-old boy with autism, was referred to me because of his hyperactive tendencies, and he attended 17 sessions of music therapy. What first struck me about James was how young he looked for his age, and how he spoke and sang in a childlike voice. As we began, James's love for music swiftly drew him into interaction with me, and he would be quick to respond. Before the sessions he would enter the room already singing our greeting song. However, his eagerness to play and sing caused him to rapidly become over-stimulated and overwhelmed, especially during familiar songs. Our interactions would quickly break down and fragment. His singing would become jumbled and slurred; he would become erratic, shout and squeal, play instruments deafeningly loudly and exhibit fixated movements. These expressions, along with his childlike voice, gave me a window into his feelings – muddled, 'unable' and lacking control. In fact, in the beginning phase of therapy James could only play at one volume and in one style: extremely loudly and chaotically.

Singing, especially of familiar songs, seemed to be what James enjoyed the most, probably owing to the safety it provided through structural form; yet it made him the most overwhelmed. As he became over-stimulated, I would stop using my voice and pick up the flute, responding with uncomplicated and grounding music until he calmed down. I also found that when we sang and played without lyrics, or played improvised melodies, he was able to express himself more freely. Sometimes I would hum the melody lines, which he would respond well to, but as the sessions went on, I found the flute much more effective at keeping him calm yet also interactive and expressive.

As I reviewed my video footage from the sessions, I noticed that when I played the flute James would frequently be looking out of the window in between playing. Outside there were big leafy trees, softly swaying around in the breeze. I noticed the connection between the gentle and calming nature of the flute and the way the trees moved. It seemed James had made a connection between what he could see and what he could hear, and in connecting these stimuli he was led to express himself in a more controlled manner. In these interactions James would usually choose to play the glockenspiel, a delicate instrument, mirroring the characteristics of my own music, and of the trees, and he would play it gently and sensitively. I felt that I was acting as the mouthpiece for our soothing sounds and landscape. Our interactions would usually sound conversational as we took turns to answer one another in our playing, and our motifs would be slow and reflective. By playing the flute we could bypass James's anxiety of using his voice, but retain a distinct melodic line. It acted as a voice, detached from ours, but allowed a form of expression still generated by breath, yet controlled and relaxed. I was modelling an alternative, soothing 'voice', which was mirrored by his own 'voice' on the glockenspiel. As these interactions kept occurring I slowly integrated my contribution, alternating between singing and flute. I would sing or hum in a similar pitch and gentle tone, mimicking the flute. My use of voice was not enough to overwhelm James, and so he would respond as if I was playing rather than singing. Gradually James started to use his voice too, sometimes in a shouty manner, but without escalating out of control as it once would have done. He went on to explore and develop a quieter voice over time.

In our penultimate sessions, James would still enter singing our greeting song, but with one significant difference; he sang in a softer tone and with more coherence. As I watched the video back and observed us singing 'Hello' together for the last time, I realised how much control James had gained over his vocalisations and other expressions. In our 'Hello' song James now sang a verse on his own as I accompanied him on the guitar, which had become the normal way for us to start. I realised that a reversal of roles had occurred. I didn't always need to be James's voice for him; he could now sing in a moderate and controlled manner, echoing the voice of the flute and glockenspiel, and mirroring the landscape he saw outside.

Vittorio and the magic flute

Caroline Anderson

I began learning the flute in primary school and played in various ensembles, and then went on to take a music degree with major performance on flute. After completing my degree I worked as a peripatetic woodwind teacher and conductor for several years, continuing with lessons and ensemble playing in my own time. We were encouraged to use our first-study instruments in classes and on placements on the music therapy training course. In fact, one of our first assignments was to write a letter to our first instrument, and this task reminded me of how familiar I am with this instrument, the hours I have spent practising, all the exams, concerts and recitals I have poured my energy and emotions into. As I have greater proficiency on the flute than on other instruments, I feel I can respond more effectively and have a wider musical range at my fingertips, while requiring less effort, so focusing more of my concentration on the client.

I shall now describe some casework with a man I worked with in his home environment.

Case vignette: Vittorio

Vittorio is a young man in his early 20s with a severe learning disability and epilepsy. His developmental age is limited by a genetic condition to around six months. He has no speech, but is expressive with his vocal sounds, and facial and bodily gestures. He does not seem interested in engaging with others, except for the few people closest to him, and often seems remote or in his own world, his body language curled up and defensive. Vittorio's parents and siblings have all studied music, and his father has worked as a professional opera singer; the house is full of live and recorded singing and instrumental music, and Vittorio clearly reacts when he hears music, especially the powerful sound of his father's voice.

Vittorio was referred for music therapy to encourage interaction and communication, to give him the opportunity of developing a close relationship with a new person and to encourage the use of his hands. Sessions took place weekly in Vittorio's home. After the initial assessment, music therapy sessions took a similar format each week, with a greeting song followed by improvisations on a number of different instruments, ending with a farewell song with piano accompaniment. The consistent structure and the familiar greeting and farewell songs were designed to help Vittorio orient himself to the session and help him feel comfortable and in control, as he responds well to order and routine in many aspects of his life.

Vittorio quickly showed his preference for the sounds of certain instruments, increasingly shaking his head rapidly from side to side, smiling, vocalising and screaming or chuckling when pleased. He was reluctant to play all but a few small percussion instruments himself. He seemed to particularly like loud and/or resonant sounds – for example, the singing bowl, which I would strike in response to his movements and we would then vocalise together – and also the piano and the flute. Vittorio had a real sense of anticipation, phrasing and both rhythmic and harmonic musical structure. As each cadence neared its end he shook both his head and the instrument he was playing faster and faster, tensing his body and giggling before letting out a joyful scream as the phrase resolved.

Perhaps owing to the classical music he listened to at home, especially the operatic arias of Verdi and Mozart, it felt to me that Vittorio had an affinity with the music of that genre – the predictable tonal structure and chord progressions, the dramatic variations in tempi and dynamics found in operatic music, the exaggerated rubato and drawn-out resolutions adorned with grace notes and trills. I improvised on the flute in response to Vittorio's playing, body movements and vocalisations, and I felt that when I adopted the classical, operatic style described above, Vittorio seemed particularly engaged. I found the flute was well suited to this style of playing; I was able to look at Vittorio whilst playing and move around if he adjusted his position. I could begin a note very quietly, then gradually increase the volume and amount of vibrato to create a dramatic swelling effect, or play a trill that increased in speed until the cadence came to an end with a shrill, loud final note. Vittorio vocalised frequently during these improvisations and I reflected his sounds in my playing; I found that as a wind instrument, the flute could imitate and relate well to vocal sounds.

With other clients, I found a major drawback with the flute was that I could not offer it to them to play, both because of the skill required to generate a sound, and hygiene reasons. I choose not to use it with some clients as I feel it would not be helpful to limit their choice of instrument, should they select it. At different times in music therapy sessions I like to have all kinds of instruments available, of different pitch ranges, timbres, both harmonic and melodic instruments; but as my main instrument, and for its versatile qualities, I find the flute is very useful in my work.

Vocal and verbal development work with young children

Jo Tomlinson

As a child I learnt the recorder from the age of five with a teacher in the village. I loved my recorder lessons and particularly remember the thrill of being presented with a wooden recorder, and the softer more pleasing tone of the new instrument. After several years of recorder lessons my teacher said I was ready to progress to the flute, and my parents bought me a truly appalling second-hand flute that was almost impossible to get an acceptable sound out of. After months of painful practice (and much chocolate bribery) I received a beautiful Yamaha flute for Christmas, which was an absolute joy to play in comparison. At this point my flute playing really took off and I later came to appreciate the fun of playing alongside other instrumentalists in school orchestras and ensembles.

Similarly to flautist Esther Mitchell, it was when I trained as a music therapist that I really recognised the value of the flute as a form of direct communication, an extension of my voice and an expressive outlet. The possibility of having a 'conversation' with children who would respond verbally, vocally or through singing in response to the instrument has been quite mesmerising at times, particularly when the intonation the child is using mimics exactly the pitch of the melodic line of the flute. The flute presents a non-threatening alternative to speech or the singing voice without direct demands being made of the listener, and in addition to this the sound is very often soothing, but can also be stimulating and exciting, depending on technique and musical style used by the flautist.

I have worked in special needs and mainstream schools for 20 years and regularly use my flute in sessions. The following case vignette presents work based in a large special school.

Case vignette: Adrian

Adrian was aged seven and had a diagnosis of autistic spectrum disorder (ASD) and epilepsy when I worked with him at his school. He presented as a lively boy with attention-seeking and sometimes challenging behaviour, but was generally cheerful and interactive. He loved music and musical interaction, and responded well to song structures, which directly supported his language development over a period of two years. During this time I encouraged Adrian to contribute to song phrases, with him initially singing one- and then two-word phrases, gradually building up over time the extent to which he could participate. Music therapist Lim (2012) uses similar techniques with children with ASD and claims that they can:

> Produce more advanced speech patterns by imitating musical patterns in a song which contains such elements of the speech patterns as vocabulary words, rhythm pattern, prosody, and form. The perception and production of musical patterns might positively influence the perception and production of speech in children with ASD. (Lim 2012, p.71)

With my focus for Adrian's sessions being to encourage him to engage in a co-operative and sustained interactive manner, and to develop his verbal skills, I found that musical exchanges with the flute provided a relaxing diversion from quite intensive verbal and song exchanges. When I produced the flute, Adrian would immediately make very direct eye contact and smile excitedly, imitating the exact pitch of my flute sounds when I played a familiar tune. Whereas when he was engaging in song exchanges with me, he was often fiddling with the beaters and avoiding eye contact, with the interaction with the flute he generally sustained eye contact and smiled throughout. It seemed to be something about the intensity of the sound of the flute, the 'almost vocal' quality that kept his attention fixed and his behaviour playful and non-defensive. The flute also appeared to be visually stimulating for Adrian, which encouraged him to make eye contact with me.

Imitation and reflection as part of improvisational play can be effective in engaging children in shared exchanges (Tomlinson 2012), and the flute is a very useful instrument for producing an echo effect when children are vocalising. This can give the child more of an awareness of the sound they are creating and the fact that this can be mirrored back and made 'conversational' can lead the child towards more effective interactive vocal exchanges. In this way the music therapist can use the flute to facilitate psychoanalytic theorist Daniel Stern's (1985) 'affect attunement' in which the 'feeling states' of the child are reflected back.

Sometimes the surprise element of the sound of the flute can almost catch the child unawares, momentarily reducing resistance to interactive play, and allowing a more flexible exchange to occur. This is particularly relevant in my work with children with ASD, where I have to work hard to encourage the child to engage with me. Often I find I start sessions primarily using the piano or guitar to accompany a greeting song, and then to support the child in their musical interaction. Moving on to the flute provides a fresh sound palette and a lighter, less grounded accompaniment. I often notice that the child makes the most sustained and intense eye contact at the moment that I produce my flute, as the sound and sight of the instrument gains their attention.

Case vignette: Ella

Ella was a five-year-old girl I worked with at her special school; she had profound and multiple learning disabilities and was very restricted in her movements and her capacity to respond spontaneously, as well as being visually impaired and epileptic. Ella had previously had music therapy with Amelia Oldfield (see Chapter 1 on the clarinet), and Ella's mother said that she had responded particularly well to high-pitched notes played on the clarinet, and would lift her head and engage through animated facial responses and vocal sounds. I worked with Ella for one year in individual music therapy sessions as part of a research project looking into the development of vocal and verbal skills in young children with special needs. I subsequently worked with Ella in a small music therapy group, which provided her with opportunities to engage with and listen to her peer group and me. During this time Ella consistently responded in a lively and enthusiastic way to the sound of my flute, nearly always lifting her head, smiling and making a range of humorous and communicative vocal sounds. There was undoubtedly something about the sound of a wind instrument played at high pitch that stimulated and engaged Ella. This increased her levels of interaction with me and encouraged her to use her voice in an expressive and communicative way. Ella's response to the flute was increased if I put my head and flute close to her face so that she could see the instrument and hear the sound more clearly.

Figure 3.3 Ella responding vocally to the sound of the flute

Case vignette: Group

Leo, Atlas and Mary attended a music therapy group at their mainstream primary school. Leo had speech delay and a learning disability and particularly needed support with verbal development. Atlas had difficulties with concentration and listening, and could be attention-seeking in the group. Mary had had recent health concerns with diabetes and coeliac disease with a lot of time off school, and attended the group to provide her with emotional support.

All three children responded well to a clear structure for sessions, with a focus on song material and fun musical games and interaction. We would always start the session with singing and playing, sitting in a circle. This would provide Leo with opportunities for contributing verbally during the songs, building up his song repertoire and word use from week to week. After five to ten minutes Atlas would start to become restless and need to charge around the room, so we would regularly march around the large hall singing and dancing, which is where the portability of my flute really came into its own. In addition to the fact that I could move around whilst playing the flute, the high pitch of the instrument enabled me to be heard when the children were playing loudly, but I could also reduce the volume and pitch while the children had their turn at leading the group. After initially sitting in the circle for piano- and guitar-based singing, the movement around the room supported by a new and higher-pitched melodic instrument refocused and energised the children, encouraging them to interact with each other in a way that fitted with my therapeutic objectives for each individual.

Flute characteristics in music therapy practice

The quality and range of flute sounds

Several flautists discussed the range of sounds available on the flute that can elicit a variety of responses from clients. This capacity for producing a range of sounds enables the therapist to both convey their own expression and reflect the client's emotional world. Through particular techniques flautists can also create unusual sounds that can gain the client's attention or reflect sounds that the client is making.

Portability of the flute

All the flautists referred to the ease of portability of the flute, which makes it such a convenient instrument to use in therapy sessions, both in terms of the therapist moving around the room and also in getting physically close to clients who might be limited in their mobility. In addition to this, the possibility of picking up the instrument and being able to play straight away, without having to warm it up or sort out a reed is an advantage. Flautists can also make use of the flute case, creating intrigue by being secretive about what might be hiding within.

Breathing / blowing aspects of the flute

Most of the flautists claimed that the use of breath and blowing into the flute can increase the client's awareness of their own vocal and speech production. Clients can mimic the therapist in blowing into simple wind instruments, providing them with an expressive outlet and a means of communication. In addition to this, the 'breathy' sound of flute playing can engage the client's interest and develop their use of eye contact.

Flute as an extension of the therapist's voice

All the flautists mentioned that the flute could act as an extension of the therapist's voice, whether this be through creating vocal-type sounds that the therapist was unable to produce, or through mimicking vocal sounds that were then less threatening to the client than the human voice.

Flute as imitator of client's sounds

Several flautists discussed the usefulness of the flute in its capacity to mirror the client's vocal and musical sounds, creating opportunities for intense interaction between client and therapist. Humour and playfulness within the imitative interaction also enhanced the communicative contact between therapist and client.

Flute as an object

Two flautists mentioned the fact that clients are often captivated by the sound and sight of the flute, and that the appealing nature of the instrument can entice clients into engaging in musical exchanges. There was also the element of the flute being a container for transference projections, with the capacity to absorb or reflect back to the client. One flautist mentioned the possibility of the client disliking the sound or sight of the instrument, and how this might impact on the therapeutic relationship.

Value of therapist having their own instrument

Two flautists discussed the positive impact of the therapist having their own separate instrument that the client did not have access to. This made the instrument special and separate, as well as taking the pressure off the client to play. One flautist did not use her flute in sessions with particular clients when she felt they would not be able to cope with the flute being inaccessible to them.

References

Alvin, J. (1966) *Music Therapy.* London, UK: Stainer and Bell.

Bruscia, K. (1987) *Improvisational Models of Music Therapy.* Springfield, IL: Charles C. Thomas.

Clarke, I. (2012) 'A Shifting Normality: (Extended) Flute Techniques in the 21st century.' In *A Flutist's Handbook: A Pedagogy Anthology Volume 2.* Chicago, IL: National Flute Association

Dick, R. (1986) *Tone Development Through Extended Techniques* (Revised edition). St. Louis. MO: Multiple Breath Music Company.

Gomez, L. (1997) *An Introduction to Object Relations* London, UK: Free Association Books

Lim, H. (2012) *Developmental Speech-Language Training through Music for Children with Autism Spectrum Disorder.* London, UK: Jessica Kingsley Publishers.

Pavlicevic, M. (1997) *Music Therapy in Context. Music Meaning and Relationship.* London, UK: Jessica Kingsley Publishers.

Sobey, K. and Woodcock, J. (1999) 'Psychodynamic Music Therapy.' In A. Catanach (ed.) *Process in the Arts Therapies.* London, UK: Jessica Kingsley Publishers.

Stern, D.N. (1985) *The Interpersonal World of the Infant.* London, UK: Karnac Books.

Sweeney-Brown, C. (2005) 'Music and Medicine: Music Therapy within a Medical Setting.' In M. Pavlicevic (ed.) Music Therapy in Children's Hospices. London, UK: Jessica Kingsley Publishers.

Tomlinson, J., Derrington, P. and Oldfield, A. (2012) *Music Therapy in Schools: Working with Children of all Ages in Mainstream and Special Education.* London, UK: Jessica Kingsley Publishers.

University of Oxford (2012) 'Earliest musical instruments in Europe 40,000 years ago.' *ScienceDaily* (27 May). Retrieved 21 October 2014 from www.sciencedaily. com/releases/2012/05/120527195720.htm.

Wilkinson, D. (2005) 'This Musical Life: Ty Hafan Children's Hospice – A Place For Living.' In M. Pavlicevic (ed.) *Music Therapy in Children's Hospices.* London, UK: Jessica Kingsley Publishers.

Wilson, R. (2013) *Renaissance Flutes.* Retrieved 21 October 2014 from www.oldflutes. com/renai.htm.

Winnicott, D. (1971) *Playing and Reality* London, UK: Pelican Books.

CHAPTER 4

The Cello

Contributors: Philip Hughes, Annie Tyhurst,
Catherine Warner (introduction and case vignette)
and Tessa Watson (introduction and case vignette)

Introduction

The early history of the cello is not entirely clear, though Stowell (1999, p.7) references a fresco decorating Saronno Cathedral that depicted a three-stringed cello in 1535. Early cellos were small, with a shorter neck, flat back and no end-pin. As instrument-making and playing requirements developed, the cello became the melodious instrument that we know today, with a range from bottom C (two octaves below middle C), up to the high notes of thumb position in the treble clef. The act of bowing gives many harmonically related overtones; perhaps this is one reason that the instrument elicits such a response from the listener. 'If any instrument has a deep and visceral appeal it is the cello. It reaches our emotions on a deep and profound level,' eulogised Yehudi Menuhin (1982, p.ix).

Figure 4.1 Range of the cello

After the Baroque period, the cello was adapted for the demands of greater projection in the Romantic era, with a longer neck, steel or silver-wound strings rather than sheep gut, and an end-pin to stick in the floor rather than its being supported by the player's calves. This allowed greater physical flexibility and the upper registers of the cello were increasingly used from the Classical era onwards. Dvořák and Elgar made great use of the register roughly between middle C and the two octaves above. The richness of tone quality here can be likened to the sound of a countertenor, evoking the beauty and uniqueness of this particular voice. It is technically more difficult to access the passages between E above middle C up to the following C or D because of the need for the left hand to manoeuvre around the neck; these leaps are often practised for hours by cellists, and the resulting power and beauty of the sound are very rewarding. 'The Swan' by Saint-Saëns is an example of the use of this register with the rising scales and elegant upward leaps; this should sound effortless but requires a good left-hand anchoring technique in order to allow this feeling of calm.

The cello in music therapy literature

The cello was used in pioneering music therapy practice; Juliet Alvin, an accomplished concert cellist, began her work in hospitals and schools by performing standard repertoire on the cello. She writes often in her seminal 1965 text about the impact that her cello playing had on the different children with whom she worked, about their varied responses and how they might react when given a chance to play the instrument. Alvin includes the children's comments about the music and the instrument. She writes: 'The children often call me "the music lady" or "Mrs Cello" because what seems to matter is the music and the instrument, and as a person I do try to keep in the background' (1965, p.103). Nordoff and Robbins (1971, p.24) refer to the use of a cello with one string, which the children played in their group sessions, and in the foreword to Nordoff and Robbins' book, Benjamin Britten writes: 'I long to introduce my friend Rostropovich to the one-stringed cello, to find out what *he* could do with it.'

Figure 4.2 The cello

The voice of the cello in music therapy

Tessa Watson

Since an impromptu performance in my junior school hall, when I was transfixed by the sound of the cello, I have often pondered its appeal. Machover (2007, p.14) writes of the likeness of the cello to a person in size and range. I often use my cello in therapy work, but occasionally have been reticent to introduce it because of issues such as competition, envy and distance that might be brought into the room with my large, curvy, deep-voiced instrument. In some relationships in music therapy, the cello is an object between us, which prevents the therapeutic contact from being established or from developing. From a practical viewpoint getting the cello ready to play can be a distraction; I have sometimes needed a musical response quickly and have not had time to take out my instrument, tighten my bow, and adjust the end-pin. It can also be vulnerable to damage at times.

Recently, I have used my cello in partnership with my colleague Minna Harman, a music therapist who plays the violin (alongside other instruments). Working with the music of adults with profound and multiple learning disabilities in a music therapy and sensory interaction group, we frequently play our stringed instruments together to support the vocal, percussion and soundbeam music of the group (Watson in press). Techniques such as double stopping, pizzicato, glissando and harmonics help to match the individual and idiosyncratic contributions of our group members in their singing and playing. The range of our instruments can reflect bass to soprano voices. The ability of our instruments to sustain continuous lines helps to maintain the music as 'going on being' (Winnicott 1960, p.591), which is particularly important when some members have significant sensory impairments. Along with the violin, the voice of the cello has come to represent the idea of a playful and expressive potential space for the group, making links between the 'me' and 'not me' experience (Winnicott 1971), and its particular sound is central to the culture of the group.

My relationship with music and with the cello has changed through different phases in my life. Playing in different ensembles and exploring a range of repertoire has brought me new ways of experiencing music and of experiencing my cello, and this has permeated and enriched my work as a music therapist. I have not always had my cello available in clinical work, and at these times I have used my other instruments – voice, piano, guitar and recorder; but working with my cello is for me to have all the colours and shades of emotion and different ways of speaking available. It feels like an extension of me, and I can empathise with the words of the renowned cellist Rostropovich: 'When I started learning the cello, I fell in love with the instrument because it seemed like a voice – my voice' (Rostropovich in Talbot 2007, p.24).

Case vignette: Tim

Tim, aged 40, had cerebral palsy and learning disabilities. He asked to come to music therapy and had a strong sense of what he wanted in his life. Tim was also struggling with issues of attachment and loss stemming from experiences in his early years. Before starting therapy he had been curious about my regular comings and goings into and out of the music therapy room with different people, and from the beginning our work was intensely about attachment.

In our first sessions Tim used the drum and cymbal and I used the xylophone and voice. Tim was excited by the way that he could use the instruments to control our relationship and express himself, and there were qualities of frustration and anger in his music, but I did not feel as though I was providing the musical support that he really needed. The next week he pointed to my cello case and asked 'What's that?'. I fetched my cello, fixed the end-pin, tightened the bow, and as soon as I began to play with Tim's music, using low, atonal and arrhythmic phrases, we had found the connection that we needed. The cello spoke the right language to explore and support Tim's feelings. As the therapy work developed, the cello supported Tim's expressions of anger and frustration, and I used techniques such as double stopping and tremolo to match the drama of his playing. The cello took a supporting line as Tim's music became more confident and individualised, with the deep notes being important in connecting with Tim's gender and identity.

Over time the cello seemed to help Tim to express himself freely, as though its sound provided him with a sense of security and reassurance. When our work ended because Tim moved away with his family, we wrote a song together about this, with the cello providing a sonorous bass line as Tim and I sang over the top. In this work, the cello was able to capture and respond to many different qualities and emotions, and its voice played a key role in Tim's therapy.

The versatility of the cello

Catherine Warner

I believe that one of the most compelling properties of the cello is the great beauty of the sound. When writing this I reflected on how often, when I have told someone what I play, they have said 'I *love* the sound of the cello'. As with other bowed stringed instruments, the acoustic profiles of the notes are complex, with similarities to the acoustic profiles of the human voice. The experience of creating sound with a bow across a string drawing out the sound is often relaxing and has physiological effects. Although the pitch range is not quite low enough for comparisons with vibro-acoustic therapy, where the pitches are around 20 Hz, those receiving music therapy with the cello have often reported that bowing on the lowest strings has made them feel more relaxed.

Aspects of the physicality of the cello can be striking. The player must sit down because of the size of the instrument. This has implications for therapeutic practice, particularly if a client wanders around and needs the therapist to respond quickly in a physical way to keep them safe. But it is physically easier as a player to accommodate the cello than the violin as the player does not need to counteract gravity to hold it. Using a relaxed arm weight can produce a resonant sound and clients who have never tried a cello have been able to manage a sonorous sound easily and independently. Symbolically the cello can evoke the sense of the instrument being rather like a person, especially with its curves. The usable pitch range is over six octaves, invoking the depth of a bass voice or a high soprano. The potential for the evocation of male and female associations can be helpful in music therapy.

Playing the cello can allow a small child to make deep and profound music. The sound can be created easily with the bow by a child standing in front of the cello, holding the bow at each end and bowing on the strings whilst the therapist sits supporting the weight of the cello and stopping the strings to change pitch. This shared playing can encourage intimate shared contact but also requires some delicate negotiation. As with other bowed instruments, there is the capacity to make crunching and squeaking noises, which again could be quite therapeutically useful if made intentionally, but if unintentional could cause frustration or even distress.

With the cello there is the possibility of playing in harmony with four strings. Some of the cello suites of Bach are able to exploit this, in particular the sixth suite in D major, which was originally written for a five-stringed cello with an extra E string. Harmonically the cello can be used a little like a guitar with the cellist plucking three- or four-note chords. It is also possible to create a walking bass that is reminiscent of a double bass, albeit less sonorous. This illustrates the range and versatility of the instrument in a therapeutic setting: a cellist can be a harmonic accompanist, singer (bass, tenor, alto or soprano) or drummer, using the instrument as a resonant sounding box.

In Baroque music the cello often takes the role of continuo in partnership with the keyboard, such as the harpsichord or organ. Here the cello reinforces the line of the keyboard music, and the keyboard provides the harmonic structure. In this music the harmony and shape of the bass line are symbiotic, inseparable, so that the two instruments are thought of as one in the form of a continuo. The continuo provides support for the voices or instruments above, and the bass line (often dynamic and involving many leaps) can propel the music forward. A steadying pulse from the continuo allows the singer to move around the tempo in an expressive and fluid way.

This aspect of cello playing has been an important part of shaping my own musical identity, as I have tried to develop an understanding of how providing a musical framework can facilitate expression and create recognisable boundaries. I have found it a pleasure to take on this role, and there is a parallel with the therapist's function of punctuating, framing, holding, returning and responding to the music of the client. So, for example, in a Passion by J.S. Bach we as continuo players have been able to interpret the very recognisable perfect cadence as anger, or as if bereft, in response to the sung role of the Evangelist, using only differences in attack and timing. The ensuing silence (especially in a resonant acoustic like a church) allows the feeling to be experienced and held before Bach's music moves on to the next aria or chorus.

Case vignette: Nico

Nico was a young man who had had a psychotic breakdown and had lost his social confidence. He self-referred with the support of his case co-ordinator and initially attended individual music therapy sessions. Following these sessions he joined a weekly music therapy group taking place in the community. Nico had been a confident bass guitar player and decided to bring his own instrument to the group.

As Nico arrived he seemed to walk only in straight lines, staring ahead once seated as if existing within a tunnel. He plugged in his guitar and began to improvise a rhythmic bass line, repeating this many times with little immediate rhythmic connection or reference to the music already being improvised by the group, again reinforcing this worry of how to 'be'. Two existing group members, sympathetic to his newness and vulnerability, adapted their darabouka drum and xylophone playing to attempt to accommodate his pulse.

Rather than being drawn to the piano to connect with this, I took the cello and plucked pizzicato notes at the cadence points to reinforce fragments of the bass line, supporting the unsteady beat Nico was creating. It felt invasive to play more of the bass line, and his music felt too fragile for any kind of counter melody at this point. He appeared to notice the way I had joined him and although he did not turn his head towards me, he smiled a little. I felt I could start to reinforce his playing and connect more with him through using the cello body as a drum, knocking the wood at its most resonant point, again only at the cadences but increasingly playing longer phrases. Nico's rhythm quickly gained a kind of muscularity and it felt possible to resume the plucked rhythmic cello line in a similar register, but with different melodic contours, as a kind of partner bass line. This gave the other group members confidence to play more creatively and the music seemed more relaxed, with Nico and the group providing each other with mutual musical support.

Nico began to elaborate his line with a few quicker fill notes and introduced some chromaticism. I felt excited by his creativity, but held this in check, staying instead with the same tempo and intensity before making the significant step of playing with the bow, which then introduced a more intimate and direct sound to the group. Nico continued playing in a similar vein, negotiating an ending with the whole group a few minutes later. My co-therapist caught my eye at this point, as if briefly celebrating a surprisingly sensitive demonstration of Nico's musical and social self. Nico said 'It was good' and turned slightly to look at other group members for the first time, at which point some of them complimented him on his playing. After listening to the group discussion he started playing a faster, confident new bass line, more elaborate and unusual in terms of phrase structure, and this was immediately joined melodically by the co-therapist on melodica in very much the same way as the bowed cello partnership at the end of the previous improvisation.

I was grateful that I had the cello as a resource; the versatility of the sound and role had allowed Nico to explore a gradual change of relationships within the music, which enabled him to connect more closely with individual group members, and to engage in subsequent discussion.

A cello in the room

Annie Tyhurst

At the beginning of my music therapy training in Bristol we were encouraged to reflect on our musical identities and early personal music histories. I had chosen to learn the cello because I had tried it when two student teachers brought their instruments into my primary school class. One had a flute, and another a cello. My father, a lover of classical music, encouraged me, enthused by his interest in Jacqueline Du Pré and the Elgar Cello Concerto.

It is fascinating to consider our musical histories, our decisions for selecting a particular instrument, our personal stories of success and failure, our reasons for becoming music therapists and our choosing whether or not to use our own instruments in therapy.

The cello, as a therapy instrument of course, features significantly in the early beginnings of the music therapy profession. I can recall being told a story about music therapist Juliette Alvin bashing on the door of Holloway Prison, demanding to be let in to play music for the inmates. This metaphoric door was to open out a whole future for the music therapy profession.

For Alvin (who was a brilliant concert cellist), the therapist's own musical instrument represented a container of projected feelings, a safe object that formed an intrinsic part of the development of relationships. Her method of 'empathic improvisation', a receptive technique involving the therapist's attempt to deeply connect through improvised playing, was a means of further trust building (Wigram, Pedersen and Bonde 2002). I have used this way of working in different settings, particularly in end-of-life care, in hospitals and with those who may have profound and multiple learning difficulties. Rather than working with music technologies, I have found it simpler to spend time sitting with and playing for clients.

An essential competence of a music therapist is to be able to play to a professional standard. Just being with or accompanying a client necessitates a secure technique with knowledge of a diverse repertoire. The therapist tunes in at a deep level. We have travelled for so long with our own instruments, and therefore feel connected and able to use this extension of self, striving to be totally in the moment with our client.

The cello in the therapy room creates a strong, human-sized presence. Its tonal range encompasses bass to soprano and its timbre can be one of great warmth. The cellist Steven Isserlis calls it 'Everyone's favourite instrument'. The possibilities for creativity are huge. I can remember being given the title of Carnival for the improvisation during my music therapy audition and deciding to exploit the cello's capabilities fully: bowing, plucking, playing *sul ponticello, col legno*, and finishing with tapping samba rhythms on its body.

Transporting the cello along with a trolley-load of instruments and a keyboard has not been one of the more rewarding aspects of being a community-based therapist. However, I am lucky having a second cello for work, so I do not have to consider the implications for sharing a beloved or particularly valuable instrument.

Case vignette: Adam

I used my cello in music therapy sessions with a ten-year-old boy called Adam, who had serious issues relating to his self-image and self-esteem. The sessions took place in his mainstream primary school. We improvised together, with him playing the cello and me supporting on keyboard. Playing the open strings (C-G-D-A) is easy, giving scope to many different chord combinations. Near the end of our time working together he asked me if he could play for his classmates. I struggled with the performance issue here but checked with his mother and teacher, and finally agreed at his insistence. His whole class came into the space and listened intently whilst he played a rock-style ballad, delivered slowly and assuredly. At the end of his performance the class inevitably applauded and I could see the 'big boys' in the class high-five-ing him. It was an empowering moment for him.

Case vignette: Sushanta

Sushanta took the cello. There was an unusual quietude in the room as I helped position it for him in a suitable playing position. I handed him the bow, his fingers grasping the end. Inside I noticed my feelings of anxiety, running a list of 'What if…?' questions. The main one, of course, was whether he would drop the cello. He didn't. He started to play, drawing the bow slowly and carefully across the D string, his head cocked, listening with a sense of wonder. I moved away towards the keyboard to give him more space, and we began together.

It was one of those magical moments in therapy. I had been working with 13-year-old Sushanta for several weeks as part of my clinical work as tutor for The Music Therapy Trust in New Delhi, India. He had seemed drawn to the sound of the cello when I had played it for him, always listening so intently. Diagnosed with autistic spectrum disorder, Sushanta was non-verbal and had a curiosity for sounds but was socially very isolated. He seemed close to his mother, who worked in the large centre for children with autism. We had been exploring instruments together, seeing if music therapy might be a way into his world.

The decision to hand the cello to him took a leap of trust, but was also an acknowledgement of where our relationship had got to. Here was a young man with potential, understanding, cognitive skills, emotional sensitivity, the ability to form relationships and sufficient motor skills to manage a complex physical task. It felt risky (it would have been impossible to get the cello fixed in India), but that moment is still imprinted on my mind.

Perhaps it had been a rather strange decision to take a cello all the way to India? No extra seat paid for on the plane for this cello; just packing it up in a hard case, sticking 'Fragile' all over it, and hoping for the best in airport baggage handling. Nevertheless, when I arrived in Delhi it felt like a familiar friend, one that had been with me for nearly 40 years.

Figure 4.3 Sushanta explores the cello

Associations with the cello

Philip Hughes

My first instrument is the violin, followed by the flute, but I took up
the cello a few years ago because I loved the tone. I find it interesting
to reflect on how I use the different instruments, and particularly
how I vary what I use as my main instrument in music therapy. I
usually come back to the violin or the flute, but I will go through
a period of using the cello, guitar, piano or alto flute, and I find
that is a useful way of refreshing my musical ideas. I have different
histories of learning this range of instruments; two relatives gave
me my first proper violin and flute when I was in my early teens,
so I associate them with those people. Also I initially taught myself
the flute, only later having several years of lessons, and I have less
experience of playing the flute in formal settings, such as orchestras.
The motivation for later taking up the cello was purely an impulse
because I related to the tone of the instrument, and my aim in
having lessons was to become good enough to attempt the Bach
cello suites. I believe it helps to be aware of these associations and
how they might influence the music we play with clients. Hopefully,
as therapists, we can separate them from our experience of a client
in a session, and find a way of playing music that relates to them.

I am still more confident technically on the violin and flute, but
I have used the cello in music therapy with two particular client
groups. Working with people with profound and multiple learning
disabilities, I found some clients responded well to the cello, as I
could find a pitch and tone that matched their vocal sounds almost
exactly, with a warm resonance. I would be playing a phrase in
response to their vocal sound, and waiting for them to respond in
turn. It was often difficult to tell whether the client was aware of
the fact that I was responding to them and trying to build a musical
conversation. As the therapy progressed, I became more confident
that they were aware of the interaction, and responding in turn.

In contrast, I have also used the cello in some work in mental
health settings, mostly secure settings. Where the clients are more
unpredictable, in an acute ward for example, I would feel more
reluctant to take my cello into the session; I would usually take my
flute and violin, but if there was a concern about a particular client

who might become aggressive, I might only take the flute, as that is obviously the easiest to move quickly out of harm's way. However, where I have known the clients for longer, I do feel able to bring the cello, and I have found that they are interested in the instrument and appreciate the different sonority.

Using any orchestral instrument in music therapy is likely to bring up the issue of using a valuable possession of one's own. Each therapist will carry out the risk assessment differently, and address in their own way the question of whether to let clients try their instrument. I have generally been happy to let clients try the violin and cello, under supervision, and based on my feeling for how they will react. I would also in principle let a client try my flute, subject to disinfecting before and after, but this is often a disappointment as the client then finds they cannot get a sound out of the instrument. In contrast, the clients are often pleased with the results of playing open strings on the violin or cello, perhaps even more so on the cello as it doesn't sound as scratchy. When I am playing the cello myself, I find I use it to provide vigorous rhythmic bass accompaniments, if the client is playing a drum or singing. I do play melodic figures as well, but I personally find playing very lively melodies easier on the violin, and that is at least partly due to my greater expertise on that instrument.

I would speculate that the low pitch of the cello appeals to some of the male clients because it matches their voice, and can make a vigorous, powerful sound; especially as many of the anti-psychotic drugs have side-effects that mean their masculine potency is compromised. This kind of speculation perhaps has something in common with Mary Priestley's writings (Priestley 1994), where she interpreted clients' choices of instrument, for instance saying that choosing the biggest drum might represent identifying with one's father. I think such choices are interesting: there is presumably a wish to make a particular kind of sound, either powerful or tentative, and that reflects something of the client's state of mind. However, these choices are also very much overlaid by the cultural perceptions surrounding the instruments; for example, a common complaint in my mental health work is that the percussion instruments are childish because they remind clients of school music-making. An orchestral instrument also clearly has its own associations for the client, possibly reinforcing the differences between themselves and the therapist, who has had the aptitude and opportunity to learn a technically demanding instrument. On the other hand, I have often found that if I can trust the client to try playing my violin or cello, they appreciate that trust and like being able to play what is clearly a 'proper' instrument.

Cello characteristics in music therapy practice

The quality of sound of the cello

All the cellists described the beautiful and sonorous tone of the cello that can 'reach the emotions' and have a profoundly relaxing or soothing effect on clients. The sound of the cello seems to be immediately appealing and accessible to a wide range of clients. One cellist described the cello as providing 'all the colours and shades of emotion' during therapy work.

The range of sounds available on the cello

Several cellists mentioned the wide range of the cello, which spans six octaves and can be used to respond to both high and low voices in the therapy context. There is also the possibility of using techniques such as double stopping, pizzicato, glissando and harmonics. The cello was described as having the capacity to provide a bass line, a harmonic accompaniment, a vocal line, or a percussive accompaniment (through drumming on the body of the cello).

The human size and shape of the instrument

Several of the cellists compared the shape and size of the instrument with a human body, which could be comforting and also absorb the transference from clients. The large size of the instrument, however, had the potential to create an obstacle between the client and therapist.

The masculine/feminine aspects of the cello

The cello was described as having a masculine sound and appearance that could be useful in responding to the voices of male clients; one cellist described the cello as representing both masculine (large) and feminine (curvy) characteristics that could provide useful associations as part of the therapeutic process.

Issues in relation to portability

The cello is a large, heavy instrument, and that has been an issue for some of the cellists in getting the instrument to the music therapy room. The need to sit at the cello can also be a disadvantage if the therapist has to make sudden movements to keep the clients safe. Several cellists mentioned the anxiety associated with protecting their instrument from unpredictable clients. In addition to this, the preparation of the instrument could inhibit the capacity of the therapist to respond spontaneously to clients.

Accessibility to clients

Two of the cellists described the way in which they had encouraged the client to play their cello, and felt that a positive element of the instrument was its accessibility. The fact that the client can sit down to play and create an acceptable or even beautiful sound instantly is an advantage. One cellist felt that there could be issues of envy if the client felt that they could not produce as beautiful a sound as the therapist.

The capacity to create bass line accompaniments

Two of the cellists wrote about the possibility of supporting the client musically through creating a secure bass line accompaniment on the cello, which could either have a steadying effect or propel the music forwards.

References

Alvin, J. (1965) *Music for the Handicapped Child*. Oxford, UK: Oxford University Press.

Machover, T. (2007) 'My Cello.' In T. Sherry (ed.) *Evocative Objects We Think With*. Cambridge, MA: MIT Press.

Menuhin, Y. (1982) 'Introduction.' In W. Pleeth *Cello*. London, UK: Macdonald and Company

Nordoff, P. and Robbins, C. (1971) *Therapy in Music for Handicapped Children*. London, UK: Victor Gollancz.

Priestley, M. (1994) *Essays on Analytical Music Therapy*. Phoenixville, PA: Barcelona Publishers.

Stowell, R. (1999) *The Cambridge Companion to the Cello*. Cambridge, UK: Cambridge University Press.

Talbot, J. (2007) 'Shaping a Century' *The Strad* (December), pp.23–26.

Watson, T. (in press) '"The World is Alive!" Music Therapy with Adults with Learning Disabilities.' In J. Edwards (ed.) *The Handbook of Music Therapy* Oxford, UK: Oxford University Press.

Wigram, T., Pedersen, I.N and Bonde, L.O (2002) *A Comprehensive Guide to Music Therapy*. London, UK: Jessica Kingsley Publishers.

Winnicott, D.W. (1960) 'The theory of the parent–infant relationship.' *International Journal of Psychoanalysis 41*, 585–595.

Winnicott, D.W. (1971) *Playing and Reality*. London, UK: Pelican Books.

CHAPTER 5

The Trumpet and the Flugelhorn

Contributors: Philippa Derrington,
Mike Gilroy (introduction and case vignettes),
Shlomi Hason and Concetta Tomaino

Introduction

The trumpet

The original form of the trumpet was the animal horn, which was played by the Romans and, further back in history, by the Ancient Egyptians and Greeks (Monks 2014). One of the earliest examples was discovered in the tomb of the Pharaoh Tutankhamun, and is thought to date from circa 1350 BC. As well as animal horns, shells were also played, and these early forms of instruments could be heard over longer distances than the human voice.

Over the centuries the horn acquired a more recognisable structure with the advent of copper and brass. We might consider its simplest form to be similar to what we know as the post horn – a single piece of tubing with a specifically moulded mouthpiece and a fluted bell area. Historically it was used to signal the arrival of the post, thus taking on a communicative role within the community.

The long, straight design of the post horn was not easily transportable or playable, hence the 14th and 15th centuries witnessed the evolution of a more folded form (Estrella 2014). With the arrival of this new malleable method of constructing and designing, came new variations of brass instruments. The early French horn, trumpet and bugle all began to realise their distinctive and individual identities, particularly with subsequent features of additional tubing and slides, and their characteristic roles within different musical cultures. The new design was compact and simple, and although harmonically limited, served a specific, functional role within its military milieu.

The evolution of the piston valve in the early 19th century continued to influence new designs. One of these was the cornet, developed originally in France. While the trumpet was widely used for fanfares, the cornet with its more mellow sound, was used for the melodic parts of orchestral works. In the UK the cornet was used more in the brass band movement, which had its roots around the same period, probably as a direct consequence of the new and varied designs. Brass bands were initially set up to consolidate industrial workforces and communities, partly as a social or competitive enterprise, but also by philanthropists, employers and companies as a means of occupying otherwise potentially misused leisure times of employees.

Although the trumpet had begun to be introduced into orchestral works during the 17th and 18th centuries, the introduction of more functional, reliable and accurate valve mechanisms that increased harmonic possibilities resulted in the trumpet broadening its appeal and potential. And it has continued to become more adaptable. The first half of the 20th century witnessed the arrival of such pioneers as Louis Armstrong, Dizzy Gillespie, Miles Davis and Hugh Masakela (Clark 2013) and their role within the early jazz movement. This fresh genre of music was played in a much less conventional style, using techniques such as 'growling' and vibrato. In addition to these techniques, numerous arrays of mutes were employed, for example, harmon, straight, cup, wah-wah, etc., offering a totally new sound.

In addition to the techniques used in jazz, double- and triple-tonguing were much utilised in brass bands and classical music. This type of technique is where the tongue is manipulated in a controlled, rapid up and down movement, and specifically where the written work is of numerous notes needing to be played at a fast tempo, and where otherwise it would be difficult to attain an accurate performance by the orthodox single-tonguing technique.

Figure 5.1 The range of the trumpet is around three octaves

The piccolo trumpet, with up to half the amount of tubing, is able to achieve greater clarity and a higher range in comparison with the standard trumpet. Most trumpets are Bb instruments, although it is common for American orchestral trumpets to be in C. The vast majority have three valves, though some models also have finger slides linked to the first and third valves, which when triggered alter any harmonic discrepancies that might occur when both of these valves are depressed simultaneously.

The flugelhorn

The term *Flug* – a German noun for wing, flight or flank – is the initial clue to its classification, linking in with the flank of an army and military connotations. Its closest relative in terms of its physical appearance is the trumpet, i.e. the instrument is held horizontally away from the lips. However, the flugel has a deeper mouthpiece, a wider tubular diameter, and similarly a wider bell area, the fluted area where the sound comes out. Because of this bell the sound of the flugel has a much more mellow timbre, less harsh than the trumpet, although having a similar range, but noticeably clearer and more pleasing in its lower range. Being part of the horn family, although it is held horizontally, its idiosyncratic timbre sits somewhere between that of the trumpet, tenor horn and French horn.

One of the features of the flugelhorn is its position in the world of brass bands, there being one in each brass band ensemble. Although certainly not exclusively so, the prevalence of brass bands is notably more apparent in industrialised communities in the UK, none less so than in the north of England. It can be seen then that the use of the flugelhorn is potentially regional, even before considering any earlier analysis of its historical roots in Germany.

For many people, including those from a musical background, the only awareness they have of the flugelhorn might be through the medium of film and theatre, notably the principal feature of the musical and film *Brassed Off.* Tara Fitzgerald plays the character of Gloria Mullins, who has been sent to the town where she grew up to assess the profitability of the local pit. She was initially greeted with scepticism and even prejudice, partly as she was perceived as an outsider from the South, but also as a female in a highly male-dominated domain. Being a proficient flugelhorn player, she eventually became an intricate member of the failing brass band, initiating a sense of purpose and aiming to breathe new life into a declining and demoralised community adapting to industrial and demographic change.

Figure 5.2 The flugelhorn

Brassed on!

Mike Gilroy

Although my primary instrument is the piano, I began playing the flugelhorn at the age of 11, when I moved to secondary education. At the time there were a number of schools and music centres that had brass and/or concert bands (the latter consisting of both brass and reed instruments). The school I attended did have an established concert band that had a twinning association with a similar band in Mönchengladbach in what was then West Germany. The regional cultural influence and prevalence of brass bands undoubtedly influenced the provision of instruments within the school, and thus the inclusion and opportunities for students to progress into the school band. During my young adulthood I continued to play the flugelhorn, and subsequently during my music therapy training through to the present time.

It could be argued that traditionally music therapy has not embraced the resource of brass instruments; this was certainly reflected in my own experience during music therapy training. The cohort of students on my course ten years ago consisted of predominantly string and woodwind players. Although this balance may currently be changing, it might reflect the traditional demographic and initially gender-biased and culturally influenced background of those practising in music therapy.

Furthermore, and interestingly, a significant proportion of my current clinical work is with young people and families from a cultural background other than Western Europe, and particularly from Asia and the Middle East. This demographic change, which is increasingly evident in many parts of the UK, may indeed provide further topical debate upon the necessity to continue to develop music therapy approaches that might be more relevant to this changing multi-cultural demography.

Instruments that require an individual to breathe in a specific and controlled way in order to produce a desired sound would suggest that the resulting sound would probably be a highly individualised tone, coupled with great expressivity. This is equally true if we consider that two pianists, for example, will create a very different sound on the same piano, owing to variations in their individual playing styles. However, it is felt that instruments that necessitate a blowing technique, and hence create a single melodic sound, can be likened to the highly intimate concept of the voice, with its idiosyncratic interactive force. Not only the sound that is created, but also the facial dynamics and body posture associated with this technique, surely add weight to this theory.

I have been fortunate to have practised in a varied array of environments and client groups, but currently the majority of my practice finds me working with neonates, children and young adults in Martin House Hospice, as well as a number of special educational needs (SEN) schools in the north of England. I often work with different members of families in the hospice, and the children I work with in all my clinical settings have a wide variation in abilities and needs, ranging from those who have very complex medical and/or social, emotional and psychological needs, through those who have mainly physical disabilities, to those who are diagnosed as having autistic spectrum disorder.

It is not only the sound of the instrument that appeals to the young people with whom I work. There are visual and palpable attributes that play an important part in the wider sensory experience. The flugelhorn is certainly not without its own idiosyncratic appeal and personality; for example, one can tap on the brass, observe and explore the movement of valves and slides, feel the vibrations of the instrument, create a range of pitch and dynamics, as well as relate to the breathing of the client with the bell of the horn.

Certainly those with a degree of visual impairment may be attracted to the bright shiny silver surface of the instrument, not only reflecting the daylight or artificial light, but also acting as a type of mirror at times. The silky smoothness of the curves, often cool to touch when first taken out of its case, adds to the wider sensory experience – particularly for little hands and feet.

Figure 5.3 Engaging in a mirroring interactive exchange with the flugelhorn
      Figure 5.4 Exploring through sound and resonance

Case vignette: Tim

Around seven years ago I began working at an SEN school that provided education for children from the age of three to 19 years.

The school had a history of music therapy provision, which was well received by both teaching and management teams.

One student who I began to work with seven years ago was an 11-year-old boy called Tim, a colourful character diagnosed as having autistic spectrum disorder, and who displayed a definite interest in music. His musical interest had been supported both in school and by his family, who were themselves eager and proactive in striving to have music therapy written into his statement of needs. I believe he had access to an electric guitar and drum kit at home, one of which belonged to his brother.

Tim had previously had music therapy with a colleague and it was initially a challenge for him to adjust to both the change of therapist and range of musical instruments that were available to him. Many music therapists incorporate the reliable and valuable media of piano, guitar and percussion, but there is an array of other instruments that we also use in our practice. I increasingly use digital technologies in my work. Alongside these, and avoiding any narcissistic spotlight on my efforts on percussion and voice – (the latter often receiving satirised comment but never rewarded with an accolade!) – is my flugelhorn.

Initially Tim appeared to tolerate most of the instruments or activities that I included, as well as initiating his own ideas and style. However, after a few weeks he noticeably began to respond negatively when I took the flugelhorn out of its hard case, and gradually even the sight of the case in the room would make him anxious. Eventually I had to make a mental note to make sure the case was not visible in the room before Tim entered for his session, particularly if I had been using the flugelhorn in an earlier session with another child. It felt as if Tim had established an important boundary, and the security that this provided him with enabled us to connect and establish a successful therapeutic relationship.

Our work together continued with absent brass, the musical content being based around the use of guitar, piano, and tuned and untuned percussion. The approach was largely improvisational, often with a strongly rhythmic emphasis. Tim often chose familiar instruments and initiated repetitive themes.

I have found when working with children with autistic spectrum disorder, that any changes often need to be introduced in a gradual and guarded but determined manner. It would be surprising for a new idea to be positively received at its inception. Tim gradually became more trusting of me and receptive to new ideas. We used to spend the majority of the time sharing a guitar, exploring as many ways as possible of creating sound from it both together and independently. One of the techniques that evolved during this period, and one that I have continued to use with many other clients, is a special Hitchcock-like nail-scraping experience along the strings of the guitar.

Around 18 months into our work I felt that Tim and I had developed a constructive therapeutic relationship, and even on the occasions when Tim was reportedly struggling in his normal classroom environment, and/or anxious about his respite stays away from home, he would consistently use our sessions appropriately to express himself, exerting his own personality within a shared environment.

I felt it was important to keep challenging Tim by broadening his receptive experience. Having established a trusting relationship with him, I decided to reintroduce the flugelhorn to see if he could begin to tolerate its presence. I began by simply placing the flugel case in the room, but at the opposite end of our usual working area. For a number of weeks Tim would display his anxiety, by screwing up his face and vocalising with a sound that clearly showed his disquiet, and after a while I would verbally acknowledge this, and move the case outside the door. This process continued for a number of weeks until Tim gradually became used to having the case in the room.

In subsequent sessions Tim developed the capacity to accept the flugelhorn's physical presence in the room, and eventually I removed it from its case. Its physical and structural attributes were the way in to a greater exploration. Just as we had explored the guitar together, the physical movement of the valves of the flugelhorn and other palpable aspects of the instrument allowed for in-depth exploration, weeks before any sound was introduced.

On the occasions when Tim would show that he wanted to put the flugelhorn away, I began to encourage him to help me return it to its case, so that he felt in control of the flugelhorn's final movement for that particular session.

Even with increasing familiarity and tolerance, the production of sound was always going to be potentially traumatic for Tim. However, I found that by singing into the bell area of the horn and getting Tim to copy me, it felt like a safe route into using the instrument for its intended purpose. Having a shared understanding not only of levels of trust but also of humour, this became a fun, as well as a safe, approach. If anything it felt strangely apt to sing into the bell, as this is indeed the authentic area of sound emission under normal circumstances! This was a great foundation for further sound exploration, which subsequently moved on to singing through the mouthpiece, leading to eventually blowing in a conventional manner.

My fears about Tim having a negative reaction to the horn were indeed realised, but with routine persistence each additional obstacle, whether it be pitch variation, volume, intensity, pressure or anticipation of the impending sound, added value to the broadened experience and levels of tolerance. Indeed, it felt as though what had initially been barely tolerable became the centre of Tim's interest.

Over the subsequent sessions Tim's interest in our sessions began to revolve more around the flugelhorn than anything else, to the point where he now actively seeks out the case and feels a sense of responsibility to bring it to me, interestingly always expecting me to open the catches. This might be a result of the discipline that I do try to promote in sessions, but may be as a sign of the respect that Tim offers the flugelhorn itself.

As a teenager who was sometimes unpredictable as well as over-exuberant, Tim was able to engage with me consistently with gentleness and sensitivity. For example, if I was blowing the horn, he would relish the opportunity, whenever I allowed him, to alter the sound by either pressing the valves or cupping his hand like a mute into the bell area. Indeed, the flugelhorn has undoubtedly been a major catalyst for a greater shared interaction in our work. This interaction has evolved through exploring the production of sound, but also through using and developing his verbal skills and discussing the names of various components – e.g. valves, mouthpiece and silver. In addition to this Tim has been able to control the dynamics verbally and with the height and direction of his hand – e.g. high, low, loud, quiet, fast and slow.

An amalgamation of local schools and the subsequent pooling of resources unearthed a number of brass instruments that had been languishing in another school's storeroom. I discovered a very tired looking trumpet and a trombone that had a slide that was totally alien to the main body of the instrument! By now, Tim's interest and confidence had totally turned full circle, and he was extremely enthusiastic to explore these new instruments as much as possible.

For the past two years Tim has progressed into a regular small music therapy group, consisting of one of his peers, his teaching assistant and myself, and while at times his increased confidence results in his being slightly intimidating, bossy or provocative, it is clear that he now relishes the opportunity to use the flugelhorn, or trombone. Tim has gained an effective technique in the use of the flugelhorn's mouthpiece. The resulting level of confidence has undoubtedly helped Tim progress on to other instruments, including the trombone, and he also regularly initiates new ideas, such as encouraging the group to play together in didgeridoo improvisations.

The trumpet shall sound

Concetta Tomaino

I can honestly say that the trumpet is the reason I became a music therapist. Although I had studied accordion for many years during elementary school, I had no plans to continue with music, having my mind firmly set on studying science and playing basketball when I entered high school. I was very upset when I did not make the final selection for the high school basketball team. My friends, who were all in the concert band, tried to recruit me because I could read music, but I had no desire to start another instrument. To maintain my accordion skills, I was still practising at least an hour a day and several hours on the weekends. My friends persisted. What would it be like to play in an ensemble? What instrument would I choose?

When I was seven years old I heard Louis Armstrong and Count Basie perform at a pre-Disney type theme park. The trumpet had such a marvellous sound but I could not imagine playing it. Now, given the chance to join the band, I thought it would be fun to learn the trumpet. The band director was not too thrilled about a girl trumpeter, so challenged me to play 'Military Escort', a popular fanfare march, on the mouthpiece alone. If I did well, then, and only then, would he let me play the trumpet. The trumpet, I soon discovered, gets its sound by the musician vibrating his or her lips into a cupped mouthpiece. The looseness or tightness of the lips provides the register of the tone, while the three valves, in various combinations, provide the exact pitch. I did so well with his challenge that he gave me a brand new cornet, and within a year I was not only playing solos but performing in brass quintets and school musicals with the band. The bandmaster had a way of challenging us to hear the music without being stuck on the notes alone. He would also often make us switch lesson books with other instruments to force us to transpose the notes. The trumpet is keyed in Bb, which means a written C on the trumpet music sheet is actually a Bb if played on the piano. For the trumpet to play along with a piano score the musician has to read a full note above. Without knowing it we were learning to transpose music and build our listening skills as part of our routine band exercises.

Eventually I made the decision to transfer from science to a music degree. I was playing with every ensemble possible, small string ensembles, jazz bands, musical theatre, chamber orchestra and opera. I had no idea what I was going to do after graduation. I did not want to teach music but now was addicted to it. I had originally gone to college to become a physician and felt guilty that I was not pursuing a career in a helping profession. During the winter break I was skimming through some old magazines and came across an advertisement entitled 'A Career in Music Therapy'. My heart started racing; was there such a field as music therapy? Could I help someone with music? I found out that there was a music therapy master's course in New York. When I met with the head of the programme and I told her my major instrument was the trumpet, she said 'There are no music therapists that play trumpet – what else do you play?' I told her I had several years of piano as part of my college studies and many years of accordion, which I had now stored away in a closet, having become more involved with the trumpet. She told me to dust off the accordion and come prepared to play it as well as the piano.

Whilst carrying out my music therapy training I secured an internship at a nursing home in Brooklyn. At this point I was playing basic guitar and piano during our music therapy classes and these were my instruments at the time I started this internship.

Case vignette: Martha

During my first week at the Wartburg Home in East New York, I was introduced to Martha, the resident pianist, who led all the musical activities at the home. Martha was 90 years old. When I was introduced as the music therapist, Martha said 'This I got to see' and she didn't want anything to do with me or my therapy sessions. The Wartburg was an interesting place as it grew out of a German retirement community of attached one-bedroom residences and a chapel. As the residents started to age, a nursing home was built at the other end, forming a courtyard between the 'well and the infirm' both physically and metaphorically. I found that the well seniors did not want to participate with or have anything to do with their 'sick' friends in the nursing home. Martha was particularly distant. My work responsibilities were part of the home's activities programme and as such I had to cover other programmes as well as work every Sunday.

Sunday services were held in the chapel – a quaint wooden structure – and Martha was the church organist. One Sunday I brought my trumpet in as I had a rehearsal immediately after work. Martha was already in the chapel and I asked if I could play the hymns with her. Martha looked sceptical, but because I could transpose I easily sight-read the music over her shoulder. She was impressed and soon I became her regular 'music assistant'. The trumpet was my way of getting connected with her and sharing music. We started what she called weekly musicals; I would give her room to direct me and arrange when I should play the melody. Although I didn't think of my rehearsals with Martha as music therapy sessions, in retrospect they definitely were. Martha, who had been very judgemental and distant, was now becoming open to new possibilities.

While I was working at the nursing home in Brooklyn, Martha had a stroke and was paralysed on her right side. She was bed-bound, extremely sad and refused to eat. Because we had developed such a close relationship she let me feed her but kept lamenting that her music was over. I brought tone chimes and placed them on her bed table to encourage her to play the chimes while I played 'our songs' on my trumpet. Her motivation and spirit slowly came back and eventually she was able to get out of bed. We returned to our weekly musicals, but this time I played the right hand of the music on the piano while she played the left.

Although I enjoyed working at this facility, the drive from the Bronx to Brooklyn was very difficult and I needed to look for a job closer to home. I saw a job advertisement posted for a music therapy position in a nursing home close to my home in the Bronx, and I was hired. My new position was as a music therapist within the social service department, which included therapeutic recreation and group psychotherapy. I was replacing a very talented pianist who had a vast repertoire. At the time I was still using the guitar to lead my sessions and it was clear that this would not work well here – I needed a more robust sound to engage the residents. It became obvious that the accordion would be a perfect instrument to use. I didn't know many songs but my supervisor challenged me to memorise a few each week so I wouldn't be limited by having to read from music sheets.

I continued to play trumpet in the evening with various bands, including a Polish polka band. By playing with so many different music ensembles, such as Latin, Polish, classical and jazz, I was expanding my repertoire of ethnic music. This strongly influenced my ability to incorporate these melodies and styles into my music therapy sessions. With many residents of Russian, Polish and East European Jewish origin, along with a few Italians and Irish, my knowledge of folk genres was extremely beneficial. Although I primarily used the accordion or piano for my group and individual sessions, I did find opportunities to use the trumpet effectively. Often it was to engage a resident who was a musician and was still able to play their instrument to some degree.

Case vignette: Sam

Sam was one of these residents. He had played clarinet in swing bands throughout the 1940s but now needed long-term care for respiratory and heart problems. Sam was very depressed at his weakened state and barely had the energy to participate in any programmes. He was referred to music therapy to improve his mood, but his family was also hoping that I might get him to play his clarinet again. Sam did not want to try because of his respiratory problems. I told him I played trumpet and played with several swing bands and knew many of the charts that he probably played. I then asked if he would like to play some tunes when he felt able. First I just encouraged him to play long tones on the clarinet while I played similar tones on the trumpet. Then we moved to short tunes. Even though his sound was weak, his fingers worked well and he started finishing the short melodies that I played on trumpet, or we would exchange phrases, which he found very motivating. His respiration improved greatly.

I worked closely with staff in other departments, especially physical rehabilitation. One of the physiotherapists had a wonderful voice and often sang to his clients while he helped them with their movements. He would volunteer to sing at special parties and I accompanied him on the piano or the accordion. Soon other staff mentioned that they played instruments. One of the accountants had played clarinet with dance bands and was eager to have a chance to play again. One of the building engineers was a drummer. I put together an impromptu band of these staff members and soon we became regulars for special events and holiday parties. I played trumpet, piano or accordion, depending on the song. Our ensemble did much to build up staff morale.

Being a trumpet player has definitely informed my music therapy practice. My performances with small wind ensembles taught me to listen, anticipate and truly synchronise with the other musicians. Such skills helped me listen closely and pick up nuances of subtle movements in my dementia patients. Trumpet players need to be able to transpose orchestral music. This skill has allowed me to transpose on the accordion with ease. Performing with so many types of ensembles has enriched my repertoire of folk music, ethnic music and classical music. Whether it was in creating staff ensembles, community music therapy programmes or supporting a patient's own music-making, the trumpet has had a very positive impact on my work in music therapy.

'In the mood'

Philippa Derrington

A flexible, dynamic, informed and sensitive approach from an essentially client-centred way of working is particularly relevant to music therapy work with adolescents. Musical improvisation is central to this, which applies as much to *what* instrument I play, as to *how* I play it. In my experience, at different times and for various reasons, I respond in the moment to what each adolescent brings, their mood and presentation. This means it is frequently necessary to play other instruments and not just clarinet or saxophone, which I am most familiar with.

Each of the following case vignettes took place in a music therapy garage, which was a space created specifically for adolescents (Derrington 2012). It is full of instruments, such as drum kits, electric and bass guitars, ukuleles, trumpets, keyboards, a violin and lots of percussion. Here, I shall highlight how the trumpet was used by adolescents and explore the reasons why. Was it simply that you could blow raspberries through it to make farting noises, or blast a fanfare for the whole school to hear? The potential of the trumpet is perhaps unexpected with this client group, but the following vignettes of students, who all have emotional difficulties, illustrate how the trumpet provided a means of connecting musically with them.

Case vignette: Clare

Clare was 14 years old and was used to keeping a lid on her emotions. She often talked about feeling numb, even when she had hurt herself. Perhaps it seemed safer for her not to acknowledge how she really felt or she did not dare to feel anything. Music therapy was a vital space for Clare to think, sing, chat and be heard. Most of all, she liked performing and being creative. Sessions felt free and spontaneous, which was at odds with her life at home, where she faced many difficulties and did not have much space to be playful.

On one occasion, Clare chose to sing along to K'naan's song 'Wavin' Flag'. To join in with her play, I brought over a big flag that happened to have been left in the room and waved along, dancing and moving to the music. As she began to sing the line 'when I get older I will be stronger' she gestured with her arms, punching the air, seeming to embody the lyrics. To reflect this show of determination and strength, I instinctively took up the trumpet because of its triumphant quality. Playing a single improvised, melodic line on it I was able to connect her music and movement, match her energy and support her expression. This in turn seemed to give her permission to express herself with more confidence.

Case vignette: Oliver

Oliver attended music therapy for two years from the age of 14. He enjoyed singing songs from musicals, which I accompanied on the piano. In addition to his ambition to be a singer in the West End, performing these songs with me allowed him to take on lead roles and characters and step into a world that he loved.

It was always important for him that the songs sounded right. This often meant a certain amount of rehearsal was needed, but he enjoyed this just as much as each performance he gave in front of the video camera. Oliver sometimes used other instruments, such as drums and bass guitar, to support his acting and singing, but it was the trumpet that provided the greatest opportunity for creative musical improvisation. He quickly learned to blast sounds, twiddle on the valves and improvise a soaring line above songs from The Blues Brothers and other musicals. When playing the trumpet, he seemed self-assured, moved freely and expressively, empowered by the sound, stance and overall feeling.

Figure 5.5 Oliver

Case vignette: Christopher

Christopher was 15 years old when he was referred to music therapy. When I met him he had recently joined the school after being excluded from another. He was resistant to most activities and classes at that time but did attend music therapy every week and talked about his situation. He generally refused to touch any instruments but one week made a throwaway comment about the trumpet. Despite his apparent lack of interest I used his comment as a starting point, using it to engage him musically. At first he resisted my attempts and disregarded the trumpet as an orchestral instrument that 'only musical people can play', going on to say 'it takes years to learn it properly'.

I showed him that by blowing a raspberry into the mouthpiece you could make a sound. I focused on the playfulness and kept chatting as we usually did. Christopher laughed at the strange, humorous noises I made using the trumpet. At first he cursed me and the 'stupid instrument', but he was obviously curious as he then picked up the other trumpet to have a go. We laughed together at the unusual sounds he could make, and this gave him the confidence to keep going in search of making the strangest possible sounds. This led to a dialogue of humorous noises using two trumpets. It was the first non-verbal exchange and served as the beginning of Christopher using other musical instruments to express himself. He had taken delight in playing the trumpet in precisely the opposite way to his preconceived notion of how it should be played.

The trumpet, triumph and despair

Shlomi Hason

I was 11 years old and a piano student in my local conservatoire when I was given the opportunity to choose a second-study brass instrument to fill up spaces in our local youth orchestra. I admired my older cousin who could play the trumpet very well, so it seemed only natural for me to play it too.

It was a torture for the young learner to get a sound out of the trumpet, and my neighbours were not very happy either. For years to come my relationship with the trumpet remained somewhat tenuous, and I recall that my fifth year was punctuated by a strong wish to quit. I had always been drawn to minor keys and mellow music but was expected to play fanfare style most of the time. To accommodate, my teacher tried to help by adding some lyrical studies to my repertoire, and I could not escape the trumpet calling for long. During my army service I had to memorise syncopated backings for some 30 military marches, as well as uninspiring fanfares. I travelled on duty with my trumpet around Israel to raise flags or fly the flag at half-mast. Despite my personal musical preference, I could not help being astonished at how a few notes played at fourth and fifth intervals, and organised in a particular way, could so solemnly dictate feelings of grief or victory in the audience.

The emotional world of my client and my emotional responses to it are at the foreground of my psychodynamic thinking. The musical elements become a symbolic communication of those feelings that are inaccessible to both of us. The choice of sounds and silences in the room conveys a narrative, often a challenging and painful one, of the client's relationship with others and with themselves. The therapist's trumpet may play a significant role in the symbolic play with the client.

Case vignette: Jennifer

Music therapy was introduced in a neurorehabilitation hospital unit for a trial period of three years. Adult clients were admitted for a short but intensive period of rehabilitation, ranging from a few weeks to three months. An interdisciplinary team offered an all-round medical intervention to minimise the loss of functions and skills and set patients on a road to recovery. The primary role of music therapy was to assist clients to process their feelings in the face of traumatic changes in their lives and accept the damaged parts of their body and identity.

I saw Jennifer for five individual sessions during her stay. Jennifer was a woman in her late 40s, who suffered a left frontal stroke, causing damage to the part of the brain that organises movements. Jennifer's right side of the body was affected as a result. She was wheelchair-bound and experienced other cognitive deficits with initiation, attention, memory, disorientation and emotional lability. On the referral form, speech and physiotherapy teams described Jennifer as being resistant to rehabilitation on account of her bouts of anger and use of abusive language.

Denial of traumatic changes after head injury is not uncommon in the first stage of rehabilitation (Van den Broek 2005). Music therapy was found to be particularly useful with defensive patients, by finding ways to harness resistance and to foster awareness of the therapeutic process (Austin and Dvorkin 1993). The desirable outcome would be an increased alliance and collaboration with the patient in their rehabilitation.

Empathic echo

I wheel Jennifer to her first session. She indicates her wish to play the keyboard. I am surprised, as most patients at first show reluctance to play or wait for me to make a choice for them. Without taking any notice of me, Jennifer attempts to play the beginning notes of the popular piano tune 'Chopsticks' or 'The Flea Waltz'. I wonder if the choice of the amusing waltz is a symbol of her longing for the exuberant and wholesome child she once used to be. Perhaps the 'chopped sticks' are the equivalent of vulnerable limbs and feeling trapped in an estranged body. She attempts to play the tune with one hand, adding the good hand, when clearly the tune demands a collaboration of both hands. As she keeps getting the notes wrong, with each mistake she emits a cry, swears, and goes back to the beginning. All the while Jennifer is barely looking at me. I offer harmony first with the guitar, then a steadfast beat with a djembe drum, but she keeps swearing, appearing to be oblivious to me and my music. I try to speak to Jennifer. I tell her that her mistakes are not so bad and that I am impressed that she can actually play, but my praise falls on deaf ears and draws us further apart. I end up feeling very frustrated, as there is no way for me to ease Jennifer's pain, nor can I escape feeling useless myself. This goes on for the entire length of our first session.

During our second session, I feel an urge to play my trumpet. The radiant silver colour and distinctive trumpet sonority are so undeniable that it immediately validates my presence, despite my previous helplessness. I phrase short melodic lines that are well-timed with Jennifer's cautious taps on the keys. But as soon as she makes another error followed by a foul swear, I deliberately fluff a note of an unpleasant quality to end with her cry. It is as though my trumpet is learning to swear through sound. Jennifer is looking at me for the first time and I feel acknowledged. 'Does she feel the same?' I wonder. An elongated silence resolves the tension and brings a sense of relief. She continues her satirical waltz, as I stretch a few drones. Another ill-tempered outburst from Jennifer and the trumpet lets out a sudden roar. Jennifer smiles at me in response, suggesting my like-minded trumpet is accepted into her world of despair.

A fluffed note, a 'kix' as my trumpet teacher used to call it, is caused by failure of airflow to hit the resonance of the pipe, causing the sound to split. For the young classical performer it meant extreme anxiety before a solo part. Now, however, it has a positive effect on Jennifer. The snide use of the trumpet seemed like an appropriate translation of Jennifer's spurts of anger into music. Presumably Jennifer heard an echo, perhaps even an empathic voice inviting her to reflect on her traumatic experience.

Mother's reverie

During her third session, Jennifer looks at me more often as she shares some thoughts about the music. It feels closer and calmer in the room. Jennifer attempts to use her right injured arm interchangeably with her left hand. With each trial I am anxious she might fail to press the key. However, by steering away from the waltz and playing improvised simple phrases, I realise she is curious to explore her affected body and is more in touch with what her hands are realistically capable of doing. Therefore she doesn't swear. Accordingly, I keep my trumpet to the realm of pleasing drones. Unresolved harmony unfolds at the meeting point between our sounds.

The dynamics in the room reminded me of Bion's concept of 'reverie', aptly described by Waddell (2002, p.30) as the 'mother's capacity to hold her baby's anxiety and her own, to go on thinking in the face of puzzling and increasingly intense protest and distress, drawing on and offering her inner resources'.

Paternal pride

> 'A key role for the father, which most men find they do intuitively, is to introduce the baby to the world.' (Emanuel 2002, p.142)

During our fifth and final session, Jennifer starts to play the C major scale with only the use of her right weak arm. I play the same scale on my trumpet, usually synchronising my notes with hers, but Jennifer then hesitates. I choose to keep my airflow going, extending her last note, and waiting for her to move to the next one. She then plays the next note and I breathe and repeat this after her. She finally finishes the whole scale and cries out to me with an exclamation of joy. 'Hooray!' I call back, feeling as proud as a father would be.

Last impressions

The trumpet is certainly not my weekly first choice in clinical sessions, and there will be weeks if not months in which it will remain in its case. In the early stages of therapy many clients express the need to merge with the therapist and to avoid seeing them both as separate beings. I have found this state of dependency to be crucial for clients to develop their own sense of identity. The therapist who possesses the trumpet and the exclusive skill to blow it may be experienced as a threat to the client whose self-esteem is low and whose trust in therapy has yet to consolidate.

Jennifer initially refused to let me into her musical space and to share her feelings. By blocking the valves only half-way to achieve the effect of in-between notes, the trumpet aptly embodied Jennifer's protest, despair and her playful nature. With its multi-faceted resonance, the trumpet thus was a powerful instrument to empathically meet Jennifer's state of being and invite her into a therapeutic alliance.

Trumpet and flugelhorn characteristics in music therapy practice

Quality of trumpet and flugelhorn sound

One therapist described the marvellous sound of the trumpet that encouraged her to take up playing the instrument in order to play alongside other musicians in bands. Two of the trumpet players commented on the capacity of the trumpet to inspire a feeling of triumph or grief, just through a limited number of notes but a particular sound that was evocative of this range of feelings. The flugelhorn was described as being more mellow and pleasing in the lower range. Angry fluffed sounds were also created by one therapist in responding to rage from a client.

Vocal quality of the trumpet

Two trumpet players described the way in which sounds are created on the trumpet as linking in with the production of singing and vocal sounds. This vocal quality could similarly be associated with the breath control of clients, and one therapist discussed the way in which her trumpet playing had a direct effect on the breathing patterns of an elderly man.

Versatility of the trumpet

One trumpet player wrote about how musically versatile the trumpet is, in suiting both orchestral and jazz genres. In addition to this, unusual techniques could be employed to create a range of sounds through vibrato, growling, and so on, which could be useful in responding to a variety of clients' contributions in therapy sessions.

Mechanical aspects of the trumpet and flugelhorn to explore

One flugelhorn player encouraged the client to explore the valves and slides of the horn, and this shared exploration overcame the client's anxiety about the instrument, consequently encouraging him to play it. Clients are also able to create additional sounds through tapping on the smooth metal and exploring in this way.

Visual appeal of the trumpet

Two trumpet players commented on the bright and shiny appearance of the instrument, which could appeal to clients and draw them into dialogue or exchanges. This was felt to be especially relevant in work with young children.

The trumpet player's ability to 'listen in' and respond in an improvisational way to clients

One trumpet player discussed the way in which her playing in bands had prepared her for improvisational playing in music therapy sessions, through having to listen and respond musically to other musicians, as well as transpose music at sight. This enabled her to respond to subtle movements and sounds made by clients with dementia.

Capacity of the trumpet to be played in a humorous way

One trumpet player described the way in which she opened up communication channels with a teenager through using the mouthpiece of the trumpet to blow raspberry noises. This became a humorous, playful exchange that engaged the client and made the instrument seem more accessible.

Creating a sense of empowerment through trumpet playing

One therapist observed that teenage clients seem to get a sense of self-assurance through playing the trumpet, both through the stance that is necessary to play and the powerful sound that can be produced.

Aspect of the trumpet/flugelhorn being the therapist's own instrument

Two therapists remarked on the fact that playing the trumpet could make the client feel threatened or separate, as the client did not have the necessary skills to play. This was overcome in one situation by the client learning to play the trumpet and being able to share in duo playing with the therapist on another trumpet.

References

Austin, S.D. and Dvorkin, J.M. (1993) 'Resistance in individual music therapy.' *The Arts in Psychotherapy 20*, 423–429.

Clark, P. (2013) *Brass history: The trumpet through the ages.* Retrieved 15 August from www.sinfinimusic.com/uk/features/guides/instrument-guides/trumpet-development-connections.

Derrington, P. (2012). '"Yeah I'll do music!" Working with Secondary-aged Students Who Have Complex Emotional and Behavioural Difficulties.' In J. Tomlinson, P. Derrington and A. Oldfield (eds) *Music Therapy in Schools.* London, UK: Jessica Kingsley Publishers.

Emanuel, R. (2002) 'On Becoming a Father: Reflections from Infant Observation.' In J. Trowell and E. Etchegoyen (eds) *The Importance of Fathers: A Psychoanalytic Re-evaluation.* Hove: Brunner-Routledge; New York, NY: Taylor and Francis.

Estrella, E. (2014) *Profile of the trumpet.* Retrieved 16 July 2014 from http://musiced.about.com/od/musicinstruments/p/trumpet.htm.

Monks, G. (2014) *The History of the Cornet, from Pre-History to the Present.* Retrieved 16 July 2014 from www.blackdiamondbrass.com/tpthist/trpthist.htm.

Van den Broek, M.D. (2005) 'Why does neurorehabilitation fail?' *Journal of Head Trauma Rehabilitation 20*, 5, 464–473.

Waddell, M. (2002) *Inside Lives: Psychoanalysis and the Growth of the Personality* (Revised edition). London, UK: Karnac.

CHAPTER 6

The Bassoon

*Contributors: Penelope Birnstingl,
Lisa Margetts (introduction and case vignettes),
Joanna Burley and Grace Watts*

Introduction

The bassoon is able to deliver enormous musical reward through a register of over three octaves, and a varied palette of tonal colour, dynamic range and contrasts of articulation.

Figure 6.1 Range of the bassoon

The warmth and sonority of the lowest register is often the foundation upon which the orchestral wind section is built, while the haunting quality of the highest register evidences a more starkly soloistic tonal world, as heard in the opening of Stravinsky's revolutionary *Rite of Spring* (1913). The middle and upper registers reveal the lyrical, singing quality of the bassoon, widely explored throughout the repertoire (see Walker and Drake 2006 for examples). Principal bassoonist of the Philadelphia Orchestra Daniel Matsukawa has been quoted as saying: 'My favourite compliment…is when someone tells me it doesn't sound like a bassoon. It sounds like a voice' (Kelley 2006). The bassoon can convey a stately dignity, as in the opening

135

theme of Elgar's Symphony No. 1 (1908), yet engage playfully with humour and flair (Perkins and New London Orchestra 2004). The instrument is capable both of a relaxed, sustained legato, and considerable agility and immediacy of attack, as seen in Mozart's elegiac and playful Concerto in B♭ (1774).

Figure 6.2 The bassoon

The early history of the bassoon is unclear as so few models survive. However, we do know that the predecessors of the bassoon included the dulcian and the curtal. The word *fagott* originated in 14th-century France as *fagot* or a bundle of sticks. Fagott, which remains the German translation of bassoon, was then used to distinguish an instrument in four joints from the dulcian, which was made in a single piece. The first person to use the term as the name of a musical instrument was Alfarno degli Albonesi, who in the early 16th century named his type of bagpipe (employing, like the bassoon, a doubled back bore) the phagotum. In the mid-17th century, the basson represented an evolution of the bass curtal, which, when remodelled to comprise four joints, arrived in England as the French bassoon. 'The old horse's leg', as it became known colloquially, had a sweet and soft tone that was equally capable of blending with other instruments, and of holding its own as a solo voice (Baines 1977).

The development of the bassoon's orchestral role may be said to have been coincident with its evolution as an instrument. Early orchestral parts served to strengthen the bass section: it is interesting that, even as late as Handel's *Messiah* (1741), the bassoon part predominantly follows that of the cellos, the basso continuo. This style of writing for the bassoon began to fade from 1760. As the standard orchestral woodwind section emerged towards the end of the 18th century, the bassoon was elevated to a melodic, soloistic role of equal stature to its fellow wind voices. Mozart, in particular, explored combinations of tone for the two bassoons of the wind section in his symphonies. During the 19th century, as the bassoon continued to develop as an instrument under the leadership of Carl Almenraeder (1786–1843), composers were able to explore the versatility of register and timbre of the bassoon to a greater extent. For example, in the fourth movement of his *Symphonie fantastique* (1830) Berlioz chooses four soli bassoons to add a dark, menacing tone to the 'March to the Scaffold'. Meanwhile, Wagner sought to push the boundaries of the bassoon register, requiring the bassoon to play an A below the usual bass compass of Bb in *Tristan and Isolde* (1865), for which a specifically commissioned, longer bell joint was used. The expressive and lyrical quality of the bassoon's tenor register was beautifully exploited by Rimsky-Korsakov in three long and important cadenzas in the Andantino of *Scheherazade* (1888). The 20th century saw English composers such as Grainger, Bax, Elgar and Vaughan Williams employing different characterful aspects of the bassoon's soloistic capacity in their orchestral writing.

To play or not to play? The bassoon and music therapy practice

Lisa Margetts and Grace Watts

'The bassoon should not be played before ten o'clock in the morning.' This unequivocal pronouncement delivered by an internationally renowned bassoonist in a masterclass (which started at nine o'clock) at the Royal Northern College of Music, where Lisa Margetts was a bassoon student, has seemed ever since to typify the particular peculiarities that have characterised a long-standing relationship with this contrary, temperamental, yet beautiful and versatile instrument. It is the bassoon's capacity to be powerful yet delicate, comforting and yet turbulent, a playful or a solemn presence, that can facilitate a particular musical responsiveness in clinical work in music therapy across a range of settings. Lee and Houde further state:

> Many clients will be familiar with the sounds of the guitar and piano, but few will have had direct experience with the more unique textures and timbres of, say, the cello or bassoon. It is the unique textures and presence of such instruments that can make them valid and potentially powerful instruments in therapy. (Lee and Houde 2011, p.399)

Music therapist Hannah Smith has described the distinctive musical qualities of the bassoon as very effective in meeting the needs of children with a variety of presenting challenges, for example in enabling creative thematic play with adolescent clients' stories and ideas in the setting of Child and Adolescent Mental Health Services.

Within the context of a child development centre, music therapist Joanna Burley describes her experience of using the bassoon with Harry, a three-year-old boy who had speech delay and co-ordination difficulties.

Case vignette: Harry

I had a total of eight sessions with Harry. It seemed that play was crucial for him, yet at nursery school they reported that he did not join in. I encouraged him to explore the instruments with both literal and symbolic play, but it was through using the bassoon that I was able to match his intensity and mirror his emotional expression using the wide range of the bassoon register and the particular timbre of the sound.

My impression of Harry was of a rather careful child who was expected to keep things in their place. During the time of our work together, a sudden change at home had a profound effect on Harry, and he brought his emotional turmoil into the sessions. As he knelt beside a glockenspiel he began to remove the individual bars, throwing them aside with increasing urgency and force; I knelt up next to him with the bassoon in place and began to follow his actions with sound, starting in the low register. I worked my way up the melodic range using slurred pairs of notes, increasing the dynamic, the tempo and the intensity as the pitch got higher, to mirror Harry's actions; as he threw the last bar on the floor I reached the top register and then plummeted to the bottom as we paused to survey the 'mess'. This time Harry had been able to vent his frustration and had been heard clearly and acknowledged by the sound world of the bassoon.

Given the potential for extensive flexibility of musical soundscapes and the emotional expression, characterisation and playfulness of the bassoon, it is interesting that some music therapists who are bassoonists choose not to use their instrument in the clinical setting. There are, undoubtedly, practical aspects of the bassoon that can provoke unhelpful anxiety in the therapist and so hinder, rather than support, the therapeutic process with clients; not least of which may be the fragility and costliness of an instrument that, if damaged, is very expensive to repair. Music therapist Hannah Smith suggests that the size and complexity of the bassoon as an object may be limiting or even daunting in work with some clients with learning disabilities. A bassoonist's playing position means that a substantial physical barrier exists across the body of the therapist, whose movement is also often restricted. Unlike therapists who play stringed or percussion instruments, wind and brass players are unable to use their voice and instrument simultaneously to respond to clients, and empathic communication through facial expression is also restricted. There is the further consideration of the unpredictable performance of bassoon reeds in different environments. This can significantly affect sound quality and intonation, provoking not inconsiderable anxiety in the music therapist, who, in being drawn away from focusing on clients to the technicalities and mechanics of the instrument, can too easily be left feeling as though they may have missed the moment to respond.

Grace Watts describes such an experience during a session with an open group for adults with acute and enduring mental health illness.

Case vignette: Mental health group

The group began by talking for about 20 minutes before one group member began a quiet, broken improvisation on the xylophone. As I put my reed onto the crook of the bassoon, I could feel my anxiety about the reed rising; could I produce a sound delicate enough to meet the patient's music and would the reed speak more freely if I began in the tenor register or the lower register? I experienced powerful feelings of inadequacy and alienation at this time as this patient was playing the xylophone. I wondered about this, in terms of countertransference; perhaps my feelings were triggered by the patient's emotional state at that moment.

Despite its temperamental nature, music therapists who have formed a lasting bond with the bassoon often describe a warm attachment to, and awareness of the effectiveness of this musical voice within a variety of clinical settings. Here, Joanna Burley describes work with a 17-year-old girl with autistic spectrum disorder who attended individual music therapy sessions.

Case vignette: Anna

It was immediately apparent that Anna wanted to express her own voice and she chose the piano to do so; she was not prepared to share this instrument on any account and initially her constant barrage of sound felt overwhelming. I needed the bassoon to establish a voice that could mirror and reflect her personal expressions. The work continued for 18 months, and gradually I was allowed to share the piano and even offer an accompaniment for her recorder playing, but the bassoon was my individual voice with which I was able to play alongside her rather than overwhelm or impose.

Hannah Smith described her hospice work with both adults and children, and the way in which the warmth and resonance of the bassoon sound can forge a beautiful connection at the bedside, offering an accessible connection with vocal sounds. Additionally the client can have physical contact with the instrument's sympathetic vibration. Older adults with dementia may be intrigued by the instrument, which may then promote reminiscence and association, while also enjoying the tactile experience of the bassoon as an object.

The physical presence and dignity of the bassoon have been found to be respectful when working with families of the terminally ill, while that same adult quality can be valuable in music therapy with adults with mental health needs. For example, in a session of the previously described slow open group for adults with mental health illness, one group member exclaimed 'Ah, a fagott!' upon entering the music therapy studio. In this short greeting, the bassoon had acted as a cultural key, telling the group something about the patient's musical knowledge and experience, as well as something about their cultural identity. Through the presence of the bassoon, a relationship began to form.

The bassoon also offers an extensive range of non-tonal sounds, from the percussive quality of the keys and the resonant wooden surface, to multiphonics in three registers that can effectively meet roughness and harshness in a client's musical self-expression.

A music therapy student group improvisation: A dual perspective

As a tutor on the MA Music Therapy programme at the University of Roehampton, Lisa Margetts has drawn upon the strength of tone, and range of pitch, timbre, dynamic and articulation of the bassoon's presence to meet and support strong, shifting feelings of students in group improvisation:

> Students and two tutors were gathered for the traditional group improvisation to mark the beginning of a new semester. There was a palpable sense of anxiety as the improvisation followed discussions about coming assignments. The music began tentatively, building quickly to strongly pulsed, loud music underpinned with energetic drumming from several of the group members. The capacity for volume, resonance and resilience of tone enabled the bassoon actively to contain this turbulent group expression without becoming overwhelmed. The large pitch range meant that the bassoon could respond to thematic material in different registers with corresponding tonal qualities; sustained notes in the lowest register could support with a solid, yet warm presence, while an edgier sound

and incisive sharpness of attack in the tenor register could meet accented drum beats. As the music became quieter, drawing to a close, previously drowned plucked string sounds emerged, together with a soft piano theme. The bassoon now became a gentle companion, responding to this altered mood from the singing tenor register.

Grace Watts shares this experience of the bassoon, in the same group improvisation, from the perspective of a member of the student group:

> The anxieties of the group could be felt as we began to greet each other again musically for the first time after the break. I found my thoughts and attention turning to the bassoon that was being played by one of the tutors. As a bassoonist, I was acutely aware of its presence in the room and within the music, and wondered how it was being experienced by others in the group. My interest in the instrument began to come to the fore, but my attention was quickly drawn back into the present moment as I heard and felt the bassoon meeting the rising affect of the group's music, the full tone being employed to contain and hold the group. The bassoon moved freely through its range of colours and dynamics, commenting and responding using articulation and phrasing as the music developed, expressing perhaps more of the palpable anxiety felt before the improvisation began. As the affect began to change to something more reflective and softer, the bassoon's lyrical, more vocal qualities sang through, offering another experience of this unique instrument.

The usefulness of the bassoon as a therapeutic instrument appears to engender divided views from music therapists, who are nonetheless agreed on the essential artistic and emotional rewards of playing this distinctive, capricious instrument. In order to reach this rich potential for diversity and expressiveness, the bassoon demands commitment of time, thought, preparation, patience and individualised, meticulous attention to detail – qualities that are simultaneously inherent in the music therapist's approach to relationships with their clients.

A gentle giant

Penelope Birnstingl

The long-standing love affair between myself and the bassoon began when I was nine years old. I started to notice it on television background music like *Noggin the Nog, Ivor the Engine* and especially in cartoons such as *The Flintstones, Top Cat* and *Popeye.* I loved the rich and characterful sound that it made. It was often used to depict amusing episodes or funny personalities, so I think I made a happy connection with it, but as I was already beginning to play the clarinet, my interest in the bassoon remained in an embryonic form. A couple of years on, I was starting to get to know classical orchestral pieces, and again loved the sound of the bassoon. When I went to my senior school I was suddenly brought face to face with the new school bassoon. It seemed to me to be wholly exotic: imposing in stature, glistening wood, silver keywork and really almost like a large tropical snake! Yes, I was just the teeniest bit scared of it. The first sounds that came from it were produced by a couple of schoolgirls aged about 12, and in all honesty I cannot imagine that the sounds were especially beautiful, but I knew that I wanted to play the bassoon from that moment, and it was just a question of biding my time until I was old enough to handle such an untamed creature.

When I did start to play, I virtually taught myself until I was spotted by someone high up in the county music department, and from then on I channelled my musical energy into the bassoon, while the clarinet sat abandoned in its case. I went to the Guildhall School of Music and Drama and thereafter the bassoon was my life and my career until I made the decision to train as a music therapist.

During my training, a lot of emphasis was placed on developing keyboard and vocal skills, so that I could not really find a way to easily include the bassoon in music therapy sessions. In any case, I was quite nervous about using it in certain settings because of the danger of the instrument being damaged, and I came to the conclusion that using recorders or a flute would be less worrying, not to mention easier to carry.

I did have one especially memorable occasion when I was working with elderly residents of a care home and, one day, my co-therapist suggested that the clients might like to see the bassoon. It was decided that I would bring it in to the next session and play it to them. I felt sure that it would be of interest and that its sonorous character would be appreciated.

We began our session in the usual manner and then I placed the bassoon, in its case, in the centre of the circle and began to unpack it piece by piece, showing the residents how beautiful and shiny it was. Most were fascinated and were keen to stroke or touch it, but I suddenly became aware that one lady was finding enough inner strength to push her chair further and further out of the circle. When it came to the point of putting the reed onto the bassoon and playing what I thought was a gentle but beguiling melody, she more or less disappeared, showing considerable alarm. She did not like the bassoon one bit, apparently taking it to be some sort of rifle! I cannot say that it was a great success to use the bassoon on that occasion, and so I rarely included it in my music therapy sessions. However, I do think that it has a place, if you can be sure that it will not be damaged, and if it seems that it would be appropriate and appealing to individuals or certain groups. I just think that you have to choose the situation carefully. At the risk of dwelling on the disadvantages of using the bassoon, I think I have to add that I personally felt that it cramped my style in many ways. If I stood up to play it, it was attached to me and not easy to put down quickly; and if I sat to play, I felt too static. I felt so much freer with the recorder or the flute.

Most of my work was with pre-school children, and the bassoon often did not really fit into that context. However, there was an occasion where the bassoon was enjoyed and valued by a group of young children and their mothers. The children were of pre-school age and had a range of disabilities. The mothers were sitting in the group with their children. I played the bassoon, showing it to them first and then gradually introducing the sounds that it could produce. I started very quietly in the mid-range notes and then began to explore the lower and upper ranges. Then I began to introduce a few familiar tunes that they knew, such as 'Old Macdonald', 'The

Wheels on the Bus' and 'Twinkle Twinkle Little Star'. The mothers spontaneously began to sing the songs and clap, each encouraging their child to do the same. The children seemed to enjoy this activity and possibly liked to hear an instrument with a different timbre. For a special occasion, such as the end of term, and where there were plenty of assistants or helpers, the bassoon, being an unusual instrument, was much appreciated.

Bassoon characteristics in music therapy practice

The quality of sounds of the bassoon

All the authors commented on the rich and characterful sound of the bassoon, and a varied 'palette of tone colours' that can be useful in meeting and reflecting back the emotions and expressions of both adult and child clients. One author wrote about the warm tone of the bassoon enhancing the therapeutic relationship in work with adults in a hospice setting. The use of multiphonics on the bassoon can respond to harsh sounds created by the client, and percussive sounds can also be achieved through the metal keys and wooden surfaces of the instrument.

The range of sounds of the bassoon

The span of three octaves of the bassoon can be used to respond to clients at a wide range of pitches. The warmth and sonority of the lower notes of the bassoon can be used to calm and soothe, while the upper register can respond to livelier, lighter moods.

The capacity of the bassoon to produce powerful sounds due to the large size of the instrument

Two of the authors discussed the 'dignity' of the instrument and the possibility of supporting with a powerful sound on the bassoon. The large size of the bassoon was discussed as potentially intimidating, but also in some contexts reassuring as clients could easily feel the vibrations.

Breathing/blowing aspects of the bassoon

One author wrote about the capacity of the bassoon to make a connection with the client's vocal sounds.

Issues in relation to portability

All the authors described the difficulties of transporting the bassoon and the physical barrier that it might create between therapist and client. Additionally, the bassoon is a valuable instrument that the therapist might be anxious about damaging in therapy sessions.

The bassoon as a reed instrument

The preparation of the reed for the bassoon presents challenges in therapy sessions, as this can reduce the ability of the therapist to respond in a spontaneous way to clients. A parallel was drawn between the attention to detail that is paid by the bassoonist to their instrument and the therapists' approach to the relationship they have with their clients.

References

Baines, A. (1977) *Woodwind Instruments and Their History*. New York, NY: Dover Publishers.

Kelley, L.C. (2006) 'Musical mission possible: Daniel Matsukawa sings out for lyrical bassoon playing.' *Overtones* (Fall), pp.12–13. Retrieved 23 April 2013 from www. curtis.edu/resources/uploads/embeds/file/Faculty/Matsukawa,%20Daniel.pdf.

Lee, C.A. and Houde, M. (2011) *Improvising in Styles: A Workbook for Music Therapists, Educators and Musicians*. Phoenixville, PA: Barcelona Publishers.

Perkins, L. and New London Orchestra (2004) *The Playful Pachyderm: Classic Miniatures for Bassoon and Orchestra* [CD]. Hyperion.

Walker, K. and Drake, J. (2006) *The Bel Canto Bassoon* [CD]. Regent Records.

CHAPTER 7

The Violin

*Contributors: Katy Bell, Nicky Haire (introduction
and case vignettes), Trisha Montague and
Sharon Warnes (introduction and case vignette)*

Introduction

The viol, emerging during the 12th century, preceded the violin and
was contemporary with it during the 16th century. Viols featured a
fretted neck, six thin strings and a flat back and bridge; the treble
and alto viols were held upright on the player's knee and bowed
with a broad bow, and the resulting delicate, soft tone meant they
were more suited to chamber music in the domestic setting than the
concert hall. The early violin proper emerged around 1550; its true
predecessors were the medieval fiddle, the rebec, and the lira da
braccio, which were played by troubadours to accompany dancing and
singing, and which shared many features with the violin, including
its regular sound holes and waisted profile. The early violin featured
four strings, a waisted body, lateral pegs and f-shaped sound holes, it
was held under the chin, supported by the left shoulder. Whereas the
viol had been the instrument of the Court, the violin was originally
the instrument of the common folk; however, its capacity for sound
projection and versatility of playing technique resulted in the violin
superseding the viol by 1700 (Diagram Group 1976).

The present-day violin has changed remarkably little from the
instruments produced during the Golden Age of violin making
(c.1550–1750), when Cremonese violin makers – Amati, Guarneri,
Rugeri, Bergonzi – perfected the form of the instrument. Further

adaptations were made around 1800, including angling the neck, lengthening the fingerboard and adding tension to the strings to accommodate the needs of contemporary music, but essentially the violin as we know it has existed for over 400 years. In addition, the bow underwent significant changes, developing from the short, unyielding bow pioneered by Corelli around 1700 to the Tourte concave bow of c.1785 that is still used today, featuring an inward-curving stick designed for good balance, capable of more powerful and varied bow-strokes. During that period, the lyrical qualities of this expressive instrument allowed for a vast diversity of musical compositions, ranging from the virtuosic concerti of the Baroque period, performed at Court, to the ballads, jigs and reels of the Celtic fiddle, leading the dancers at a ceilidh.

The violin is an instrument that is equally at home in solo, chamber or orchestral music; in the symphonic repertoire it is generally the string section (and the first violins in particular) that carries more of the melodic line than any other section of the orchestra. The violin has often been likened to the human voice in terms of its range and expressive capabilities. This may be due to the possibility of vibrato, and of slight expressive adjustments in pitch and timbre achieved through minute adjustments of the left-finger positioning, and the placement, pressure and speed of the bow on the string. Each violin sings with a unique voice as individual as the human voice.

> [The violin] is one of the most perfect instruments acoustically and has extraordinary musical versatility. In beauty and emotional appeal its tone rivals that of its model, the human voice, but at the same time the violin is capable of particular agility and brilliant figuration, making possible in one instrument the expression of moods and effects that may range, depending on the will and skill of the player, from the lyric and tender to the brilliant and dramatic. (Boyden *et al.* 1980, p.1)

Figure 7.1 Range of the violin

Angus and his traditional Scottish music

Sharon Warnes

I think it may have been the human element to the violin's voice that initially attracted me to the instrument; when I heard the violin's lyrical, sparkling brilliance in Vivaldi's *Four Seasons* as a child, I was inspired to learn this most technically demanding, but ultimately rewarding instrument. I have been a professional violinist since 1991 and have combined performing and teaching in a wide diversity of fields, including concert halls, schools and prisons; however, it is perhaps only since graduating from the music therapy training course at Anglia Ruskin University in 2005 that I have come to truly appreciate the therapeutic qualities inherent in the violin.

Case vignette: Angus

I first met Angus at the residential care home where I run individual and group music therapy sessions for residents. Diagnosed with dementia in his early 80s, Angus, now 84, was living in the care home and struggling to settle into his new life there. Confused, anxious and distressed, he came to the group session with his wife Mary, who hoped the music would help to calm and soothe Angus. Initially resistant, refusing to sit and uttering distressed little cries, it was only when Angus heard the traditional Scottish ballad 'Ye Banks and Braes' played on the violin and sung by the therapist and other group members that he was able to settle, sitting with Mary to sing many of the songs he recognised from childhood such as 'My Bonnie Lies over the Ocean' and 'Skye Boat Song'. Watching the bow move across the strings, Angus occasionally lifted his arms as though conducting the music, a movement I mirrored with the bow, lifting it up to conduct with him whilst continuing to sing.

Scottish music, and the violin in particular, had special resonance for Angus, who grew up in Scotland listening to traditional Scottish folk music, in which the violin plays a leading role. He also attended ceilidhs and took part in Scottish country dancing, later moving to England where he continued to sing in a choir for 30 years and listened to both classical and Scottish dance music for pleasure. Over the next six months, I saw Angus regularly for both group and individual sessions, working with him in his room when he was too tired, ill or frail to attend the group.

Our second meeting took place in the corridor where Angus was walking: he appeared anxious, disorientated and unsure where to go. I sang 'Ye Banks and Braes' as we walked to his room; once there I reminded Angus of the forthcoming Burns Night, which elicited his exclamation 'Oh yes!' as I started playing improvised and pre-composed Celtic jigs, reels and songs on the violin. Angus sat, sometimes clapping along to the beat (for example in the tune 'Mairi's Wedding'), singing 'Charlie Is My Darling', or just listening appreciatively, smiling with eyes closed, to music that prompted memories of past dances, happy occasions redolent with positive associations.

Although Angus responded to other musical genres and instruments during sessions, it was the violin that evoked the strongest reactions. The violin's versatility came to the fore in our individual sessions in Angus's room, where volume control was essential, so that other residents were not disturbed. Varying the bow-stroke and lightening the pressure of the bow produced a soft, gentle sotto-voce effect which could soothe and relax Angus, sometimes to the point of sleep. Occasionally I sang and played a melody simultaneously, or harmonised with myself, playing a counter melody on the violin whilst singing the tune, adding harmonic depth and interest to the sound; the violin is not exclusively a single-line instrument. Alternatively, chords could be strummed by either Angus or me, if I held the violin like a guitar as we sang together. Plucking pizzicato notes on the strings with the left index finger provided a contrasting timbre at low volume, creating bright, short staccato sounds. The practice of double-stopping, where two or more strings are played at once using the bow, produced a rich, resonant sound in which the strings' vibrations could be felt by Angus as well as heard, if he reached out to hold the scroll of the violin as it was played.

Angus came to recognise me through my violin's voice; arriving for the group session one week in a state of some confusion, on hearing the violin playing he exclaimed 'Oh! I know you!' and quickly settled down to participate in singing, conducting and listening to music. Sometimes this violin voice – so closely resembling the human mezzo-soprano voice with the same lyrical, tonal and emotionally expressive qualities achieved through bow-control, vibrato and phrasing – moved Angus to tears. Once, a rendition of 'Loch Lomond' saw him wiping away tears whilst repeatedly saying 'It's lovely!'.

The last time I saw Angus in his room, he was poorly with a chest infection. I sang and played the Scottish pieces we had shared together over the previous six months. Angus's breathing was laboured but he was aware of my presence, opening his eyes, gripping hold of my hand as I took his, moving it to and fro as if he were guiding me around the dance floor at a ceilidh. He died two days later.

How does being a professional violinist compare with being a music therapist using the violin?

A performer seeks to communicate, and in the concert hall this is usually a one-way process: the player performs, imparting their interpretation of a composer's musical text to a receptive, listening audience. In music therapy, communication is always at least two-way, and in a group situation, often more complex; the therapist must be sensitive to the needs of the client(s) and attuned to the myriad communications present in the room, endeavouring to engage with whatever is expressed through primarily musical means. Throwing away the script of pre-composed, established music to explore the idiom of improvisation liberates the music therapist from the tyranny of printed sheet music and the potential for getting it 'wrong', and this has had a profound influence on my professional playing career. I now worry far less about making musical 'mistakes', and frequently incorporate improvisation into recital programmes. Working with older adults with dementia in music therapy provides opportunities for both improvised and pre-composed music: singing, playing and hearing familiar songs and melodies evokes many and varied emotional responses whilst helping to orientate people in the here and now. I have had to learn to research and expand my repertoire of music to cover most of the 20th century. Once again, the violin proves very versatile in that if someone starts singing an old song that is unknown to me, I can usually follow the melody line, plucking quietly if necessary until I have established the tune in my head and fingers.

Bridging the gap

Katy Bell

Creatively exploring an instrument over many years and thinking about different types of music, as well as our relationship with it, has many parallels with the journey of an evolving therapist. As a violinist, one of the groups I belong to is a string quartet: four string voices attuning and engaging in a musical conversation that can be infused with infinite nuances of communication. It is a trusted forum for play; within the structure of the music there is room for experimentation, reflection, fun, repetition (often for pleasure) and careful working-out. The directness and (perhaps because of this) the sincerity of the string voices, is affirming and enriching. It is truly a shared cultural experience (Winnicott 2005, p.138), and the sense of validation through playing, with people I trust and like, could be described as a sort of transformation; it is certainly enlivening and reparative.

As therapists, our primary concern is one of establishing a relationship or shared experience with each client. As musicians, we can use our instruments in a variety of ways to enhance this process. In the study that follows, this was done by physically, as well as musically, drawing the clients together.

I have a violin that I use specifically in my music therapy work. The bow in particular is vulnerable – not only through its slender shape but also because of its attractive swooshing movements. I take the instrument out of its case when I arrive and keep it on top of a high cupboard until the right moment in a session – if that moment arises – when it can be quickly reached. Occasionally when I play, a child will simply tell me to stop, will disengage or will take the bow away from the strings. At other times a child might be intrigued (and we can make a game) or mesmerised (and I can play for the child), but commonly the violin and music associated with it seem to inspire young people to move around.

The following case vignette briefly traces the development of trust and subsequent changes between two children with very different disabilities who shared a weekly music therapy session at their special school – as well as the therapist's violin.

Case vignette: Emma and Rashid

Emma was an eight-year-old girl with cerebral palsy and severe visual impairment, which rendered her effectively blind. Unable to use her legs, she spent her time in a wheelchair or lying on a soft mat in school. She shunned physical contact and had developed a habit of screaming when she was bored or disliked an activity so that, in order to minimise distress to the class, she was often transferred with an adult to an adjacent room where she would settle. At times, of course, Emma was genuinely unwell or in pain, but it was difficult to gauge the extent or severity of her discomfort.

Rashid was a seven-year-old boy with autism. He was in the same class as Emma. Although he often became stuck in repetitive counting games, he seemed to have a warm interest in others but lacked the confidence and skills to develop relationships with his peers. He was interested in and wary of Emma, often asking why she was crying and when she would get better.

Both children responded well in the classroom to music and Emma's parents used classical music to soothe her at home.

Emma and Rashid were referred for music therapy by their class teacher, who had concerns that, for different reasons, they were becoming isolated from their peers. Emma spent much of the school day out of the classroom, and when she was in, she was unable to pick up visual cues or invitations to play with her peers; Rashid could not find a way to creatively interact with his classmates. The two spent break times alone or with adult company. For this reason we decided to try six assessment sessions with the two working as a somewhat unlikely pair. Initial aims for music therapy included establishing a trusting relationship, developing new ways for emotional expression and interaction, and encouraging communication.

Early sessions were planned carefully so that Emma could start in a calm way with opportunities to engage through music and sounds, and Rashid could settle into a safe framework that would eventually accommodate some change. To this end, Emma would arrive first with an adult and the two would listen to Tchaikovsky's *Nutcracker Suite* while I collected Rashid from the class. By the time he reached the room Rashid was often smiling in anticipation of meeting Emma, and as the weeks progressed Emma also began to await Rashid's cheery greeting. She would turn her head to one side and listen carefully as he approached, vocalising gently and waving her arms as he said 'Hello, Emma!' At this point Emma's assistant would leave so that the two children and therapist remained.

Voices were used a great deal in this work, alongside small percussion instruments and guitars, and I was aware of providing a continuous melodic joining-up that ran through the sessions. This was partly to maintain the engagement of both a static child and one who was inclined to wander (although Rashid always seemed to have an ear bent in our direction); it was also a way of narrating for Emma what was going on. I had been wary of playing my own violin – although both children had taken turns to play a half-sized violin – as I misguidedly felt that if I needed to quickly give a hand to either child the melodic continuity would be lost for the other.

One week the issue was resolved by playing a recording of the folk song 'Cockles and Mussels'. Rashid rapidly picked up the chorus of the song and, in order to bring Emma into the music, I picked up my violin and began a counter melody close to her chair. Emma reached out to hold the scroll of the instrument and began to vocalise falling thirds. Rashid noticed the new vocalisations immediately and came to stand close beside Emma. He swayed with the music as he sang, then he gently placed his hand on my right elbow, helping me to bow. For moments while the song lasted it seemed the three of us were held together not only through the music but also through the physical act of playing and through the shared vibrations of the violin. There were broad smiles as we reached the end of the piece and an urgent request from Rashid to play it again, which we did in just the same way. The song 'Cockles and Mussels' became a staple of the sessions.

Sharing the violin to bridge the gap between Emma and Rashid became a turning point for the pair in music therapy. During the weeks that followed Rashid was increasingly able to offer Emma different objects and even hold her hand to sing 'Goodbye' without the wariness on both sides that had coloured their contact up until that time. Rashid also seemed less inclined to wander. In her turn, Emma allowed Rashid to take her hand and would lean his way or even reach out to him as he approached her chair. She began to express herself through a more creative range of vocalisations.

Months after the music therapy had come to an end a new teacher observed that Rashid would approach Emma in the playground to ask whether she wanted to 'play Cockles and Mussels' with him. Emma would smile and wave her arms, then Rashid would take one arm gently and move it backwards and forwards, as if bowing, while he sang 'Alive, alive-oh! Alive, alive-oh!'.

Thoughts about my relationship with the violin

Nicky Haire

I am a music therapist and a violinist. I use all kinds of instruments in my work, but the violin has been a constant in my development as a person, a musician and a music therapist. Over the years I have developed a relationship with it and I am as comfortable with it as I am with my voice. I know it as a partner in this sense in many musical settings, not just in a music therapy context. I feel comfortable when I am playing the violin. I can be freely creative with it and it provides me with the most capacity for musical variation, including style, harmony and expression. I don't have to think when I play it; I can listen and respond immediately to a client.

I work in two special schools as a music therapist and I also run weekly social music groups for elderly clients with dementia in two care homes. In both cases I use my violin regularly. I have a specific instrument for therapy work as it feels important to make a distinction between performance and therapeutic interactions; being able to share the instrument freely is essential in my work.

Stylistically the violin is a hugely versatile instrument. It enjoys a place in most forms of music. In a therapy session, I find it lends itself to playing *with* clients. When I play, my whole body is involved. I am able to face clients and give eye contact and I am mobile, so can engage physically using movement and gesture. During my social music groups with elderly clients, I can walk around the group and interact with people individually and musically in a way that I find less easy when I am playing the piano, guitar or drum, for example. I can also sing and play at the same time and, as I explore in the following four short case vignettes, the actual instrument can provide a connecting bridge between my music therapy clients and me.

Case vignette: Jason seeks out the violin

An inquisitive face appeared at the school music room window one day. I had been playing the violin while I waited for my next session, but I stopped and welcomed the pupil into the room. It was Jason, a 19-year-old with mental health issues and learning difficulties. He had been drawn there by the sound and asked me if I could play something fast so he could dance. I did so and he began to move quickly without inhibition in a jig-like way.

When I asked his teacher about referring him she was enthusiastic because Jason could become highly anxious. During those early sessions, he had a strong desire to play the violin. We had two violins in the music room, and when I handed him my own instrument he understood that this was a sign of trust. I am sure that this had a huge impact on the course of the therapy; he came to trust me and the improvisations and interactions that followed on lots of instruments were involved and meaningful for both of us.

Case vignette: Anna is visibly lifted by our playing

Anna, aged 11, has profound and multiple learning difficulties. Her head hangs so low over the soundhole of the guitar that her nose touches the strings. She is completely absorbed by the instrument, which fits neatly on her wheelchair. She begins to strum the guitar sporadically. I follow her and introduce a melodic line on the violin, observing her emotional expression. I am using a strong tone, really digging into the strings with full bows, and she begins to move back and forth. I develop the melody I am playing according to her movement and also take the rhythmic impetus from this. As I begin to play faster and faster I add more to the musical texture, with double stops broadening the music. Anna seems to be punctuating the melodic line on her guitar. There is a real drive forward in the music. It is not clear who is leading. Suddenly Anna lifts up her head and plays the guitar in the same rhythm. We are both completely in tune with each other and connected in music. It is an intense experience full of joy and life.

Case vignette: William reaches out

For William, who was six years old and on the autistic spectrum, the violin was an exciting instrument, but he was slightly nervous about all the instruments in the room. He felt safe when he was in control. Sometimes he would watch from the corner of the room as I played gently, following his movements. On occasions when I took the violin to join him going round the room, he would indicate for me to stop playing. As our therapeutic relationship developed over two years, William became more assured in the sessions. He began to use his voice and join me in playing together, expressing himself with the various instruments on offer. However, he was still physically distant. Towards the end of our sessions, one day, completely unexpectedly, he reached out and touched the bow as I was playing. I was astonished. He had created an actual bridge between us. Over the following weeks, it happened again and William began to gain in confidence, now holding the bow and pulling downward a little. I felt that he knew the importance of that physical connection.

Figure 7.2 Nicky playing her violin in a music therapy session in a school

Case vignette: Bringing the violin to group work at a care home for the elderly

During a social music group at one of the care homes I work in, just after I have finished leading a selection of known songs on the piano with the residents, I take up my violin. Someone says 'Oh, my dear, a violin!' I begin to play and one resident imitates the movements I make, others listen, some sing along, some play along with small percussion instruments, and one turns to her neighbour and comments on the tune I am playing. I walk round the room and every resident – even if their eyes are closed and they look asleep – is tapping their foot or moving their leg in time. The whole group is joined by the music, alive with it. I then make a connection with a resident and he gets up to dance, helped by a carer. I keep playing, repeating the song as the resident has begun to sing. It is an incredibly touching moment. I feel as if I am dancing with both the resident and the carer as they swirl round. The resident wants to keep dancing and singing but he becomes breathless and needs to sit down. As he does so, his fellow residents clap and he smiles happily.

I always think very carefully about using the violin in my work as a music therapist. Is it musically, stylistically or physically appropriate here? Will a client immediately feel de-skilled because I can play the violin better than they can? Will it be damaged? For a teenager who only listens to Hard Grind, dubstep or hip-hop, is a violin in a session immediately going to deter them? This was not the case with Jason. For William the fact that the violin has a bow, a separate part of the instrument, enabled him to join with me. With Anna and the elderly group, I believe something about the sound as well as the movement and rhythm of the playing engaged them.

As these case studies show, the versatility of the violin is to be celebrated. This is true not only in musical styles but also in its physical features. The way it nestles under your chin, resting on your collarbone, means it resonates physically when played. When holding it I am reminded of a mother cradling a child and this sense is often observed in how clients carefully hold it or play it with me. Yet, along with many clients I work with, I am struck by the contrast between the gentle intimacy of the instrument and its dynamic strength – physically, acoustically and dynamically. How such a beautifully crafted intricate instrument can be so robust and used in such a playfully accessible yet intimate way is a constant surprise to me and the clients with whom I share it.

Thoughts about my use of the violin in forensic music therapy

Trisha Montague

When I started work as a newly qualified music therapist in a medium-secure hospital in 2003, it seemed an unlikely setting for a violin.

I thought an instrument so fragile and precious, one that seemed to me to symbolise the elitism of Western classical music, would be incongruous and at risk amongst such a patient population, many of whom had committed acts of violence against people (murder, rape) and property (arson, burglary). I could not easily imagine how I would make musical connections with patients more familiar with hip-hop, ska, reggae and heavy metal. I feared scorn and teasing. The teasing happened as much from staff as from patients, but I enjoyed the humour and the curiosity: 'You got a gun in there?' takes on a particular resonance in this environment.

My years of education and practice as a classical violinist using strict musical notation had started to change in 1986 when I discovered the world of traditional fiddle music. I left the world of Beethoven string quartets to explore the world of Scottish strathspeys and Irish reels, Klezmer freylekhs, Swedish polskas and Appalachian bluegrass.

The discovery of unusual scales, chords and rhythms, the percussive potential of the bow and the violin's wooden body were exciting; they each allowed something much freer to evolve in my playing for which the versatility of the 'fiddle' proved ideal. They also helped to prepare me for working as a music therapist, particularly so with the diverse population found in a forensic hospital.

Many patients I have worked with are familiar with drum kits, acoustic and bass guitars; congas, maracas and large xylophones are popular and easy to play, and occasionally the microphone is used for rapping. Instruments that can be hit and shaken are used to express and release pent-up energy, anger and frustration. I have consequently been surprised and charmed by the curiosity of patients hesitantly asking to 'have a go' on the unfamiliar, awkward violin. I have also been moved watching big hands that have caused destruction and hurt, carefully picking it up and asking for help to draw the bow across the strings.

In that moment what comes to the fore is the capacity of many of these patients for gentleness and sensitivity, courage and vulnerability. Their awareness of being entrusted with something fragile and valuable is evident. There is mutual trust: my trust in them to treat the instrument with care, and their trust in me not to mock them.

Figure 7.3 The violin

The following two case studies illustrate the importance of the violin, as well as its symbolic significance, in my work.

Case vignette: Considering Ron's relationship with me and my violin

Ron, a 53-year-old Irishman, has been attending music therapy regularly for the past three-and-a-half years. His long-term mental illness, drug addiction and depression are incapacitating. He is emotionally cut off and declines all other activities offered to him. Many sessions are spent sitting together in silence after some brief shared improvisation on big xylophones. The violin has rarely been played in his sessions, although it is always available and ready if needed. At the end of each session, Ron removes the shoulder-rest and puts the violin and bow away, carefully covering it up before closing the case. When returning together to his ward, he often carries the violin case while I open doors and gates, dismissing any jibes from other patients we meet on the way. Smiling, he hands it back to me to take to a group therapy session on a different ward.

I have wondered what the violin and I represent for Ron. Am I the absent, missed mother, or former wife? Is he being a helpful child or a protective partner? The transference is strong, but any attempts at putting words to his feelings and actions are met with a silent shrug. What is clear is his symbolic expression of the importance of his relationship with me, shown very poignantly in his safekeeping of the instrument he knows to be special to me.

Case vignette: Making contact with Jal

Jal is a 32-year-old refugee from the Middle East who arrived on the acute admission ward a year ago. He presented with a complex history of mental illness and a borderline personality disorder. His early traumatic history includes abandonment by his mother and growing up with a violent father. He came to the hospital after committing a very violent offence.

Jal showed an interest in music therapy and so I agreed to meet with him on the ward, offering a trolley full of instruments. He paced the ward proclaiming his delusional beliefs about the world around him, ensuring that other people, as well as his own disturbed and intrusive thoughts and memories, were kept at bay. However, when I started to sing and play the djembe, he broke off to listen and briefly joined in on the large xylophone.

In the second session I started to play the violin while Jal walked around the room gesticulating and talking loudly. He stopped and began swaying to the music as I played. He then asked if he could try to play the violin himself. He sat on the floor while I helped to position it under his chin and showed him how to move the bow across the open strings. I accompanied him on the xylophone, picking out the same range of notes he was playing. His playing was cautious and gentle; he looked at me intently and then closed his eyes and after a few minutes handed the violin back to me and asked me to play it again. As he listened, I noticed tears welling up in his eyes. He said he 'had a dream that took him back'. He did not expand on this, and on this occasion I simply acknowledged that something painful had been touched by the sound of the violin.

In subsequent sessions he has spoken more about his 'sad' childhood. It is clear that the intimacy of playing together and the soft, emotive sound of the violin have triggered deeply painful memories for him. It has allowed him gradually to emerge from the disturbing, delusional world that has been protecting him, and seems to have offered him a space to reflect on his losses and his past.

A year later, the symptoms of Jal's mental illness have reduced. When he listens to me playing the violin, he closes his eyes and sometimes recalls more traumatic incidents from his childhood. Other weeks he will sing or dance around the room. His exact mirroring of my physical movements when I am playing other instruments suggests a wish for closeness and a lack of separation. However, some weeks he struggles to manage the constancy, predictability and intimacy of the therapeutic relationship, and therapy sessions can be followed by a distancing on his part and a refusal to attend. This is understood in part as a need to protect himself from unbearable feelings that link to his disturbed past, his isolation and his mental disorder, as well as to his forensic history, which includes his own potential for violence.

Violin characteristics in music therapy practice

Therapist's own instrument

All the therapists are also performing violinists and all expressed a special affinity with the violin. They commented that their clients recognised them through their violin; that this was part of their identity. A work violin was, however, considered essential, not only because of the expense and vulnerability of their performance instrument but also to make a distinction between their performance and interactive therapeutic work.

Mobility and portability

The usefulness of being able to take a violin to the bedside to play quietly with a patient or to take onto a forensic ward, or wherever the client was situated, was expressed by all the therapists. The violinist is also able to face clients whilst playing and give eye contact, as she moves around, so she can engage physically using movement and gesture.

Encouraging movement and dance

All of the therapists noted how they themselves move freely whilst playing and that the violin music also seems to inspire their clients to move and dance around. There is a rich variety of violin music associated with a wide range of dance styles.

Eliciting vocalisations

All of the violinists felt that the tone quality of the violin was similar to the human voice and all have successfully used the violin to encourage clients to vocalise or sing. One therapist felt that this voice-like quality may be due to the violin's vibrato and to the way a player can make slight expressive adjustments in pitch and timbre with minute adjustments of the left-finger positioning and also by the placement, pressure and speed of the bow on the string. Also, each violin has its own unique voice; much like the human voice. Being able to sing and/or harmonise with their violin playing was also considered important.

Bridging the gap

Creating a circle between the therapist, patient and the instrument; two of the therapist's note how the violin could provide a connecting bridge between their clients, the music and themselves. One therapist noted that the separateness of the violin bow (not being part of the actual instrument) enabled her client to share the playing.

The violin's versatility in improvising and working out songs sung by clients

One therapist explained how she could discreetly follow the melody line of an unknown song, plucking quietly if necessary until the tune is established. The violin is described as a versatile instrument, enjoying a place in most genres of music.

The violin's gentleness and vulnerability

All of the therapists described offering clients their violins to play in sessions and how this was perceived as a sign of mutual trust, hugely important for the therapy. For one therapist, cradling the violin was reminiscent of holding a baby. Another therapist described the need for gentleness and sensitivity, as well as quiet playing, whilst working in a patient's bedroom at his end of life; the violin was particularly suitable for this work. The fragility of this instrument, in stark contrast to the violence of the offences committed by those in a forensic setting, was also considered to be important.

Conducting the music using the bow

This was mentioned by one of the therapists as a useful part of her work with a particular client.

Association with particular styles of music

The violin plays a leading role in Celtic dance music, ceilidhs, music for Burns Night and other traditional celebrations, as well as in Irish reels, Klezmer freylekhs, Swedish polskas and Appalachian bluegrass. Its association with a diversity of music from classical string quartets, chamber music and orchestral playing to less formal social events and family gatherings gives the violin a wide appeal.

References

Boyden, D.D., Schwarz, B., Woodward, A.M., Marx, K. *et al.* (1980) *The Violin Family*, in The New Grove Musical Instrument Series. London, UK: Macmillan.

Diagram Group (1976) *Musical Instruments of the World*. New York, NY: Paddington Press.

Winnicott, D.W. (2005) *Playing and Reality*. London, UK: Routledge Classics.

CHAPTER 8

The Viola

Contributors: Angela Harrison and
Oonagh Jones (introduction and case vignette)

Introduction

Historically, the viola has been left in the shadow of its siblings, the violin and cello. Played like a violin but tuned a fifth lower in pitch, composers of early orchestral music rarely gave the viola the important melodic lines; instead they used the instrument to provide depth of harmony and tone. Violists (as a consequence of having been considered lesser violinists) have often found themselves in the unenviable position of being the butt of musicians' jokes.

However, by the end of the 19th century Lionel Tertis (1876–1975) commanded a new respect for the viola. His beautiful tone and expressive playing inspired composers such as Bax, Bowen and Bridge to write solo and chamber music for the viola, particularly exploiting the instrument's mournful expressive qualities. Walton's Viola Concerto written in 1929 and later Bartok's Viola Concerto (inspired by William Primrose 1904–1982) demonstrated that the instrument was not only capable of a great range of expressive sonorities but could also be played with assured virtuosity. More recently violists including Nubuko Imai (b.1943), Yuri Bashmet (b.1953) and Tabea Zimmerman (b.1966) have continued to inspire composers and listeners alike, and the viola is now taken seriously as a solo instrument. British viola player Lawrence Power quoted in *The Guardian* says:

> I just love the viola; I find its sound very touching, because it's very close to the sound and the range of the human speaking voice. It can sing, or be dramatic, and it has a lot of emotion in it when it's played well. (Service 2008)

It is this expressive, yet intimate sound quality of the viola that I have found useful in making connections with clients in music therapy.

Figure 8.1 Range of the viola

Using the viola in music therapy

Oonagh Jones

Case vignette: The Cinderella of the orchestra joins the party

Bryan is about 30 years old and lives in a small care home. He has many challenges in life, being registered blind and hearing-impaired. He also has cerebral palsy and spastic quadriplegia. Bryan relies on others for all of his needs. He was referred to music therapy as his carers were concerned that he was so deeply isolated from others. Much of his day is spent sleeping and he rarely engages in meaningful activities.

We are part-way into the session today and Bryan looks as if he might drop off to sleep. He sits in his wheelchair facing me, his carer alongside. I offer him a tambourine to play and he grunts and mumbles, pushing the tambourine away and then pulling his hands away. I decide to play to Bryan rather than offer other instruments, hoping the music might enliven him. I pick up my viola and begin a simple lilting tune in 6/8 time, quite lively, in an effort to lift his energy levels. I leave brief pauses, assessing whether Bryan is reacting in any way, whether he is listening. I provide a little extra texture and warmth in the harmony with some double stopping. The improvisation is loosely structured with a clear major tonality and occasionally repeated motifs. However, it is open-ended and flexible in relation to Bryan's body movements, facial expressions or grunts. There is little to go with at this point, so I feel like the improvisation is essentially my music, with some prior knowledge (from earlier sessions) as to what style of music might reach Bryan.

Not long after beginning to play I notice that Bryan is now vocalising and filling the gaps that I leave in between phrases. At this stage his sounds are low in pitch and indistinct, as if he is grumbling or mumbling something, clearing his throat even. I respond to these sounds by creating more space in the music for Bryan. I simplify the music, creating open phrases and using fewer notes, but reflecting Bryan's pitch and timbre. His sounds become clearer and I feel the improvisation is becoming more of a duet rather than me playing to Bryan. Using held notes and simple phrases, I create a more structured and predictable framework within which we fall into a turn-taking pattern. I question at this point whether I am simply fitting in to Bryan's natural breathing pattern or if he is responding to me. I shorten my phrase lengths and he follows suit. I subtly adjust the timing and he does too. He definitely is listening and responding. I begin to vocalise too, and the viola becomes the accompanying instrument, providing a secure bass. The improvisation continues, focusing on shared vocalising and turn-taking. We reach a level of interaction that is possible for Bryan only through music.

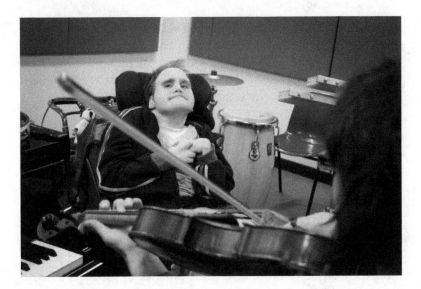

Figure 8.2 Bryan listens and responds to the viola

Bryan's carer commented:

> I never thought that music therapy could evoke such a response.
> It has become a unique way for Bryan to express himself. When
> Bryan hears the music played directly to him he engages and
> can control the session. He is able to escape and connect with
> the world around him in a way that we never thought possible
> for Bryan. To see him engage is absolutely inspiring.

So why did I choose to play the viola at this point in the session and
what is it about the viola that seemed to elicit the best response from
this very disabled and isolated man?

As a student at Nordoff-Robbins (2002–2004) I focused on
learning the musical skills I would need as a music therapist primarily
at the piano. However, as a first-study viola player I was not entirely
comfortable with this, which led me to explore the therapist's choice of
instrument in my master's dissertation. Now, after ten years of clinical
experience, I find that what I discovered through that investigation still
holds true:

> I would suggest that when the therapist needs to focus on
> connecting with the client they [the therapist] might choose
> the instrument instinctively and it is likely that they would
> choose an instrument that they feel most expressive on. (Jones
> 2004, p.58)

That day with Bryan, I chose to play the viola knowing it was my best
hope of making a musical connection. I have found that within the
varied range of clients I see, I use the viola most with those who have
the greatest disabilities and are the most difficult to reach. I think there
are two main reasons for this: attunement and musical inspiration.

Attunement

I have found that I have a natural inclination to leave more space
when I am using the viola. I wait and listen more keenly, allowing
more time to reflect, and there is consequently more space for
the client to respond and guide the improvisation. Perhaps this is
because the viola is a single line instrument, but it could also be
that I am inherently more confident and technically assured playing
the viola than other instruments. It is possible to sustain a note on
the viola, which means I can keep a thread of sound going, yet at

the same time wait for the client. I can be more flexible in terms of timbre; for example, I could match Bryan's vocal sounds on the viola, incorporating varieties of pitch and tone. I can instinctively attune, responding to the subtle changes in dynamics, timbre and pitch. This is due to a combination of the nature of the instrument and my previous musical experiences on the viola.

Musical inspiration

For clients who have greater barriers to communicating and making music, the therapist has to offer more ideas and needs a richer internal musical landscape from which they can choose something meaningful for the individual client. The subtle gestures and sounds a client makes are the seeds that help the therapist create an improvisation that is meaningful to the client. While I have studied the piano, and in particular improvisation techniques on the piano, I have internalised a wider range of viola music, be that solo, duo, chamber or orchestral music. Experiences such as accompanying singers in operas are remarkably similar to accompanying the (sometimes unpredictable) vocal offerings that a client brings to a session. Of course, these skills transfer to any other instrument a therapist uses but the transfer is most instinctive to the therapist via the first-study instrument.

When reviewing the relevant literature for my dissertation in 2004 it was evident that very little had been written by music therapists about the instrument they used in sessions. An exception to this was Amelia Oldfield, who had written about her work using the clarinet. While she writes about the practical advantages of using this instrument, it is her final reason that resonates most strongly with me:

> Perhaps the most important reason for using the clarinet in my sessions is that it is my first instrument, which I love and feel a great affinity for. I am more likely to be able to communicate effectively with this instrument than on any other. (Oldfield 2003, p.37)

Symphonist to therapist

Angela Harrison

The point has been reached where I have been practising as a music therapist for more years than I spent as a full-time professional musician, playing viola with the Hallé Orchestra. My identity as a viola player and the relationship with my viola endure, and whenever I play it is as if I have never been away. The intense physicality of the instrument, while increasingly challenging, remains enchanting to me.

My motivation for a change of career was the need to explore my own creativity after so many years of recreating the works of others and to build on my experiences, which had shown that interactive music-making can be a compelling catalyst for change. Whilst in the orchestra, I was inspired by numerous world-class musicians, and although my attempts to emulate their technique were often unsuccessful, on occasion I was surprised and delighted to 'rise above myself'. I never lost my fascination for, and the exhilaration of, being in the midst of a large group of people, all dedicated to the task and together creating something greater than the sum of its parts.

Figure 8.3 Angela Harrison with her viola
Photograph by Simon King

I have described my transition from symphonist to therapist in a number of talks and here I present a few reflections, each performance (P) idea having a therapy (T) parallel.

(P) Patrick Ireland, my viola tutor at music college, I found to be a master of communication, seemingly at one with his viola, and he explained this in terms of the completion of a perfect circle. As I understood his description, he meant the incorporation of the viola within the sensitive, connective pressure between the ball of the left thumb (supporting the instrument) and the middle section of the right forefinger (resting on the bow). Thus the viola and bow become extensions of the player's arms, making an extraordinary conduit for musical expression.

(T) When I now invite a client, young or old, to share an instrument with me it could be said that we are meeting one another in the completion of that same circle. An example is working with a guitar, offering it up to clients with the chords formed by my fingers and the strings awaiting their touch. As they reach out to strum, my hand falls into the rhythm of their movements and my singing acknowledges our shared creation in which we are co-dependent.

(P) The task of mastering an instrument to the point where expressiveness can flow takes many years of painstaking, repetitive practice, and I still remember the moment at which the viola yielded to my influence and became a part of me, a new voice.

(T) This came to mind during my work with a young boy, Robert, diagnosed at the age of three as being at the severe end of the autistic spectrum. His family, resisting the suggestion that Robert was uneducable, chose to seek out a combination of behavioural therapy, nutritional treatment and weekly music therapy. We had been working together for several years when Robert suddenly leapt in the air, crying 'I'm free' and glanced over his shoulder at his discarded 'autistic self'. From this point on, his therapy moved towards a conclusion, and while autism is still very real for him, Robert has far more control over his life. He too, by repetition and patient application, gained the skills required to communicate more effectively, not only through music but in all areas of his life. For Robert, these skills included listening, the processing of information and the ability to draw on memories to give context for sensory input. Robert and I agree that it was music therapy that helped him to internalise what he had learnt, enabling him to meet new situations with growing confidence. Robert has just completed his second year at university, giving full rein to his exceptional musical ability.

(P) The viola section plays such a crucial role in orchestral music, and in my experience our significance only really becomes apparent when we are asked in rehearsal *not* to play. Suddenly absent is the velvety, rich quality of tone that is so distinctive and that deepens the emotional impact of the music. Violas are often given a flowing line that moves towards and away from the melodies of the more dominant instruments, creating and resolving dissonance and adding colour and texture to the music.

(T) It is my belief that my therapeutic skills reflect on me as viola player and this is the person that my clients meet, whether or not my viola is present. The underlying processes seen within an orchestra or string quartet, where the viola enriches harmonies and weaves melodies between the other players, can be brought into play in the therapy room.

The following case vignettes will show how the same processes can be harnessed using spoken language or melodic vocalising and also give an indication as to why I rarely introduce my viola into therapy sessions.

Case vignette 1

For one term in a special school, a small group of teenagers with Asperger's syndrome met with me every week to make music and share their experiences. Each had limited use of expressive language, so as we began to talk I wove an intuitive narrative (the viola's melodic meandering) around their factual contributions, which resulted in us all having an experience of free-flowing conversation. The young men began to listen to one another and discovered shared interests as they spoke enthusiastically about their love of films, books, outdoor pursuits and food preferences (Harrison 2012).

Case vignette 2

In the same vein, during a period of work on the acute ward in a psychiatric hospital, I used my viola to bring cohesion to the fragmented contributions of the patients, who were having difficulties with motivation and in ordering their thoughts and movements. There is something so appealing to me about the intimacy of the viola's sound emerging from the centre of a musical experience, be it orchestral, chamber music or improvisations in the course of my work. It therefore came as a rude awakening to hear one group member asking me in strong terms not to get my viola out of its case as the sound was so terrible to her ears, draining her of energy and hope. When some time later one of my clients had an unexpected seizure, in part attributed to the stimulation of my playing, I decided that even though my instrument was an integral part of me I could go it alone and still make an impact.

Case vignette 3

My voice lies within the range of my viola, and I have found that meaningful connection can be made with one young woman in therapy using wordless songs, improvised as if on my viola. The guitar provides accompaniment but also acts as a valuable barrier between us, ensuring space between us. My client is unable to use language to express the impact of early childhood trauma yet can vocalise with me, blending our sounds to find healing and release.

My final analogy for the orchestral life is one I have often described (Harrison 2006, 2011).

> (P) When working with great conductors, players may watch them discreetly and adjust the dynamism of performance to match their movements and non-verbal communications. Their bodies become the transmitters of musical meaning, and, having interviewed a number of conductors, I am encouraged to

believe that gesture and levels of vitality authentically represent their interpretation of the music being played. There is great variety in the extent to which a conductor is demonstrative in performance, but even when the gestures are minimal the usual positioning of the violas at the centre of the string section puts us at the perfect vantage point for such discreet awareness and response. Working with conductors with charismatic presence, I have often experienced a sense of deep connection whilst playing which is not created by eye contact or overt communication, but by a synchronising of dynamic energy and vitality.

(T) When working with young people on the autistic spectrum who initially do not want to play an instrument, I have found great value in reverting to the role of the orchestral player, albeit at the keyboard. By subtly connecting with the child (as with a great conductor) and improvising a musical soundtrack that relates to the pace and energy of his or her movements, the child receives audible feedback, moment by moment. This may mean responding musically to the rhythm of rocking, to moments of stillness, to the tapping of beaters or to jumping or stamping. Based on my understanding of Daniel Stern's work on vitality affects, I propose that the use of such a mirroring technique can contribute to the development of a sense of self, without which relationship with others is difficult – if not impossible – to achieve (Stern 2010). I have seen children progress from this phase of therapy to one in which I am acting as accompanist to their tentative solos, then to joint improvisations where we are both confidently presenting and sharing our music.

Playing the viola requires broad shoulders, literally and metaphorically, a thick skin to withstand the endless jokes and nerves of steel to cope with the rush of adrenalin when fearsome solos loom. Gaining this resilience can only be seen as excellent preparation for life as a music therapist and I count myself extremely fortunate in having two careers that have proven so fruitful for me and for others in concert halls around the world and therapy spaces across North Yorkshire.

Viola characteristics in music therapy practice

Similarity to the human voice

Both therapists mentioned that the viola was similar to the human voice – one stating that the range of the instrument was similar to that of her own voice – and they have both used the viola to encourage clients to vocalise. This voice-like quality may be due to the way an experienced player can make slight expressive adjustments in pitch and timbre using tiny adjustments of the left finger positioning and also by varying the placement and pressure of the bow on the strings (similar to the violinists' comments). One of the therapists talked about weaving a narrative (the viola's melodic meandering) around the sporadic factual contributions of a group of young people with limited expressive language; this had resulted in an experience of free-flowing conversation.

The viola's melancholic tone quality evoking strong emotional responses

One therapist explained that it was the viola's rich, expressive, yet intimate sound that initially drew her to the viola and that it was this quality she found most useful in her music therapy work. The second therapist also described the distinctive velvety, rich quality of tone, which she feels deepens the emotional impact of the music. However, although this was noted to bring cohesion to a fragmented group, it was also suggested that the viola's tone quality could evoke strong emotional responses from clients, which could be negative as well as positive.

Making a circle of communication

In a similar way to the violinists' explanation of 'bridging the gap', one of the violists talked about the perfect circle formed from the ball of the player's left thumb (supporting the instrument) to the middle section of the right forefinger (resting on the bow); the viola and bow becoming extensions of the player's arms. In music therapy, when a client is invited to share the playing, it could be said that therapist and client were meeting one another in the completion of that same circle and this could provide a conduit for musical expression.

Similarities to the viola's role in an orchestra

Both therapists mentioned that the viola is rarely given the important melodic lines in orchestral music but instead is used to provide depth of harmony and tone, weaving in and out of the main melodies. Violas, although not the dominant instruments in an orchestra, were considered to be crucial in providing the fullness of sound between melody and bass line, creating and resolving dissonance and adding colour and texture to the music. The link was made between the role of a violist in an orchestra and that of a music therapist in a session; striving not to dominate or show off but to enrich the music of the whole group and to provide depth and cohesion.

References

Harrison, A. (2006) 'Conductors Uncovered – Learning from Orchestral Experience.' In *The Sound of Music Therapy: Papers from the BSMT/APMT Annual Conference*, held on 17–18 March 2006 at the Resource Centre, London, UK.

Harrison, A. (2011) 'Developing Through Music.' In C. Rose (ed.) *Self Awareness and Personal Development: Resources for Psychotherapists and Counsellors* (pp.73–89). Basingstoke, UK: Palgrave Macmillan.

Harrison, A. (2012) '"Music, My Voice" Projects for Children: the Development of One Aspect of a Community-based Music Therapy Service in York and North Yorkshire.' In J. Tomlinson, P. Derrington and A. Oldfield (eds) *Music Therapy in Schools: Working with Children of All Ages in Mainstream and Special Education* (pp.117–132). London, UK: Jessica Kingsley Publishers.

Jones, O. (2004) *'I didn't know you could do music therapy on a viola!' Exploring the Music Therapist's Choice of Instrument and the Influence It Has on the Music Created.* Unpublished master's dissertation available in the Nordoff-Robbins library, London, UK.

Oldfield, A. (2003) *Music Therapy with Children on the Autistic Spectrum: Approaches Derived from Clinical Practice and Research.* Unpublished PhD thesis, Anglia Ruskin University, Cambridge.

Service, T. (2008) 'Joking Apart.' *The Guardian* (15 August). Retrieved 22 October 2014 from www.theguardian.com/music/2008/aug/15/classicalmusicandopera.

Stern, D.N. (2010) *Forms of Vitality: Exploring Dynamic Experience in Psychology, the Arts, Psychotherapy, and Development.* Oxford, UK: Oxford University Press.

CHAPTER 9

The Harp

Contributors: Rivka Gottlieb, Anna Lockett
(introduction and case vignette) and
Holly Mentzer (harp therapy and case vignettes)

Introduction

There is something visceral about the sound of the harp. The sound
of gut string and resonating wood is not just musical notes; it's an
echo of something ancient, something that resides deep within
our collective memory. The first reference we have of the harp is
in Egypt 3000 BC in the form of a hunter's bow (Rensch 1989).
In 1500 BC the Asians created a more angled harp, which had the
triangular shape that we are more familiar with today. There are a
number of references to the lyre in the Bible, particularly in Kings
chapter 1, recounting history between 960 and 560 BC; David
played his lyre to King Saul, who was said to have a troubled soul,
and the music helped calm him. At this point in the states of Israel
and Judea the harp was becoming a celebrated musical instrument
used by the Jews.

The harp circulated around Persia and India, and there are
statues of people playing the harp in temples in India, during the
Tamil dynasty around 500 BC. Indeed the harp was the first musical
instrument played by the Tamil people, and Tamil Sangam literature
from 200 BC documents this type of harp-playing.

The monastic movement used the harp as a vocal accompaniment
The spread of the harp mirrored the movement of the monks using
the Roman infrastructure: to Ireland and Scotland, where the harp

became important in the Gaelic countries. During the sixth century
St. Columba stressed that the Christian faith be communicated
through poetic hymns and music, including the harp. The triangular
'harpa' brought from Eastern Europe was the chosen instrument of
the bards, who carried with them the tales and lineage of tribes,
noblemen and great battles. Is it any wonder that when the English
tried to stamp out Gaelic culture in Ireland from the 16th to the
18th century, the first thing they did was to ban the playing of
the harp? For the Irish, the *clarsach* (Celtic harp) was a symbol of
national identity, an icon of the old Gaelic order. Fortunately, some
of the old tunes were saved and are still with us today, along with
the revival of a particular sound – the modal scales, as well as the
jigs, reels and slow airs.

Harpists playing diatonic harps with a single row of strings
adapted to increasingly chromatic music by retuning scale patterns
or shortening (stopping) strings to produce the desired alteration of
pitch (Rensch 1989). The origins of the harp with double or triple
rows of strings are vague. The Spanish *arpa doble* began to appear
in paintings and court documents in the 14th century. Claudio
Monteverdi scored for the *arpa doppia*, a harp with at least two rows
of strings, in his 1607 opera *Orfeo*. It was not until the 19th century
that Sébastien Érard developed the orchestral classical harp known
as the double action harp (1810), which is still used today for
classical music. Through technological advances he was able to make
the harp fully chromatic, like the piano. It was then that composers
could really use the harp to its full potential in compositions such as
Symphonie fantastique by Berlioz (1830) and *Danses sacrée et profane* by
Debussy (1904).

Interestingly, specific professions distinct from music therapy
have evolved in the USA for harpists. Holly Mentzer has provided
information on these under the general heading of 'harp therapy'.

Harp therapy

The soothing sound of the harp has been associated with healing
and spirituality for thousands of years, and it is thought to have
unique healing properties due to the acoustic properties of the
instrument (Gardner 1997). Harp therapy is a term that applies to

the various therapeutic applications involving harp music, but differs from music therapy in the degree of direct patient interaction and clinical intention. In music therapy the relationship between client and therapist is central, with the therapist using a systematic and purposeful approach to treatment to meet the goals and objectives of treatment (Bruscia 1998). Other uses of music in medicine are as an adjunct to patient care without specific treatment goals to improve how the patient feels during medical procedures or other clinical situations, and emphasises the patient's relationship to the music rather than the therapist.

A therapeutic harpist receives training from a therapeutic musician training programme on how to interact with patients and conduct their work in an institutional setting, and is awarded a certification credential unique to the programme. Healing Harps, founded in 1983 by Ronald Price, was one of the first organisations concentrating on the healing components of the harp. Price found that playing the harp eased the tremors caused by his cerebral palsy, and started the organisation to help others suffering with other diseases, learning disabilities, and emotional problems resulting from trauma (Laney 1994).

Over the past three decades several harp therapy and music-thanatology training and certification programmes have flourished independently (see Table 9.1, in Appendix 9.1). Training emphases vary between programmes, but all focus primarily on offering individualised bedside therapy sessions through a combination of classroom training or distance learning in addition to clinical internships. More information on harp therapy is included in Appendix 9.1.

Music-thanatology

Music-thanatologists provide prescriptive bedside vigils using harp and voice, synchronising the music to observed physiological change (Schroeder-Sheker 1994, 2001). The music-thanatologist is primarily concerned with allowing the patient to make a more peaceful transition towards death and provide emotional and spiritual support to the patient and family members who may be present (Aragon, Farris and Byers 2002; Freeman et al. 2006). The patient's changing condition, observed through verbal and non-verbal communication, can influence the musical prescription, such as by using minor intervals or modes if a patient is tearful (Freeman *et al.* 2006). Although this approach emphasises that it is prescriptive in nature, there is little interaction with the patients who receive the music, which is usually unfamiliar music to allow the dying person to unbind from life. The harp is ideal for bedside music at end of life because it creates the needed depth and warmth through reverberating strings with an appropriately non-invasive tone (Schroeder-Sheker 2001). More information on music-thanatology training and research is included in Appendix 9.2.

Using the harp with children with autistic spectrum disorder

Anna Lockett

I started learning the harp at the age of 12, after convincing my parents that it was the only instrument for me. My parents were initially keen for me to play the flute, but after hearing Marissa Robles performing on the harp I was totally inspired by the sound and sight of the instrument, and felt compelled to learn how to play it.

I have no doubt that the instinctive response to the sound of the harp is what is experienced by many of the children with autistic spectrum disorder that I have worked with. A lot of these children seem to prefer a space that is quiet and free from what they often experience as the crowded arena of their lives. So my first aim within a music therapy session is to provide that momentary reprieve. The music room is quiet and peaceful; I am alone with the child, and there is no other noise or movement or visual stimulation other than their own sounds and movements. Perhaps this is why it has never been a problem getting a child with autistic spectrum disorder to music therapy.

Once we are in the music room there is no spoken interaction. I simply use the harp as a response to whatever the children are doing. For example, my playing may mimic their body movements or it may imitate their vocal sounds. This seems to unravel their chaotic world and helps them to simply focus on their own movements and vocal sounds.

I always start gently, with soft melodies and repetitive tunes because, like all of us, children are reassured by familiarity. But the quest is not merely to placate the child with repetitive sounds. The next stage is to increase our musical engagement and provide social challenges where the child can step out of solitude and repetition. With a simple choice of instruments in the room, I wait for the child to tap a drum, or blow a whistle, whatever it may be. I then answer that sound with another sound, like a question and response. My purpose then is to engage them further, increasing the interaction between us. This process helps the children to develop their social skills. The child and I are responding to each other, not with words but with music. Within this circumscribed space they can grow in confidence and move out of their world of isolation.

Case vignette: Peter

I have worked with Peter for nearly a year. Life for him as a child with autistic spectrum disorder is full of unwelcome distractions. His favourite place is a quiet room with a ball but he also loves to come to music and is always glad to see me. It will take about ten minutes for Peter to settle into the session. Slowly he will notice the harp and will start to brush his fingers across the strings before moving away. Like a game of hide and seek he will then find that sound again and perhaps this time engage further by playing individual notes. After a year of music therapy sessions, the time that Peter spends interacting musically with me is increasing. This engagement has important ramifications for Peter as he learns to find this kind of interaction non-threatening. This may be a process he can take with him into the classroom, but the creative act of making his own music produces something meaningful and tells us what Peter is capable of and what he is feeling.

But let me return to the harp itself and its unique features. The sound of the harp comprises elements of nurture that have carried through the centuries from King David to the bards of England and beyond. It has provided solace and tranquillity, an invitation to be captivated by the language of music as it speaks to and reflects the mood of the listener in the same way as an empathetic conversation. I often find myself using the harp's soundboard as a percussive instrument. Interestingly, drums are as ancient as the harp and rhythm plays a huge part in music therapy. The combination of these two ancient sounds, the harp and the drum, can be a powerful therapeutic tool because they are sounds we are immediately comfortable with and perhaps trigger something deep within our unconscious memories. The sound of the harp can be reassuring and comforting. The purity of its transcendental sound lures you into a place removed from the turmoil of the world around you. Time and again, I have discovered precisely why this is so important for a child with autistic spectrum disorder who needs both a stimulus and an anchor in order to cope with the challenges of life.

Strings attached, maybe: Thoughts on the harp in music therapy
Rivka Gottlieb

Figure 9.1 Harp in my living room
Photo by Carlos Reyes-Manzo

One cannot deny the power and majesty of the harp, especially a gilded full-size concert harp like the one in my living room. It can seem overpowering and perhaps overwhelming in a small room, and yet there is something magical in its warm, soft tones that can reach deep inside one. And yet I have struggled with using the harp in my clinical work, not for lack of interest or conviction that it is a very powerful tool, which it undoubtedly is, but for far more mundane and practical reasons. It is large and cumbersome to move around, potentially both vulnerable and dangerous in some settings, and very expensive.

My gorgeous gilded concert harp has been my constant companion for over 25 years. Its monetary value is not my only concern. What if it gets damaged? What if a client pushes it over, throws something at it or, worse, gets hurt unbalancing the huge, awkward thing? Pianos are solid and a lot less movable. I have experienced percussion and wind instruments of all shapes and sizes being thrown, bashed, whacked and destroyed in sessions. I have often had to remind employers that part of the music therapy budget needs to be assigned to replacing and repairing instruments. But my harp is too precious to risk and to me, is irreplaceable – apart from which, surely my concern for my instrument would get in the way of my therapeutic focus on the client. So using my own harp is something that has rarely happened, although in the children's hospice where I worked the children were so unwell that the risk of damage to the harp was minimal. Harps are very expensive, even the smallest Celtic or folk harps, and unfortunately I have not (yet) been able to persuade an employer to buy one for music therapy. I have considered buying a small harp myself to use at work, but the cost has so far put me off.

There are a number of important considerations when thinking about including a harp in music therapy. There is the instrument itself: harps come in a range of sizes, from small lap harps, to free-standing lever harps, to large pedal harps; they vary tremendously in sound, feel and tone quality, with some sounding quite harsh and brittle, while others have a warmer, more rounded sound. Some modern instruments are more robust than others, while older instruments might be wholly unsuitable for therapeutic work as they may be too delicate, as is the case with my very first harp, an 1850 Erard double-action Gothic pedal harp – lovely to look at and beautiful to hear, but so fragile, it is virtually unplayable now. A lap harp is very portable but may be difficult for a client to balance and co-ordinate, and the sound produced may not be as good as that of a larger instrument. A free-standing lever harp on legs or small pedal harp would be my preferred choice as these do not dominate the room. These instruments are more portable than a concert harp yet have a reasonably wide range, can produce a clear, warm, even, rich sound, and should be robust enough to withstand a bit of rough handling. In addition, these days, even electric harps are available for those who are more technologically adventurous.

When considering which instruments to use for each clinical session, many questions arise regarding the inclusion of a harp. Will the client feel intimidated by this beautiful and unusual instrument? Or will he or she find it intriguing and beguiling? Thinking about the shape and tonal quality of the harp, for example, and how this could be construed as feminine or masculine raises another set of interesting questions explored by Ian McTier (2012) in relation to the use of the double bass in music therapy.

What about the therapist as harpist? By that, I mean the iconic imagery and connotations that harpists evoke, for example angels or King David soothing King Saul. The idea of the harpist as healer perhaps needs to be thought about in relation to how a client might perceive the therapist. Likewise, the power dynamic that a proficient harpist therapist might unwittingly set up; the harp is one of the hardest instruments to play, and even just plucking a string can feel quite painful to a non-harpist as harpists develop hard skin on their fingertips over time. These are considerations worth pondering; but ultimately, if I had a suitable instrument at hand, I would not hesitate to add the harp to my musical toolkit. Although the sounds the harp produces are often thought of as ethereal and gentle, in reality it is a remarkably versatile instrument that can be rhythmic, playful, even harsh or jazzy too, making it easy for the therapist to respond to changing emotional dynamics in the therapeutic space. Is that, perhaps, part of the harp's magic?

In the following case vignette I shall describe some music therapy work in a children's hospice where the harp provoked a particularly powerful response from a child.

Case vignette: Letty

I worked with Letty only once, as is often the way in children's hospices where a child comes in for respite care infrequently, on an irregular basis. In this situation each session needs to be thought about as an entire piece of work.

Letty suffered from a life-limiting condition that meant she was unable to walk or sit unaided and could not communicate verbally. She was in constant physical discomfort, and probably in pain for much of the time. When I first met Letty, she seemed isolated and withdrawn, and not really interested in the world around her. She was carried from her wheelchair into the small music room and was placed gently on her back on a mat on the floor. My co-therapist and I placed wind-chimes, suspended on a stand just above her and positioned them so that she could reach them with her fingers should she choose to. We were told by staff who knew Letty that they did not think she would play. The harp was beside Letty, and I wondered if the tall, imposing nature of the instrument was frightening as she was lying on the floor with her head turned away. When I started playing gentle, delicate sounds, her reaction was immediate; she turned her head to look at the harp, and her face opened up with an enormous smile. Moments later, she responded musically trying to reach the wind-chimes and managed to make some small, tinkling sounds with her thumb. The moment was extraordinary, and everyone in the room, including members of Letty's care team, was moved and struck by how powerful and transformative the experience was. It is one that has stayed with me for many years.

'My guardian angel'

Holly Mentzer

I was first introduced to the notion of using the harp as a therapeutic instrument when a harpist and friend from my conservatory training at the Juilliard School obtained her certification from Bedside Harp (see Table 9.1, in Appendix 9.1) and began volunteering in a local hospital. An old cassette copy of 'Rosa Mystica', composed and recorded by music-thanatologist Therese Schroeder-Sheker, reawakened an earlier curiosity about the field of music-thanatology, but ultimately I decided to pursue a degree in music therapy. During my training at New York University, it became clearer that playing the harp was leading me towards focusing on oncology and palliative care, which resonated with my earlier interest in music-thanatology. Although the unfortunate truth of working in a cancer hospital is that we frequently do play music at the bedside for *dying* patients, we are also very much concerned with using music to help the *living* cope with the sometimes overwhelming experience of being hospitalised for cancer treatment.

As a music therapist practising in a cancer hospital, I have a wide range of reactions from patients who first experience the harp as a therapeutic instrument, ranging from the guarded or inappropriate ('I thought I died and went to heaven') to the exaggerated or near-magical ('I think of you as my guardian angel'). More frequently the response is somewhere in the middle, and almost always it is received, in the right context, as an invitation to be temporarily transported away from what can be a dehumanising experience to a more beautiful and peaceful place. Patients bring their own memories and associations to the harp, sometimes from spiritual or religious beliefs, or perhaps remembering a harp played at a family wedding. It may be a non-threatening way to introduce music therapy because it has such an immediate visual appeal and is innately soothing.

I derive pleasure from playing the harp because it is cradled against the chest, allowing me to feel the same vibrations that are projected towards the patient. When medically appropriate, I may invite the patient to strum the harp or even position it in their lap. The harp I use at Memorial Sloan Kettering Cancer Center is a Christina Therapy Harp, made by Triplett Harps. In addition to its resonance and portability, it is visually beautiful, with a carved Celtic design. The acoustic properties of vibrating strings and resulting overtones provide something uniquely different from an electronic keyboard or guitar. The harp has allowed me to connect with certain patients in a way that traditional music therapy instruments do not invite because of its aesthetics and what it may symbolise.

Case vignette: Richard

Richard, a 54-year old man with multiple myeloma, was referred for music therapy for anxiety and depression. During his first hospitalisation for an allogenic stem cell transplant, our music therapy sessions typically involved the patient and his very musical family singing popular and folk songs and playing instruments as an outlet for creative self-expression and to support family bonds. He played the guitar as a young man, so our initial sessions always utilised the guitar simply because it linked with the music that was appropriate at the time. His transplant course was unremarkable, and he achieved remission and was discharged.

Two months later he was re-admitted to the intensive care unit for complications from his transplant. He experienced periods of steroid-induced psychosis, paranoia, delusions and mood disorder, and became verbally abusive to staff. During this period of mood disturbance, I brought music therapy students Kelli Rae and Julian to join me for a music therapy session. Typically I would let Richard lead the direction of our sessions because his thoughts were frequently rapidly changing, and he would often spontaneously break out into singing his favourite songs. But today, something was different. He did not indicate any preferences, and told me to pick a song. Feeling unsure of my direction, I chose a familiar popular song that he had sung with me during previous sessions, but he abruptly interrupted me and said: 'I'm sick of that shit. I can't stand what they play on the radio any more. I want some real music, classical music! Play 'The Ode to Man' [sic].' He hummed J.S. Bach's 'Jesu, Joy of Man's Desiring'. I decided to take out my harp to recreate the Bach for him, thinking the gentleness of 9/8 time would offer a soothing lullaby-like quality that would be calming. It worked! He scolded: 'Why didn't you tell me you played the harp before?'.

After he seemed more grounded, I began to hum and play Beethoven's 'Ode to Joy', unsure if he was trying to ask me for the Beethoven when he was singing Bach, and more unsure of whether to try to continue calming him, or to match his underlying mood. Richard started to conduct, and directed Kelli Rae and Julian to join me on drums and in singing. He waved his arms to indicate he wanted us to play louder and faster. It was quite exhilarating, but frightening at the same time. I wanted to calm him back down, so afterwards I played a soft Bach cello prelude on the harp. He put his head in his hands and began to cry. I had never seen him show such vulnerability before. After the music ended, he said through his tears: 'Thank you, thank you, you have no idea how much I needed that.'

When we left the session, I noticed my face was flushed and my heart was beating faster. It was almost as if his 'steroid rage' was contagious. I felt so grateful for having the presence of mind to bring the harp into the room to provide the music he craved at that moment, and also for having Kelli Rae and Julian witness how powerfully he reacted to guiding his own intervention in choosing music and an instrument that addressed specific emotional and physiological realms.

Case vignette: Orly

Orly, a 43-year-old Israeli woman with recurrent thyroid cancer, heard my harp for the first time through the curtain of her shared hospital room. Her moans would periodically penetrate through the strains of old hymns that her room-mate requested – 'Amazing Grace', 'The Old Rugged Cross', and 'Sweet Hour of Prayer'. Her mother begged me to come back the next day to play the same music for her daughter because she saw how much it helped soothe her suffering. Being sensitive to cultural differences and religious beliefs, I explained that I was playing Christian hymns for her room-mate, and asked if perhaps there was other music she would prefer. Her mother shook her head, 'It does not matter, it is universal because it is so soothing. Please come tomorrow.' I peeked in at her daughter, seated in a chair, eyes closed, the gauze around her throat tinged pink and yellow with discharge and blood, and her pain seemingly quieted for the moment.

Session 1
The next day, I came as promised, and offered her mother a book of Jewish music that might be more familiar to her. Her mother got excited seeing so many familiar songs from her childhood, and I began to accompany her on the harp while she sang to her daughter. We saw her fingers begin tapping to the music and Orly started to smile. Her mother whispered 'Look!' when her daughter silently moved her lips to the music. She would never speak using her vocal chords again, but she could not be truly silenced for long. Her mother confided to me afterwards that Orly was a special education teacher who loved her work, and was very saddened by the loss of her voice. How would she work? How would she communicate with the children who already faced such difficulty with their own communication?

Sessions 2–4
Orly began to engage more actively by choosing songs for us to sing for her by pointing in my book. I began to get more of a sense of her vivacious personality and her desire to connect, watching her

programme accreditation in 2008 (www.therapeuticmusician.com). A survey conducted in 2012 by the NSBTM found that 74.9 per cent of therapeutic musicians played harp at the bedside, primarily in hospitals, hospices and nursing homes. Harp therapists may also provide services for children with special needs, people with Alzheimer's disease, in intensive care units, or during childbirth. Although several harp therapy programmes offer certification that meets the NSBTM-accredited certification programme standards, others have opted not to join for various reasons, such as the preference openly to include spirituality as part of their practice.

The International Harp Therapy Program (IHTP), founded by music therapist Christina Tourin in 1994, was one of the first four therapeutic musician training programmes accredited by the NSBTM in 2008. Training is offered through a combination of class modules and internet-based learning, and emphasises playing harp music to match the patient's breathing and heart rate, mood and preference in music, and may also involve interactive work in which the recipient might play the harp (www.harptherapyinternational. com). Founded by Laurie Riley in 2002, the Clinical Musician Home Study Course (CMHSC), directed by Dee Sweeney since 2007, offers independent study by distance learning to singers and instrumentalists who may play acoustic stringed instruments, woodwind instruments, flutes and portable keyboard instruments (www.harpforhealing.com). The third of the original accredited members, the Healing Musician's Center (HMC), founded by Stella Benson, currently offers webinar training through affiliation with IHTP and CMHSC (www.healingmusician.com). The fourth original accredited member, Music for Healing and Transition Program, Inc. (MHTP), provides classroom modules for training in different cities throughout the year, and emphasises providing live music to the ill and dying to facilitate and promote healing or assist in transition from life to death (www.mhtp.org).

Table 9.1. Harp Therapy and Music–Thanatology Training Programs and Certifications

Program	Year Founded	Program Director	Training offered and Certification	Member of NSBTM
Bedside Harp®	2002	Edie Elkan	CHT (Certified Harp Therapist) CMHT (Certified Master of Harp Therapy)	No
The Chalice of Repose Project	1992	Therese Schroeder-Sheker	CM-Th (Certified Music–Thanatologist) Contemplative Music Program; Music–Thanatology Program	No
Clinical Musician Certification Program	2002	Dee Sweeney	CMP® (Certified Music Practitioner)	Yes
Healing Harp Therapy Program®	2007	Rei Tokoro	CMP®	Yes
International Harp Therapy Program	1994	Christina Tourin	CTHP (Certified Therapeutic Harp Practitioners)	Yes
Lane Community College	2007	Jane Franz and Sharilyn Cohn	CM-Th (Certified Music–Thanatologist)	No

Music for Healing and Transition, Inc.™ (MHTP)	1995	Melinda Gardiner	CMP®	Yes
Music–Thanatology Association International (MTAI)	2004	Collective of 9 founding members	CM-Th	No
Therapy Harp Training Program, LLC	2013	Lynda Kuckenbrod	CHM (Certified Healthcare Musician)	No
Vibroacoustic Harp Therapy® (VAHT®)	2006	Sarajene Williams	VAHTP (Vibroacoustic Harp Therapy Practitioner)	Affiliate Member

Appendix 9.2: Music-thanatology training

The School of Music-Thanatology at the Chalice of Repose Project began in Missoula, Montana, and graduated its first class in 1994. Founder Therese Schroeder-Sheker defines music-thanatology as a sub-specialty of palliative medicine and is profoundly influenced by the Benedictine Cluniac tradition of monastic medicine (http://chaliceofrepose.org; Schroeder-Sheker 2001). The programme offers a Contemplative Musicianship Program and Music-Thanatology Program through a combination of distance learning, web lectures, and intensive residences. Certification is offered by the Music-Thanatology Association International (MTAI) or Chalice of Repose after completion of training and performing 50 supervised music vigils. The Music-Thanatology Association International (MTAI), founded in 1999, created a published set of musical and clinical standards and competencies leading to certification in 2004, including medical competencies focusing on anatomy, physiology, pain and symptom management at end of life (www.mtai.org). A music-thanatology certification preparation programme in Portland, Oregon, affiliated with Lane Community College, began offering weekend didactic sessions and supervised internships in 2007, and qualifies its graduates to apply for certification from the MTAI (Hollis 2010).

Research

Some pilot studies conducted in hospital and hospice settings by certified music practitioners and music-thanatologists suggest evidence that supports the use of harp therapy. Live therapeutic harp music at the bedside may be beneficial in reducing pain, shortness of breath, and anxiety (Aragon, Farris, and Byers 2002; Lewis *et al.* 2003; Sand-Jecklin and Emerson 2010). Live harp music reduced salivary cortisol excretions and respiratory rates associated with stress in convalescent premature infants (Block, Jennings and David 2003) and increased weight gain in stable premature infants (Kemper and Hamilton 2008). Dying patients were observed to experience decreased levels of agitation and breathe more slowly and deeply after receiving an intervention of live harp music (Freeman *et al.* 2006), and patients in an intensive care unit reported reduced perception of pain after receiving live harp music at bedside (Chiasson *et al.* 2013).

Further research is needed to rule out selection bias, potential response bias, effects of pharmacological intervention, and to determine if the response was due to the live harp music or presence of a compassionate therapeutic musician. Another potential area for study could include comparing using patient-preferred musical selections to music selected by the practitioner, or to compare recorded harp music to live harp music (Aragon *et al.* 2002).

References

Aragon, D., Farris, C. and Byers, J.F. (2002) 'The effects of harp music in vascular and thoracic surgical patient.' *Alternative Therapies in Health and Medicine 8,* 5, 52–54, 56–60.

Block, S.M., Jennings, D. and David, L.R. (2003) 'Live harp music decreases salivary cortisol levels in convalescent premature infants.' *Pediatric Research 53,* 4, 469A–470A.

Bruscia, K.E. (1998) *Defining Music Therapy.* Phoenixville, PA: Barcelona Publishers.

Chiasson, A.M., Linda Baldwin, A., McLaughlin, C., Cook, P. and Sethi, G. (2013) 'The effect of live spontaneous harp music on patients in the intensive care unit.' *Evidence-Based Complementary and Alternative Medicine.* doi:10.1155/2013/428731.

Freeman, L., Caserta, M., Lund, D., Rossa, S., Dowdy, A. and Partenheimer, A. (2006) 'Music-thanatology: Prescriptive harp music as palliative care for the dying patient.' *American Journal of Hospice and Palliative Medicine, 23,* 2, 100–104.

Gardner, K. (1997) *Sounding the Inner Landscape.* London, UK: HarperCollins.

Hollis, J.L. (2010) *Music at the End of Life.* Santa Barbara, CA: Praeger.

Kemper, K.J. and Hamilton, C. (2008) 'Live harp music reduces activity and increases weight gain in stable premature infants.' *Journal of Alternative and Complementary Medicine 14,* 10, 1185–1186.

Laney, M. (1994) 'The Healing Power of Harps.' *Chicago Tribune* (11 December). Retrieved 23 October 2014 from http://articles.chicagotribune.com/1994-12-11/features/9412110424_1_harp-french-horn-cerebral-palsy.

Lewis, C.R., de Vedia, A., Reuer, B., Schwan, R. and Tourin, C. (2003) 'Integrating complementary and alternative medicine (CAM) into standard hospice and palliative care.' *American Journal of Hospice and Palliative Medicine 20,* 3, 221–228.

McTier, I. (2012) 'Music Therapy in a Special School for Children with Autistic Spectrum Disorder Focusing Particularly on the Use of the Double Bass.' In J. Tomlinson, P. Derrington and A. Oldfield (eds) *Music Therapy in Schools.* London, UK: Jessica Kingsley Publishers.

Rensch, R. (1989) *Harps and Harpists.* Bloomington, IN: Indiana University Press.

Sand-Jecklin, K. and Emerson, H. (2010) 'The impact of a live therapeutic music intervention on patients' experience of pain, anxiety, and muscle tension.' *Holistic Nursing Practice 24*, 1, 7–15.

Schroeder-Sheker, T. (1994) 'Music for the dying: A personal account of the new field of music-thanatology – history, theories, and clinical narratives.' *Journal of Holistic Nursing 12*, 1, 83.

Schroeder-Sheker, T. (2001) *Transitus: A Blessed Death in the Modern World.* Missoula, MT: St. Dunstan's Press.

CHAPTER 10

The Guitar

*Contributors: Steven Lyons, Jonathan Poole,
Caroline Long, Alex Street (introduction and
case vignettes) and Prodromos Stylianou*

Introduction

The guitar has evolved in form, structure and sound over many centuries into an instrument of incredible character and versatility. Early harps and lyres, pictured and described in Greek mythology and early religious documents, developed into fretted instruments, initially with gut frets before metal was used, offering increasing melodic and harmonic possibilities.

From the Middle Ages many types of stringed instruments are documented, but by the Renaissance three types of vihuela were in use: the vihuela de arco (bowed), vihuela de penola (played with a plectrum) and vihuela de mano (played with the fingers). The vihuela differed from the lute in that the back of the instrument was flat, as oppose to curved, and the sides were contoured in a similar fashion to the modern acoustic guitar. The Spanish have been acknowledged as the inventors of the vihuela, also referring to it as the viola.

The 16th-century vihuela had a four-course arrangement, meaning that it had four pairs of strings. The body was only a third the size of the modern classical guitar and the tuning was a fourth higher. From the 17th century many manuscripts for solo, five-course guitar have been preserved from Italy alone, but the total repertoire of pieces for solo guitar in this period far outnumber all those available for lute or keyboard.

The modern guitar's dimensions and construction emerged in Spain towards the end of the 18th century. But the string arrangement and tuning found today has vaguer origins, with some suggesting that it first came about in either France or Italy, towards the end of the 18th century. This led into the period of Fernando Sor and Mauro Giuliani, who enthralled early 19th-century audiences with their compositions and performances, and developed technical studies that still remain at the core of many students' formative repertoire today. At this time too, Luigi Boccherini placed the guitar within the classical ensemble and orchestra, composing guitar quintets, including *The Fandango*, and symphonies, which surely inspired the much later Rodrigo's *Concierto de Aranjuez* (1939) for classical guitar and orchestra.

In the 20th century Andreas Segovia, inspired by the playing and compositions of guitarist Francisco Tárrega, embarked on a lifelong journey that elevated the classical guitar to the international stage by rapidly expanding the repertoire, inspiring compositions such as *Douze Etudes* by Villa-Lobos, and breaking new ground with his technique. Segovia's contribution arguably paved the way for such great virtuosi as John Williams, Julian Bream, Sharon Isbin and Ana Vidovic. But the 20th century also saw the development and expansion of the guitar into other forms and genres. Spanish flamenco guitar playing was already well established, with Paco de Lucia carrying the tradition forward and becoming the most commercially successful guitarist of this genre from the 1970s to the present day. In France, and later the United States, Gypsy jazz flourished in the hands of Django Reinhardt, playing his specially designed Maccaferri guitar, built with an internal sound chamber to project his complex and fast melodies across noisy clubs. Reinhardt began using an electric guitar in the 1950s, but prior to this Charlie Christian brought the electric guitar to prominence as a solo instrument, also playing a key role in founding bebop jazz. Before John Lee Hooker became one of the best known exponents of the Delta blues, there were many such guitarists dating from the early 20th century: John Henry Barbee, Ishman Bracey and Robert Johnson, to name but a few.

Inspired by Charlie Christian, B.B. King and others, Chuck Berry became the most important founding-figure in rock guitar. The electric guitar went on to gain the most enduring iconic status across the world as a musical instrument used in commercial music, driven by the music and associated imagery of artists such as Jimi Hendrix, the Beatles and the Rolling Stones. But the acoustic guitar still remains the point of entry for guitar tuition in the majority of cases and is more often used in music therapy, offering greater portability, accessibility and flexibility.

The standard tuning for the six-string guitar, starting from the sixth (lowest) string, is: E2, A3, D3, G3, B4 and E4. It is also possible to use alternative tunings on the guitar. In the classical repertoire by far the most commonly used is the 'dropped D' tuning, where the sixth string is tuned down from E to D, producing a richer bass, which is utilised in compositions as an ostinato, while the main melody plays on the first and second strings. A well-recognised example of this is *Capricho Árabe* by Francisco Tárrega (1892).

Figure 10.1 Range of the guitar

The guitar is used by many music therapists as a simple way to accompany songs by strumming a few chords. Indeed in most music therapy training courses students are expected to learn basic guitar techniques. Some music therapists also take advantage of the fact that the open guitar strings are tuned to form a pentatonic scale, making the strumming of open guitar strings a good starting point for vocal improvisations in this same scale. In this chapter, however, first-study guitarists will explore how to use the guitar in more sophisticated ways, using their intricate knowledge, expertise and love of the instrument to interact with a wide range of different clients.

Playing, moving and sharing the guitar

Steven Lyons

I began playing the guitar in various bands as a teenager. At first it was about the social experience of getting together with friends and working out songs we liked. It was mostly playing by ear, improvising and playing around with musical ideas. Guitars featured in the music we liked and they were portable. I went on to study the guitar at university, where I developed an interest in finger-style guitar, exploring various tunings and constructing interesting solo arrangements. The guitar is such a versatile instrument used in so many different styles of music. I associate it with rock, blues and jazz, where it has played a prominent role in establishing the musical genres. But the guitar has also opened up my interest in music from other cultures such as flamenco, where it provides the accompaniment to singing and dancing.

In my clinical work I tend to use a classical nylon-string guitar, which is light to carry. I try to incorporate different techniques, including using a plectrum at times to add volume, especially when playing single melodic lines. The guitar is useful in that it can provide melodic, harmonic, rhythmic and percussive elements to a musical accompaniment. I work with clients who have communication difficulties, primarily with a diagnosis of autism. With young children I often find that the guitar is the instrument they are most drawn to as they come forward to strum the strings or tap the body around the sound hole for a percussive effect. For the older children and adults I work with, the guitar can provide an initial meeting point in terms of shared interest. The popularity of the guitar also makes it a unique starting point to explore social interaction and cultural identity.

Case vignette: Aiden

One particular case I can think of where the guitar played an important role was with Aiden, a man in his 50s. Aiden had spent years in institutional living environments, and much of his interaction was one-sided. For example, he would lick, poke and draw attention to himself, but only accepted limited reciprocal behaviour. His autism, learning difficulties and institutionalised lifestyle made continuity, stability and routine particularly important. I worked with Aiden for about a year. He was a very complex character with a strong sense of mischief and fun, but apparently simple tasks could confuse him.

On first meeting Aiden, the thing I noticed was that he never stopped moving. He continually walked around the room, was very tactile and liked to smell and taste most things he picked up. He also had a range of obsessional behaviours, including a need to open and close the door several times. I accompanied his footsteps using creeping melodic lines on my guitar, which he seemed to respond to. Each time he came towards me in his circle he would strum the strings of the guitar before moving on again. Occasionally we would break into more rhythmic strumming, and Aiden would rock back and forth in front of me clapping his hands and stamping his feet.

By incorporating Aiden's movements I tried to explore different rhythms, melodies and emotional themes. I found it useful to think of providing music to a dance where I had to match and synchronise with Aiden, but I also had to provide a framework. By introducing a scale or mode to work in, our interactions developed a different intensity. Quite often I found we would be in A minor or E major, but Aiden appeared to appreciate dissonant chords, as well as percussive tapping and slapping of the strings. As our work developed together I would often play a sustained dissonant chord and wait. Aiden could quickly become impatient at the pause in the music and approach me, vocalising his frustrations and pulling my hands towards the strings. This allowed us to develop some vocal interactions as we struggled with the guitar between us. Sometimes I would continue to play, but other times I would let our struggles develop, encouraging Aiden to voice his disapproval. These vocalisations would then inform the melodies, musical keys and emotional themes on the guitar, which changed to suit his vocal range.

Throughout our work together Aiden continued to hand me the guitar at the start of the session and didn't really want me to try anything else. I'm not sure if he came to associate me with the guitar, making it difficult for him to accept anything else or whether he just liked the guitar. Nevertheless, the guitar helped provide opportunities to explore the reciprocal interaction that he struggled with.

For me as a practitioner, working with Aiden made me appreciate the sensory qualities of the guitar more and the different textures of sound that could be achieved by the vibrations of the strings and the percussive effect of the body. It also reminded me that unlike some other more delicate instruments, the guitar is essentially a tough and robust piece of wire and wood that lends itself well to sharing.

Using the slide guitar in music therapy: 'Does this mean I'm clever?'

Jonathan Poole and Caroline Long

This contribution was written jointly by the music therapist Jonathan Poole and the music therapy student who was on placement with him at the time, Caroline Long. Jonathan talks about his particular relationship with the guitar at the beginning as he is a first-study guitarist.

Playing the guitar has always been much more than just a hobby that I use to pass the time: it has become a part of my identity. I began playing the guitar when I was about 11 years old, inspired by the sound of the electric guitar and the people who played it. It formed a significant part of my development during my adolescence, and was the source of many of my achievements and failures during that time. Playing the guitar gives me the freedom to express my emotions beyond my linguistic capabilities. It provides me with a musical mirror through which I can explore my personal growth.

The guitar is a versatile instrument: it can be used to play chords and melodic lines; it can be bowed, strummed or plucked with fingers or a plectrum; it can be tapped or struck for percussive effect; and it can be played with a slide.

Little has been written about the use of slide guitar in music therapy. The short case vignette below provides some qualitative evidence and insight into why playing the guitar with a slide might be useful in music therapy.

A guitar slide is usually a tube made of metal, ceramic or glass that is worn on a finger of the fret hand and gently pressed against the guitar strings. There is also a steel bar slide used for playing lap steel guitar (with the guitar held horizontally, strings facing upward). The guitar slide is held against the strings with enough force to make sufficient contact with the strings and smoothly alter the pitches of the notes played. However, the player must be careful not to apply so much force that the strings make contact with the fret board. Doing this will not produce a smooth glissando. When the slide is positioned directly over a fret, this allows the player to produce the note at that fret. Positioning the slide between frets produces notes that are slightly sharp or flat.

Using a slide to play the guitar offers the player a different range of possibilities compared to fretted playing. For example, it provides the opportunity to use portamento and glissando playing similar to violin, it allows for broad vibrato, and it has a singing quality emulating the human voice. When playing the slide guitar, players can rely more on their ear and their intuitive feel for where to go next in pitch; it frees the player from the fear of technical musical inadequacies. The case vignette focuses on the use of slide guitar in music therapy to overcome issues of being judged, which can inhibit engagement. It provides an example of how the slide guitar empowered a young man to explore pitch and briefly to relax and contribute more of his own opinion in music therapy. This case vignette aims to present a slide guitar as an accessible playing technique that promotes confidence in both the client and the therapist. It is hoped that clinicians will become more aware of slide guitar and consider using it in therapy sessions.

Case vignette: Dave

Dave, a young man in his last year at college, had a diagnosis of autism spectrum disorder, attention deficit disorder and obsessive eating disorder. He was tall, with a large frame and a gentle demeanour. He attended group music therapy sessions as part of the preparation for the transition from a special needs college to further education and to life after college. The group, named the 'Leavers' group, comprised those learners who were leaving that year. The objective was to provide a therapeutic space for leavers to prepare for a significant ending in their lives. The music therapy consisted of weekly, 45-minute sessions with opportunities for improvisation, playing pre-composed songs, songwriting and discussion. The session was co-facilitated by the music therapist (Jonathan) and the music therapy student (Caroline) on placement.

Dave had good musical ability, with a strong sense of rhythm, melodic and harmonic awareness and competent aural skills, and was able to learn simple phrases by ear. He was comfortable using the piano and drum kit and had explored the violin and electric bass. During group discussions, Dave was quiet and allowed his peers to take up leadership roles in all activities. When asked what he wanted to do or what he thought about what others said, he would withdraw, shrug his shoulders and often respond with silence. He had been known to leave lessons and wander round the college in order to avoid being challenged. When the group improvised music together, Dave's musical voice was more present and he showed more confidence. When his peers played, they individually tended to resist following the group rhythm or harmonic framework, playing on their own agenda. Dave's peers often played songs they had learned in music lessons. This resulted in several different songs being rehearsed simultaneously by each of the group members. Perhaps their need to be in control and their reliance on pre-composed, pre-learned material indicated their anxiety about improvisation. Pre-composed material can provide familiar resources that support engagement and provide a springboard for improvisations. When the group members' attention was drawn towards their anxiety about improvisation, they chose to avoid discussion, mirroring their reluctance to discuss other issues and feelings.

In contrast to his presentation during group discussions, Dave played musical instruments with more freedom and curiosity. He seemed more comfortable with the medium of music and improvisation. He gave consistent eye contact, smiled, and responded to musical gestures. He also seemed aware of the music-making of his peers, as well as that of Jonathan and Caroline.

Dave seemed to find musical interaction more comfortable than verbal interaction. There was an increase in his use of eye contact and in his use of musical exchanges. Over the course of therapy, Dave had had the opportunity to play the violin – an unfretted stringed instrument. He said that he had played the violin on a previous occasion when a visiting orchestra had given a workshop at the school. In this Leavers group session, he played it with keen enthusiasm and seemed comfortable with the instrument, producing a satisfactory tonal quality. Later, Dave played the electric bass and, after that improvisation, said that the music reminded him of music from a Western-style film, a scene in a ghost town.

In a subsequent session, Dave attended without his peers; they chose not to come. He was happy to play music throughout the session but showed a marked change in facial expression when asked any questions about his feelings. He lost his smile and animation, looking downcast and depressed. As soon as he engaged with an instrument, he cheered up. He joked about having a 'jam' – with 'toast' – and the therapists continued the joke. He chose the guitar. The music therapist unscrewed the top of a reed horn and showed Dave how to use it like a slide. Dave seemed to find this interesting and used the slide for the whole of the improvisation. He used the full range of pitch offered by the guitar, sliding up and down the strings, alternating between playing legato melodies and rhythmic phrases. The music therapist supported with the drum kit, alternating between providing grounding rhythms, matching Dave's expressive dynamics, and synchronising with his rhythms. The music therapy student sang and played the piano. Dave smiled and gave plenty of eye contact throughout this improvisation. He interacted with both Jonathan and Caroline, who both agreed that there was a sense of congruence in the music. When the music-making finished and Dave was asked what he thought, he did not speak and he presented as withdrawn.

The following week, Dave arrived without his peers again. Once in the room, Dave, Jonathan and Caroline sat in silence for a short while. This offered Dave the opportunity to talk about anything on his mind. He did not make use of this, preferring to play music for most of the session. After the first improvisation Jonathan tried to initiate a discussion about the mood in his classroom, but Dave did not respond and played the guitar over Jonathan's talking. For the first improvisation Dave played the electric guitar, Jonathan played drum kit and Caroline sang into the microphone. There was limited musical interest, and both Jonathan and Caroline later agreed that they became quite bored, and wondered how the session was going to be filled. Caroline was about to go to the piano, but Jonathan went and then changed his mind, and Caroline also decided against it. The improvisation turned into a known song, which Dave played repetitively. After a brief discussion – in which Dave avoided talking – Jonathan showed Dave how to practise the riff he was playing. Then Jonathan suggested they all had a go on different instruments. Dave went to the piano and Jonathan took the bass. Caroline began with the floor xylophone and then moved to the glockenspiel. Dave wanted the glockenspiel to be 'miked up' so that Caroline could be heard, so Jonathan arranged two microphones over it. This was experienced as more satisfying than the first improvisation.

In this session, Dave presented as being in an avoidant mood, resisting all attempts to discuss anything and drowning out Jonathan by playing over him when he tried to start conversation.

However, he enjoyed musical, non-verbal dialogue and said that he liked the freedom of playing 'random notes'. He was also much more directive about what Jonathan and Caroline played.

On a later occasion, Dave arrived rather hurriedly without his peers, joking with Jonathan and Caroline about his desire to hide from somebody. He was known for hiding around college. The three of them sat for a little while talking mildly. It was mentioned that it was Caroline's last day for the group due to the placement ending. Dave said that he would miss Caroline and said: 'Gone but not forgotten.'

He decided he wanted to play loudly on electric guitar. Jonathan adjusted the amplifier and then asked Caroline to give Dave the copper slide. Jonathan went to the drum kit and Caroline decided to listen to them. Dave started with his back to Jonathan but soon moved to another chair in order to see him. Dave smiled and exchanged plenty of eye contact with Caroline. Eventually Caroline joined them by singing into the microphone. This was a long improvisation, lasting for about 20 minutes. It was very clear in this session that Dave liked to play and was reluctant to talk. At the end of the session, Dave shook hands with Caroline and said goodbye. Before leaving, Dave asked Jonathan whether he thought Dave was skilled as a musician and asked: 'Does this mean I'm clever?'

Dave often presented as withdrawn and unresponsive when attempts were made to engage him in meaningful conversation about his life, opinions and feelings. The use of the violin awoke his curiosity and imagination in music therapy. This led to him playing the guitar with a slide, giving him further experience of playing without feeling judged or needing to conform to a rigid technique. For Dave, it was also a novel and exotic way of playing the guitar. Perhaps the use of the slide freed him from any preconceptions he had gained about playing musical instruments in previous musical experiences. This might have released him from feeling judged, which was a significant barrier to his expression. As a result, Dave seemed more able to give his opinions and to express his feelings.

The use of the slide can attract clients to explore the guitar through its exotic appeal. The slide can also overcome restrictions of learned finger patterns and scales and provide a connection with the human voice.

Classical guitar within music therapy

Prodromos Stylianou

Thinking back to my childhood, joyful and distressing moments have always been accompanied by music improvised on my guitar. Since I was six years old, the guitar has been an important aspect of who I am as a person, and I have had the identity of a 'classical guitarist'. When I hold the guitar a unique bond is created. Our two bodies (the guitar's and mine) connect and together they create something exquisite. The correct co-ordination between the left and the right hand contribute to the sound quality produced by the guitar. The proper body stance demonstrates confidence as well as the relation a guitarist has with his instrument.

The body posture of holding a guitar is very similar to a hug. Both are comforting, supportive and provide companionship. A hug can be a safe place for people, and the guitar can grow to become a safe place for the guitarist. As a music therapist, I have often noticed that patients playing the guitar hug their instruments.

When I perform with my guitar it feels like the whole world is in my fingers. The guitar is very responsive as an instrument and every touch produces a sound that can be alternated according to the nature of the fingernails, to the pressure I apply to the instrument as well as to the place in which I position my fingers on the neck of the guitar. I believe that the guitar is the only instrument in which the physical contact between the instrument and the performer can change the sound quality and characteristics of the sound to such a great extent.

Case vignette: John

John was a young boy of eight who had been diagnosed with autism spectrum disorder at the age of three. John was non-verbal, and communication throughout his life had been very difficult. His only contribution to decision making was occasionally to express his preference through singing sounds. John was very active and often hostile to anyone who tried to engage him in any way. His special needs teacher had referred John for music therapy, in the hope that this would help with his communication skills as well as help him to engage with other people around him.

During the initial music therapy assessment John immediately connected with music-making. He made many vocal singing sounds and played the drum set, at the same time as rushing around the room. John appeared to be very energetic, playing a number of instruments at the same time. He would hold as many instruments as he could in his hands and then throw one on the floor and laugh.

When John first started therapy he would run into the music therapy room eager to start the session by playing the drums. At this stage John was quite aggressive and would hit and pinch me at every opportunity. These difficult behaviours also occurred with his family at home, and I discussed what boundaries should be set in the therapy session. For example, if John became aggressive, I would calmly stop what I was doing and turn away to help him to understand that this behaviour was inappropriate. I would also be alert to how physically close we were to one another, making sure we were both comfortable and at ease with our proximity.

Initially, John was primarily interested in playing the drums. He demonstrated an excellent sense of rhythm and his playing was musical. I found it exciting improvising with him. At times, however, John seemed to become over-aroused and stimulated, and I tried to create a calmer musical atmosphere in the hope that he would relax a little. To do this I chose to interact with him through playing the guitar. This was partly because of the interest John had previously shown in the guitar and partly because I felt I could affect the mood in the room through this playing. I also related John's wish and need to touch and hold the guitar to his need for a hug and physical warmth.

I started improvising classical melodies on the guitar: *Asturias*, *Recuerdos de la Alhambra*, *Cavatina*, using different tempi and dynamics, according to John's movement as he wandered around the room and played the drums. It felt like the music was touching his psyche and heart. John stopped running around the room and concentrated on my fingers and the sounds that were filling the room. After a short time John's fingers came closer to the guitar and I offered him the space to touch and play the instrument and explore the sounds that could be produced. He gradually took the opportunity to discover the instrument by tapping it, strumming the strings and trying to produce sounds.

Classical guitar melodies then became part of all the music therapy sessions. John would sit still, concentrating on the music that was being created. He gradually figured out that the style and mode of the music would follow his hand movements and this made the musical improvisations even more interesting for him. He started being the conductor of the music. He would move his hands slowly and the music would be minor and quiet, or else he would move them fast and the music would change to major and loud. His interest grew even more when he gradually became able to control his fingers to play some notes on the guitar using both hands. He found that very exciting, and this put a huge smile on his face.

Almost two years after the start of the therapeutic relationship John is no longer hostile towards me. I am no longer afraid to work opposite him, and I no longer worry about being pinched or hit. The guitar, rather than the drum, has now become his favourite instrument. His family have been very encouraged by his interest in the guitar and impressed by his ability to relax when surrounded by guitar music. They have bought him a guitar to use at home.

Classical guitar playing became a pivotal part of John's life owing to his need to bond and communicate with other people. My expertise with the guitar and the classical repertoire provided a supportive and secure space for John to be taken notice of, as well as to express his creativity. That became possible with my adaptation of the music to his movements and by encouraging him to conduct my classical music performances. Using other, non-classical, styles of music or different instruments might also have worked, but my expertise in both the therapeutic relationship and the guitar as an instrument with its vast possibilities when using classical technique made it my obvious first choice.

The guitar is part of who I am. I can be creative, supportive, engaging, melancholic, and joyful with it. It follows me everywhere I am and I take it everywhere I go.

The two guitarists as warp and weft

Alex Street

Figure 10.2 Strumming and singing together

'Warp: the yarns arranged lengthways on a loom through which the weft yarns are woven.' (*Collins Dictionary*)

I bought my first guitar when I was 11 years old. Having attempted several chords illustrated in the accompanying book, I realised that I would like some lessons. The Elvis Presley, Beatles and Sex Pistols songs that I had hoped to master remained beyond my reach for a while longer as I inadvertently stumbled into the classical repertoire in the capable hands of my German classical guitar teacher. Inevitably, the allure of amplifiers and electric guitars interrupted this initial two-year period and allowed me to enter into the world of Jimi Hendrix, Eric Clapton and, more importantly for me, improvisation and experimental recording.

A third phase in my development as a guitarist occurred after several years of performing in bands, song-writing and recording. One spring morning, whilst I was working as a sound engineer, I heard the guitarist from a band called The La's playing in the studio courtyard. The piece that inspired me to begin exploring the classical repertoire again was *Recuerdos de la Alhambra* by Francisco Tárrega. I would even go as far as to say that this experience eventually led me to complete all of my Associated Board grades, perform the repertoire on a small and thoroughly enjoyable scale, and study at the Guildhall School of Music and Drama as part of my music degree. Later, it became a key part of my music therapy training, as my two guitar teachers at the time helped me to explore my relationship with the instrument by approaching pieces from a purely musical perspective and with much less emphasis on technique. This process led me to become much more connected with the guitar, allowing me to play with more expressive range, both as an improviser in clinical situations and when playing repertoire.

I still enjoy playing the classical repertoire. I love the rich tone of the classical guitar when the fingernails are shaped and hit the strings just right. This type of guitar is my preference in clinical music therapy work, but I also enjoy improvising on steel-string and electric guitars, and recording, performing or simply jamming with other musicians whenever possible. The guitar has become an old and trusted friend of mine. It can frustrate me as I wrangle with technique when attempting Walton's *Bagatelles* or the Bach lute suites, but it will always sit close to me and listen to what I have to say, letting me connect my inner workings with the outer world as I pluck and strum.

Case vignette: Oscar

Oscar was 13, diagnosed with Asperger's syndrome and in a mainstream secondary school, when he was referred to me for music therapy. Despite the best efforts of school, family and social services to support Oscar, he was struggling to cope with the educational demands, classroom dynamics and everyday social complexities that he experienced within his school.

The deputy head of music at Oscar's school first approached me to discuss his referral to music therapy. She conveyed that his parents felt that he might be motivated by music-making, and that he liked the guitar. The teacher explained to me about Oscar's anxiety levels, and that he struggled to let staff and peers know how he was feeling and what he needed in order to cope and progress in school. I was then able to highlight some areas in which music therapy might be of use, principally in facilitating music improvisation in order to develop a non-verbal dialogue, allowing Oscar to express his mood and feelings, and feel listened to, understood and less anxious and isolated as a result. The teacher explained that Oscar wished to bring an electric guitar that his parents had bought him; thus the seed was planted that we would begin our sessions using guitars.

When I met Oscar for the first time he looked pleased to see me, but was tight-lipped, eyes flitting to and from mine, with a rigid posture and very few words spoken. When he did speak, his words were mumbled and accelerated, almost mono-tonal and very quiet. At his most anxious, Oscar would appear absolutely physically tense and unable to speak a single word.

Oscar liked the guitar, and listened to music a lot. From our first session together, it did not take long for our musical dialogue to emerge and develop. But his electric guitar was replaced by one of the school's classical guitars very early on. Electric guitars can be problematic, particularly at the beginner stage. Unless it is of quite high quality, costing at least two or three hundred pounds new, there will inevitably be problems with tuning and intonation. Electric guitar strings also break more easily than classical ones and, of course, they require connection to an amplifier using a reliable and durable lead, the latter often causing the biggest problems. For Oscar, using an instrument that regularly presented most of these problems, including finding a school amplifier that worked correctly, meant that he quickly turned his favour towards the infinitely more accessible school classical guitars.

Oscar always initiated our improvisations. He played the guitar with an astonishingly rich and varied range of dynamics, tempo and rhythm, mainly produced through strumming the open strings using various right-hand finger combinations. In some improvisations Oscar played one string only, using thumb down-strokes, then switched to index or middle finger flicking up and down across the first and second strings. In this way he produced steady, pulsed rhythms that could be bursting with energy, calmly flowing, or meandering solemnly. Then Oscar would initiate an increase or decrease in tempo, or lead us into a *fortissimo* crescendo, playing across all six strings before fading our music softly into silence. There were moments when Oscar would pull on the strings, making them snap percussively in different rhythms against the fingerboard. He moved with increasing fluency around the guitar, switching right-hand finger techniques to create different colours, textures or timbres. He played *sul ponticello*, strumming and plucking near to the bridge of the guitar, creating a tighter, thinner, more tense sound; or moved towards the sound-hole to produce a more neutral timbre; or softly stroked the strings, *sul tasto*, over the fingerboard, producing a full, rounded, more relaxed tone. This was Oscar's evolving musical language on the guitar, developed at his own pace, over time and as the result of our regular improvisations.

Strumming the open strings using up- or down-strokes, in various combinations of single strings, two or three simultaneously, five strings playing down-stroke from the A-string bass, etc, produces variations on a single chord, but not clear harmonic progressions. Improvising melodies over strummed open-string combinations is, therefore, well suited to modal styles of playing. Any mode can be used, depending, in respect of this case vignette, on the perceived mood evoked by Oscar's playing.

Starting with the open fourth or fifth string, using the Mixolydian mode (the same as the diatonic major scale but with a flattened seventh) or the open sixth string using the Aeolian (the same as the natural minor scale) is a simple and effective way to accompany open strumming by creating quite melodic riffs and material. In contrast, tension can be created using the Locrian mode beginning on any open string and playing the semitone, tone, tone, semitone, tone, tone, tone pattern all the way up that string, perhaps suited to louder, faster and arrhythmic strumming passages.

Oscar's style of guitar playing acted as the pedal on the loom that spun the threads of my ostinatos into melodic phrases and variations. The textures and fabric of our interwoven melody and harmony were interpretations and translations of Oscar's moods and inner dialogue. At times the music we wove together was quite Stravinskian, with a raw, pulsating drive to it. Whilst playing together, I would sometimes hear echoes of Leo Brouwer, whose works, such as *El Decameron Negro* (1996), take short ostinato phrases, gradually extend them melodically and interject them with splashes of rhythmic colour. Oscar would begin with a rhythm, tempo and dynamic, and we would depart, sometimes with great confidence and at other times tentatively, on our journey together. As we responded to one another in the music, Oscar's rhythm guitar and my melodic responses evoked a series of subtly shifting, in-the-moment moods. At times when I offered a verbal reflection on our music, he would confirm that he was feeling calm, or angry, confused or tired and vacant, enabling him to acknowledge how he was feeling and to share these feelings more directly with me using words.

Opposite (Figure 10.3) is an excerpt taken from one of our sessions, in which Oscar initiates with almost inaudible strumming, building into *mezzopiano* (*mp*) at a steady pulse of approximately 160 beats per minute. From the point at which he reaches *mp*, I enter with a semibreve phrase, which then develops into brief quaver and crotchet ostinatos, weaving in and out of Oscar's strongly pulsed and steady playing. The dynamic phrasing of my melody is prompted by Oscar's sometimes subtle shifts in dynamic as he strums, enhancing this weaving effect. Towards the end of this excerpt Oscar changes rhythm from straight crotchets to a quaver crotchet pattern, possibly in response to the rhythm used in my melody. The excerpt ends with a space left in my playing, in order that Oscar can hear himself clearly, with his newly established rhythm. In the second half of this four-minute improvisation, Oscar changes to a rhythm using minims, effectively halving the tempo from the initial speed.

It was clear that Oscar was able to translate much of his inner world, his thoughts and feelings, into his own musical language and share this with me, thus alleviating the pressures, which he experienced daily within school, of trying to find ways of telling people that he was feeling anxious or frustrated, and of explaining why and what he needed to help him cope.

We improvised together in this way every week, without interruption. Oscar always appeared very comfortable and at ease holding the guitar and never considered using any of the percussion and drums that were available, or the piano, despite my making him aware of these possibilities. His choice in using the guitar each week never became a concern, as his repertoire of playing techniques expanded continuously; there was no 'stuckness', and he clearly identified with this instrument. Our routine of entering the room, taking up our guitars, sitting and waiting for the first sound to be played provided a clear framework for Oscar, within which he recognised that he could interact and communicate with me safely and reliably when he was ready.

Figure 10.3 Excerpts of Oscar and Alex improvising

In some sessions, before we began playing I would comment on how he appeared to me, always monitoring his capacity to talk about or describe his mood and any causes of anxiety. At times his responses would comprise several sharp exhalations, tutting and sighing, or he would respond, through tight jaw and gritted teeth, 'I just don't know, I can't say it.' These responses really emphasised how much we needed simply to play, and connect through improvisation.

Oscar's breathing and posture would frequently become more steady and relaxed during and after we had played together. He would respond with a comment about the music, after I had made one, but he rarely initiated his own feedback. When he did comment, his voice was clearer, with more projection and less tension in his vocal chords and facial muscles. The dialogue that we engaged in each week was improvised via our own musical syntax, which we both recognised. Oscar's responses to my playing were usually instantaneous, showing that he was listening closely and ready, willing and able to respond. When he changed register, intensity, dynamic or rhythm, I could follow or contrast, and the flow of our dialogue would be uninterrupted. This trusting relationship reinforced Oscar's confidence, our mutual understanding of one another and awareness of these potentials.

Three years later, as he began college, Oscar would telephone me himself to arrange external music therapy sessions in which he talked freely about the music he was passionate about and described the ways in which he wanted to remix many of his favourite tracks on CD, which we then did together using a computer and music software over several weeks.

Case vignette: Carl

About ten years before I met Oscar, I spent some time teaching the guitar to a little boy, Carl, who was ten. He was very quiet, never asking questions or initiating any comment, and when I would ask him something his answer was brief and very softly spoken. Carl went to a mainstream school and had no diagnosis. At the time, I was not a music therapist and had not even decided to train as one, but as part of my music degree I had taken a ten-week module in music therapy and I had written my dissertation on music therapy techniques in mainstream primary school music education.

As we proceeded from the early stages, in which Carl quickly and easily learned how to pluck the strings and fret notes, to the beginnings of sight-reading, I noticed that he was becoming distracted and a little tense. He struggled not only to translate and co-ordinate the written notes into sounds, but also to sustain his attention on this process. I arrived one day for our lesson and noticed some small dents in the front of his guitar. We continued to work on some basic pieces until one week, when I noticed that the small dents had become larger and there were deeper cuts into the wood, where the top meets the side of the instrument, as if it had been bitten. This was a clear indication that Carl was becoming very frustrated with what we were doing with the guitar, and the marks were, in fact, his teeth marks.

The lesson proceeded, but with a new direction. The music that we had been working on previously was not placed on the music stand, instead I moved the stand aside and asked Carl to choose some notes using his left hand on the fingerboard and to play whatever he liked. He began to play two notes on the first (E) string: E and F. I waited, then I replied, playing the same notes, but then adding one more, G. Carl added this note and as he played I gently strummed a C major and then a G major chord over his melody. I suggested that he could play each note as many times as he liked and in any order, and to try adding some more notes on the second string. Carl did this with quickly growing confidence.

The following week, we continued to improvise in this way, Carl appeared relaxed and noticeably more engaged and motivated than he had been over the previous lessons. This became the structure of every weekly lesson, and the guitar suffered no more injury. Quite soon after moving forward in this way, we also began to write the notes that Carl played in a little manuscript book that I gave him. This approach effectively gave a manageable pace to his learning and access to the language of music, both as a medium through which we improvised together and as a written form through which he could capture his ideas, share them, revisit and develop them. Carl regularly played his compositions to his parents, and they expressed their pleasure to me in hearing them.

After a year of teaching Carl, I was forced to stop as I had to move some distance away from where he lived. About ten years later, Carl's mother contacted me and I was very happy to hear that he was in the second year of his music degree, studying composition, singing, playing guitar, double bass and piano, as well as playing in various, regularly performing ensembles. She also shared with me that Carl was on the autistic spectrum, but that this had not been explored or confirmed until shortly after our lessons had ended.

At one point, the guitar had become a kind of menace, an instrument of torture that brought distress and displeasure to Carl. He briefly vented his frustrations at not being able to understand the musical language that I was trying to impart to him by causing damage to the instrument. The therapeutic relationship, both with the instrument and with me, began when Carl was guided towards free playing and the manuscript put aside as self-expression was facilitated. The next stage was for us to begin recording Carl's musical phrases, melodies and all the things from his creative mind that began to enter our shared world. We did this by notating and developing his ideas. Perhaps this experience of 'making things work' with the guitar and with me had a greater depth of meaning as an experience of discovering ways of communicating, resolving conflict and building relationships for Carl, that will operate and endure both within his musical world and in his general life.

Guitar characteristics in music therapy practice
A familiar, 'cool' instrument
Unlike many of the instruments mentioned in this book, the guitar is familiar to all and, because of its association with pop music and bands, is often immediately a very appealing and desirable instrument. In several of the cases described, the clients very clearly chose the guitar above all the other instruments.

An instrument that clients can play themselves and develop basic skills on
In all of the case vignettes, clients were invited to play the guitar through strumming or tapping. In three cases clients played their own guitars in more sophisticated ways, sometimes dialoguing with the therapist who was also playing a guitar. In one case the use of the slide on the guitar enabled a client to play more easily.

The accessibility of the acoustic guitar
Unlike many other instruments described in this book, there are usually guitars available to play in most schools or institutions, and reasonable instruments can be purchased at affordable prices. Several of the guitarists mentioned how being a guitarist was an identity they readily took on as teenagers. Some of the clients mentioned in this chapter also had their own guitars and wanted to take on this identity. In one case the parents of a child were delighted to purchase a guitar for their son as a result of interest generated through the music therapy sessions. Electric guitars were also used and written about. However, unlike acoustic guitars, they are more expensive and less easy to transport and set up. One writer mentioned the pitfalls

associated with low-quality leads, non-functioning electric guitars and amplifiers, as a particular source of frustration for the child he was working with. For this reason most of the music therapists tended to use acoustic guitars more often than electric ones.

The acoustic guitar is resilient and less delicate than many of the other instruments described in this book

Guitarists will often be using instruments belonging to the institution and will not be nervous about the safety of the instrument. This means they can be relaxed about clients handling and playing the instrument.

Figure 10.4 Creative ways of playing the guitar

The versatility of the guitar to be both an accompanying rhythmic instrument and to provide a melody line

All the therapists used the guitar both to accompany their clients through strumming chords and as a way to play tunes. The fact that the guitar can do both these things very easily and is associated with both roles was mentioned as a special feature of the instrument in music therapy. In one case the music therapist was able to help a child to start improvising by accompanying with chords and encouraging the child to pick out individual notes. This then enabled the child to be free and creative in new ways.

The association of the guitar with singing

The use of singing or vocal sounds with the guitar was mentioned in all the cases. Sometimes the music therapist sang with the guitar and sometimes the client was encouraged to vocalise. By singing straight into the guitar, the voice can be amplified in quite dramatic ways, which can be useful at times.

The variety of tone colour

Several guitarists mentioned the advantage of being able to vary sounds through using a plectrum, fingers or nails to produce the notes. A note of caution though: some clients may enjoy posting the plectrum into the guitar hole, which might be a disadvantage.

The guitar as a way of accompanying movements

Two of the clients described in this chapter were very active and moved around the room a lot. Both therapists used guitar playing to accompany and effect changes in the clients' movements.

Pentatonic tuning of the open strings

This was mentioned as an advantage by most of the therapists, enabling improvisations to occur, or to be started more easily. The possibilities of different types of tuning for the strings were also referred to.

The way the guitar is held when it is played

Several authors mentioned the importance of the guitar being held near the body and being hugged by the player. The fact that the vibrations of the wood can be felt as the guitar is played was also thought to be significant.

Portability of the acoustic guitar

It was mentioned that the acoustic guitar is light and easy to carry around, particularly in contrast to the electric guitar with its heavy accompanying amplifier. Several guitarists mentioned that their instrument was always there by their side even if it was not played.

Special qualities of classical guitar music

Two guitarists wrote about the calming effect they felt classical guitar playing could have in their work. There was an element of surprise here as clients were not initially expecting the guitar to produce this kind of music. Interestingly, none of the guitarists mentioned the fact that the acoustic guitar was quite quiet, which is a feature that many classical orchestral players of other instruments might associate with the acoustic guitar. Perhaps this is because the guitar in therapy will be used both as a classical instrument and an accompanying rhythmic instrument, and it will not appear quiet when it doesn't have to compete with an orchestra.

References

Coelho, V.A. (2003) *The Cambridge Companion to the Guitar.* Cambridge, UK: Cambridge University Press.

Denyer, R. (1994) *The Guitar Handbook.* London, UK: Dorling Kindersley.

Turnbull, H. (1974) *The Guitar: From the Renaissance to the Present Day.* London, UK: Cox and Wyman.

CHAPTER 11

Lower Brass (the Trombone and the Euphonium)

Contributors: Trygve Aasgaard (trombone introduction and case vignettes), George Murray (trombone case vignette) and Helen Mottram (euphonium introduction and case vignette)

The Trombone

Introduction

The trombone is one of the wind instruments that has changed its shape the least during the past four hundred years. It is basically a long brass tube with a mouthpiece at one end and a far larger opening, a bell, at the other end. Like all brass instruments, sound is produced when the player's vibrating lips cause the air column inside the instrument to vibrate. Most trombones have a telescoping slide mechanism that varies the length of the instrument (and the air column) to change the pitch.

During the Renaissance and Baroque periods, the various families of instruments were characterised as either 'soft' (e.g. string instruments and recorders) or 'loud' (e.g. trumpets or shawms [early oboes]). Trombones or sackbuts, as they were then called, could be either 'soft' or' 'loud', depending on the setting in which they were played.

The term 'sackbut' was primarily used within English, French and Spanish realms until the end of the 18th century. In German-speaking countries the name of this instrument has always been *Posaune*, and in Italy *trombone* has a 500-year-long history. They were more delicately constructed than their modern counterparts and feature a softer sound, blending well with the human voice. Today trombones are based on originals from the 16th or 17th century.

The total range of a trombone is more than two-and-a-half octaves. While the lowest note of the tenor trombone's range (excluding fundamentals or pedal notes) is E2, the instrument's upper range is theoretically open-ended. Modern tenor trombones are often equipped with an extra attachment of tubing – about three feet or one metre in length – thus giving the player the option to lower the fundamental pitch from Bb to F. The smaller alto trombone is pitched a perfect fourth or fifth higher than the tenor trombone. Bass trombones have a wider bore and larger bell to aid the production of a fuller, weightier tone in the lower register. Like a stringed instrument, a trombone can play a true glissando – this is done by moving the slide without interrupting the airflow. Distinct notes are played by moving the slide in seven different positions (which always have to be adjusted during performance for fine tuning) and through changing the airflow with the lips.

During the 19th century, after the invention of valve systems (usually with three valves) for various brass instruments (e.g. trumpet, French horn), trombone and tuba instrument makers developed trombones with the slide mechanism replaced by valves. A Bb tenor valve trombone uses the same fingering as the Bb trumpet. Fast musical figures are often easier to execute on a valve trombone than on a slide trombone. The sound, however, is more open and distinct on a slide trombone. Valve trombones can be heard in brass bands and jazz settings, but very seldom in the symphony orchestra, where the trombone section usually consists of three musicians, the first playing tenor or alto trombone, the second playing tenor, and the third playing bass.

The various trombone pitches are in the same range as the cello and the bassoon. Often, the three trombones play harmonies together. While the trombones in the symphony orchestra have grown in size (i.e. getting a larger bore) since the middle of the 20th century in order to produce a big, colourful and brilliant sound, there are musicians, especially on the jazz/pop scene or in brass bands, who prefer instruments with a more mellow and sweet tone and a lighter style of playing.

Figure 11.1 Alto trombone range

Figure 11.2 Tenor trombone range

There are currently two brands of plastic trombones on the market, pBone and Tromba. Plastic is a cheaper and more robust alternative to brass instruments and is manufactured in several bright colours. Because plastic trombones are very light, children have far fewer problems holding the instrument in the correct position while blowing. The sound is not bad, but slightly dull and dry. Both tenor and alto plastic trombones are available. Tromba also makes a tenor, Jazzbone, where the slide is half the length of an ordinary tenor trombone. Few children below 12 years of age are able to reach even the sixth slide position on a tenor trombone, thus the Jazzbone certainly makes it easier for younger people to master the instrument.

Trombone parts are typically notated in bass clef, though often in the classical repertoire are also written in the tenor or alto clef. The trombone is not usually considered a transposing instrument (a C played on the trombone sounds like a C played on a piano). In brass band music, however, the tenor trombone is treated as a transposing instrument in Bb and reads the treble clef.

The current trombone solo repertoire (with or without accompaniment) stretches from the simplest arrangements of popular music to virtuoso avant-garde compositions. Since the early days of jazz, the trombone has been used to outline the chords, play countermelodies and to improvise. Also in Latin-American music, funk and (the less-common) rock horn sections, trombones play an important role.

The trombone as a way of life among other musical instruments

Trygve Aasgaard

My father, Roar Aasgaard, was a very versatile musician and trombone teacher at the Oslo Conservatory of Music (the forerunner of the Norwegian Academy of Music). I simply grew up playing the trombone, which felt the most natural thing to do. From the age of 12, I played the trombone and the piano in various jazz and dance music bands. As a student of music at the University of Oslo, I got my first sackbut and became passionately interested in early music. I was also spending much effort and time as a member of the First of May Recorder Quartet (with the music therapy pioneer and scholar Even Ruud). Years later I established the Oslo Baroque Winds, where I played tenor zink in addition to alto and tenor sackbut and performed with the Norwegian Baroque Orchestra. The tenor zink (tenor cornet/lizard) is a Renaissance instrument. It has a curved shape like a flattened letter S, with finger holes like a recorder and with a wooden mouthpiece a little smaller than that of the alto trombone. It is rather difficult to play in tune in the lower register, but has an angelic and clear descant. I have used the tenor zink sporadically in music therapy settings as a supportive lead instrument in sing-songs, especially in ballads, or in mini concerts with early music where the audience have often been engaged in clapping hands, stamping feet or playing finger cymbals. Many young service users have commented on how 'cool' this instrument sounds. I was also involved in many big-band projects as a musician and arranger.

Trombone players are still rare birds in the world of music therapy. As a music therapy student at the Guildhall School of Music and Drama in 1970, I never thought of using my horn in practice, although I had both trombone and piano lessons included in the syllabus. The music therapist's tool of the trade at that time was the piano, with almost no exceptions, other than our principal Juliette Alvin's cello. Some years later, however, I had my first trombone experiences of assisting teenagers in a youth psychiatric institution in making music together. Since then, my music therapy practice with trombones has primarily taken place in hospice and hospital settings. Even if the piano and other keyboard instruments always constituted the main instruments in my work, there have been few days when a trombone was not used at all.

My favourite instruments are the contemporary King 3B or Bach Stradivarius tenor trombones, which are extremely effective when playing in bands with service users, hospital doctors and nurses. In my individual music therapy sessions, however, I have preferred using an Egger alto or Meinl & Lauber tenor sackbut. One reason for this is that, as indicated in the introduction, sackbuts have less volume than contemporary instruments; the mellow sound of these small-bore trombones blends particularly well with the human voice, even if only one person is singing. Another practical reason for my extensive use of baroque trombones is that I needed to practise a lot; for several years I was performing and touring extensively with early-music ensembles at the same time as working as a music therapist. Including these instruments in my music therapy practice was an enjoyable and convenient way of warming up for later concerts.

Another practical consideration for all music therapists considering using the trombone in their clinical practice is that like all other wind instruments, trombones are potential bacterial traps owing to the small reservoirs of moisture that easily develop within the instrument. The inner tubing of the trombone slide and mouthpiece must therefore be frequently cleaned with antibacterial detergents. This is necessary in all music therapy settings, and particularly so when working with service users with potentially lowered immune systems (e.g. related to cancer diseases and treatment). Many young people want to have a go at trying to play or just making a sound on the trombone. Here, it is important to be a little strict with children eagerly demanding to blow your horn. One way around this may be to keep a plastic trombone to hand to the client, which can be thoroughly cleaned after each use.

A trombone may be used to play the melody or a bass line (or anything in between) in many different genres and settings. In music therapy, an effective trombone player must be able to read and transpose music from various clefs, improvise and play quite freely, and make up instant attractive and functional bass lines.

A small Baroque trombone (sackbut) has been useful in individual bedside sessions where I have been playing for very sick patients.

Once a middle-aged woman, dying from cancer, but unable to move anything but her eyelids and tongue because of serious multiple sclerosis, whispered after I had played and improvised over one of her favourite jazz tunes: 'If I had been able to move my hands, I would have been clapping just now!'

The value of experiencing live music – as listeners or participants – simply because we are humans must not be underestimated by music therapists. In many different clinical fields I have arranged small concerts with trombone(s) accompanied by piano or in wind ensembles. Here, the type of instrument is far less important than the musician's musical and communicative skills. It is always encouraging to play for people who have had very little experience with classical music, but who say they are 'lifted' by a performance. When playing the trombone in various groups, music very often has to be especially arranged as the existing repertoire for trombones in the field of chamber music is not extensive.

Examples of individual work

In the music therapy room, I have often collaborated with patients wanting to play an instrument better or to be accompanied on songs they wanted to sing. Clinical improvisation has always been on the menu, but some patients have been particularly interested to learn, or simply take part in, jazz or rock improvisations. One patient, a 42-year-old woman and Church of Norway minister, improved various skills in playing jazz on her flute. She was often supported by a music therapy student on guitar or piano and by me playing the trombone. At other times, we were able to enjoy ourselves through playing improvised flute and trombone duets.

A daughter recommended that the music therapist at the hospice should see her mother. The lady in her late 60s had responded more with anger than with sorrow when being informed that she had an incurable and rapidly progressing cancer disease. For days she had been banging her fist into pillows and on tables. She clearly felt that life was unjust. I asked her if she, perhaps, would like to improvise a little with me on the conga drums, and she actually seemed to like it. At our next session she was offered a full drum set, which gave her the opportunity to accompany my trombone solo. After ten minutes, our roles were switched; the patient, suddenly and surprisingly let go with rather wild and dramatic outbursts on the drums and cymbals. After a few seconds of bewilderment, I began playing a steady rhythmical pulse on the trombone. The big movements of my right arm (on the slide), probably also supported the ground beat of the heavy drumming. The trombone slide may well serve as a baton or as a visual illustration of essential features when improvising music in this way.

Figure 11.3 and 11.4: Sensing the vibrations

If the opening of the bell is placed directly on a person's skull, this person will experience the vibrating instrument and airflow created by the blowing, as a strong tickle. I have done this with children with severe hearing loss, and they often seem to appreciate this physical way of enjoying the music. Once I was presented to a seven-year-old girl who was partly blind and almost completely deaf in addition to having severe learning difficulties. Her preferred way of communication was tactile, and she liked to be cuddled and stroked by people she knew, but would easily get frightened by unfamiliar situations. Very, very slowly I approached her, talking softly and letting her touch me – and then the trombone. After some time, I placed the bell of the trombone close to one of her hands and blew carefully, and then, after many minutes, I repeated the procedure placing the bell on the top of her skull and varying the tones (and thus altering the vibrations). After a couple of repetitions she started to smile and wave her hands, and I was quite sure she, at that moment, was experiencing in a seemingly pleasant way, what music could be.

Case vignette: Selma

In a few cases, I have deviated from the rule of refusing to let clients touch the mouthpiece with their lips. During a four-day family gathering arranged by the Norwegian Society for the Support of Children with Cancer, I met a 13-year-old girl called Selma who had had a long history of battling with a rather uncommon form of cancer. All the children and teenagers present, except for some brothers and sisters, had problems related to earlier radiation treatment. Selma was not good at mixing with other young people; she persistently claimed that no one understood how sick she had been and how special she was now. She looked healthy but clearly had some communication and learning difficulties. Selma seemingly wanted to stay special, but also to be visible in the group of families and professionals in the beautiful hotel in the mountains. She told me that she was not a patient any longer and that she had just started playing a tenor horn in her local school brass band. Now she really wanted to try out the trombone; perhaps the two of us could play something together at the scheduled concert for the parents?

After a thorough cleaning of a small alto trombone, I taught her some basic tromboning. She produced a quite nice and focused sound; the mouthpiece was not very different from that of her tenor horn at home. However, Selma could not yet read music. We decided to go for a blues in Eb for two trombones where I played a melody and Selma accompanied me playing fundamentals in the three necessary chords: Eb and Bb in first position (without using the slide) and Ab in third position. I conducted her by pointing my trombone slide downwards, straight, or upright, to indicate which note she should play. After practising for two days our duo received rapturous applause at the concert. Selma had played her part remarkably well. She really appeared as someone special among the other children. After this presentation, she seemed to relax a little more in the company of the other youngsters.

Processions

Musical processions through hospital corridors serve many purposes. They can provide a spectacular way of informing, collecting, inspiring and leading young patients from different wards to an upcoming event, like the weekly Musical Hour, which takes place in some paediatric departments of Norwegian university hospitals. My choice of instruments is dependent on which other musicians are available on that particular day. On many occasions I have led the procession while playing the trombone at the same time. The trombone has the advantage of being loud and dramatic, and can be played at the same time as I walk. For one hour every participant is a potential singer, musician or actor rather than a patient, parent, nurse, physician, student or therapist.

The participants are first of all patients: some in wheelchairs, some in beds, many with infusion pumps. But also relatives, students (of various kinds) and people working in the hospital – altogether 20 or 30 people – may be present. Sometimes a dozen (young and old) start the event by marching or wheeling through the corridors playing and singing. In front walks the music therapist in top hat, blowing his trombone. As a rule, more and more participants join the line of musicians as the procession slowly proceeds from the eighth to the fourth floor of the paediatric department (Aasgaard 2004).

Unlike with any other wind instrument, playing a trombone necessitates relatively big right-arm movements because of the slide. A walking trombone player exemplifies the idea of music as sound in motion. Like health, music is not a thing but an ongoing process, and a trombone can be a good way of demonstrating music as the quickening art, in other words a way to get people going both mentally and physically.

The trombone as 'a thing for firing musical material'

George Murray

As a musician, I view myself primarily as a trombonist, who also plays the piano and sings a little. I have increasingly seen the value of singing as it is so direct. I am though, at heart, a trombonist. I feel it is probably my most authentic voice, and as a result, the one many of my clients seem to respond to most; it is a very direct way of forming connections with clients.

Case vignette: Betty

Betty is someone who is very responsive to the trombone. She is in the late stages of dementia and has a number of other health problems, and she needs a lot of care and support in the residential home where I see her. She is still a very articulate woman who has a love of words and speaks several languages. Her very successful career involved acting, and the teaching of English and drama. Betty's partner died and she has no children. Music has been an important part of her life; her mother and father played music and she likes to sing. She is an only child; she is loud and is comfortable with an audience. She is also a feisty person who can swing rapidly between keeping staff at the home on their toes and offering disarming charm.

Betty attends weekly music therapy sessions of around 45 minutes each. The sessions involve a fluid mix of conversation, songs, a little improvisation and occasionally Betty drifting in and out of sleep.

Music allows Betty to connect to different kinds of memories and conversations, acting as a kind of emotional key for unlocking memories and associations (Damasio 2003). Her ability to describe her immediate experiences clearly whilst having such a hazy sense of time and place is unusual. She has described my trombone as 'that thing for firing musical material in a military setting', succinctly conveying something about the identity of a trombone being both military and comical in a single short phrase. Betty has spoken about wishing there was a machine on her bedroom wall that people could just look at and it would tell people how she is. Despite having a sense of struggling to explain herself as she would like to, she is still able to communicate a lot about her experiences. Often the words she uses seem to convey more about the situation she is in than the 'correct' words she appears to be looking for (Kitwood 2002), for example, referring to her wheelchair as a 'plinth', perhaps telling us a lot about how she feels about her wheelchair with just one word. At one point Betty had an issue with her health, which meant she was spending more time alone in her room than usual and less time interacting with other residents. During this period she complained of feeling lonely and 'semi-detached'. Betty often describes a mixture of memories, her internal dreamlike world and what is immediately in front of her. I think the ongoing physical presence of the trombone acts as an anchor, keeping something constant about the nature of the therapeutic relationship for both Betty and me. Perhaps this helps create a sense of safety, a secure base (Bowlby 1988) that seems to allow Betty to speak so freely and articulately about her experience of having dementia.

When I play the trombone it changes the way Betty relates to me in the here and now. It allows her to see me as a fellow creative person, and therefore an ally in a world that can be confusing and difficult for her to understand. I think the creative nature of the therapeutic relationship helps Betty to connect with her previous roles as a teacher, writer and actor. Creativity is an area in which she is confident, whereas in the home as a whole she has less authority and is very reliant on the carers to support her with even the simplest tasks. I think the experience of being in a context where she can feel more in control must be very important for Betty at this point in her life.

Music helps Betty to connect to her important relationships. Perhaps partly as the result of being someone who needs a lot of looking after, she has a sharply focused sense of needing to look after others. Betty often talks about her need for connection with others. Recently she has begun to say she would really like to have a baby. The home often gives her a baby doll, and it seems to give her some comfort. Perhaps it acts as a transitional object (Winnicott 1971), reassuring Betty, who has such great needs of her own, that there is someone smaller and more vulnerable than herself. Her interactions with the doll feel reminiscent of the way even very small children act as mum to their own small dolls.

Betty's need for attachment is reflected in the way the trombone features within the therapeutic relationship. For example, she often sings Brahms's Lullaby in German as I play the trombone. Usually a parent sings a lullaby whilst a child listens or, hopefully, falls asleep. In this case though, Betty and I are both singing and being sung to. This seems like a musical reflection of her need to both be looked after and to look after others.

Betty's focus on her parents is reflected in the music and the use of the trombone within the therapeutic relationship. She often talks about her father, who sang in a 'lovely light tenor voice'. She links this with singing the song 'Mein Papa' in German. The lyrics of this song are about someone remembering their father who was a clown. The trombone has associations with the circus and the male voice and therefore seems to fit the sentiment of this song well.

I play trombone in Betty's sessions because it feels like the most direct way of connecting with her. A lot of the work seems to be about finding connections – Betty's connection with me in the therapeutic relationship, her connections with her family, her connection with the music and the trombone in the here and now, and her connections with her own memories. With Betty, it often feels like these connections may be fleeting and fragile; inevitably there is a sense of what is lost and yet this also brings into sharp focus the value of what is left (Yalom 2008).

The Euphonium

Introduction

Figure 11.5 The euphonium

Figure 11.6 The baritone, the euphonium's smaller relative

The euphonium (with the exception of the slightly bigger tuba which sounds a fifth lower), is the lowest voice of the brass family and the chief tenor soloist in military, concert and brass bands. It is often referred to as the 'cello of the band' due to similarity in timbre and place in the ensemble. Orchestral use is rarer, but the euphonium (under the pseudonym 'tenor tuba') features in several significant works by Gustav Holst, Richard Strauss and Dmitri Shostakovich. The instrument consists of approximately nine feet of brass tubing with a cone shaped bore that widens gradually from the mouthpiece to the bell.

Figure 11.7 Range of the euphonium

The euphonium derives its name from the Greek word *euphonos*, meaning 'well-sounding' or 'sweet-voiced', and it traces its ancestry back to the late Renaissance serpent, so-called for its snake-like shape, a bass wooden relation of the cornet originally used to accompany bass and tenor voices in church choirs. Players at the time required an excellent sense of pitch as intonation was a problem – 19th-century musicologist Charles Burney compared the tone of the serpent to that of a 'great hungry or rather angry Essex calf' (cited in Bowman n.d.).

The modern euphonium began its development in the early 18th century, at a time when most string instruments were being perfected and most wind instruments were still in their infancy. Composers were starting to experiment with the sudden key changes and chromatic melodies pioneered by Beethoven, but the only fully chromatic brass instrument available was the trombone, the slide being the only method of achieving a complete chromatic scale. In response to this need for greater harmonic flexibility, instrument makers started to experiment with adding keys and valves to trumpets and bugles, and the serpent was eventually superseded by the ophicleide, patented in 1821. Taking its name from the Greek *ophis* (serpent) and *kleis* (keys), the ophicleide had nine keys, came in various sizes and was an amalgamation of a modern-day bassoon and a baritone saxophone. The ophicleide appeared in the 19th-century orchestra as well as military bands of the time, and some well-known works to feature it include Mendelssohn's *An Overture to a Midsummer Night's Dream* and Berlioz's *Symphonie fantastique*.

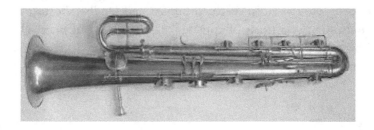

Figure 11.8 The ophicleide

Advances in technology, the invention of the piston valve and the development of the brass band movement led to 'a flurry of brass instrument innovation' (Winston Morris, Bone and Paull 2007, p.2) in the first half of the 19th century, culminating in the first piston-valved, tenor-voiced brass instrument in 1843 in Germany, with other countries rapidly following. The first British version appeared in 1874 and the modern-day euphonium and its slightly smaller relative the baritone have changed very little since then. During the Industrial Revolution most mines and mills hosted a brass band for their workers. This amateur brass band movement developed rapidly, and by 1893 there were 40,000 amateur brass bands in the UK (Childs 2005), which helped to ensure the euphonium's place as a desirable solo instrument in brass and military bands. In 1891 a journalist from *The Daily Telegraph* likened the sound of the euphonium to a foghorn, saying it was 'enough to make a Quaker kick his mother in law' (Childs 2005). However, in 2004 a journalist from *The Times* suggested the sound was 'as flexible and as agile as a trumpet, capable of producing a superbly focused glowing tone' (Childs 2005), showing positive changes in prevailing attitudes towards the instrument.

The euphonium in music therapy, a large transitional object

Helen Mottram

Having played the euphonium from an early age and had many of my early musical experiences shaped by both solo and group playing, there was never any question that I would use it in sessions when I started my music therapy training. As a student on placement I used it successfully with both children and adults with profound and multiple learning disabilities. The euphonium has several alluring sensory qualities – it is big, bright and shiny, vibrates when played and is capable of a wide variety of sounds and potential 'vitality affects' (Stern 1985), from low, deep and gruff sound qualities and timbres through to high, soaring, melodic ones – and it seemed to hold large appeal for people with very limited movement and impaired sensory functioning. In a group of adults with profound and multiple learning disabilities, several of them would reach out to touch it as I played, or put a hand down the bell to feel the vibrations of the sound. A child with no spontaneous movement would follow it around the room with his eyes as I moved whilst playing, working hard to maintain his focus on it and trying to vocalise in response to the sounds.

In an in-patient setting with a group of adults with severe mental health needs the euphonium also proved a useful tool. A boundary of the therapist being the only person allowed to play it had to be established from the beginning, which prompted a small amount of envious grumbling but was accepted quite quickly, possibly being overridden by curiosity at what the instrument could do. During group improvisations it provided a useful grounding bass amidst the often chaotic music, taking on either a rhythmic or more melodic walking bass-line role. At the same time it possessed the flexibility to alternate between this and a more soloistic function when required, and when the co-therapist took over the bass line on another instrument I was able to engage the group members in dialogues and duets.

After I qualified as a music therapist, my attempts at using the euphonium in my work with children in both special and mainstream educational settings immediately presented problems –

inevitably they wanted to handle it and play it themselves, and after an incident where a child dropped an egg shaker down it and it became stuck I stopped using it for a long time. Eventually I invested in a very cheap baritone, a slightly smaller cousin of the euphonium. The euphonium's size and its position in front of the face as it was played had at times seemed like a drawback of using it, feeling a little like a barrier between myself and the client. I was sometimes aware of feelings of putting a skill that I possessed and they didn't quite literally between us. Dominic Davies describes the idea of a powerful 'majority culture' in therapy with gay and lesbian clients, and writes: 'it will be important for such therapists to consider the implications of this power in the light of the relative powerlessness and low self-esteem that many…clients experience' (Davies 1996, p.26), and I felt very aware of what I perceived as a power imbalance. This, however, felt like less of a problem with the baritone – its smaller size and thinner bell, as well as my reduced anxiety about allowing children to handle and play it, meant it felt immediately more accessible and comfortable to work with.

In a mainstream setting it proved useful in many ways. Jenna, a very quiet, slight, withdrawn and anxious ten-year-old girl was referred for her near mutism and very clear unhappiness in the classroom setting. She found the process of starting to play in music therapy very difficult, needing much time and 'continual positive regard' (Rogers 1961) from the therapist to be able to engage in the process of musical play. When I introduced the baritone to our work halfway through our year of working together, it felt like a very non-threatening means of initiating interaction. Jenna would ask to clean it and oil the valves and slides before eventually moving on to attempting to play it. Rather than worrying she wouldn't get it right, as was characteristic of her, she seemed reassured that she wasn't expected to make a good sound and was able to relax and enjoy the humour of some of the sounds she did produce. Winnicott (1971) describes the importance of creating this psychological space for play to develop, and the baritone seemed to have a crucial role in this.

Case vignette: Leon

Leon, a five-year-old boy in a mainstream setting, was referred owing to his elective mutism and withdrawn behaviour in school and was initially seen by a student music therapist. In his early sessions he sat rigid in his chair, pointing at instruments continually but showing little interest when they were offered to him. After several weeks the student brought her French horn to the session in an effort to lessen the focus on the silent but very controlling demands Leon was making and as a way of offering a point of mutual interest. Leon was immediately intrigued and moved from his chair to examine it closely. Over the weeks he grew in confidence in the sessions, starting to explore the instrument in various ways, including trying to hit the bell of the French horn with a beater, seeming to think it was a cymbal. He also started to experiment very cautiously with using his voice to laugh very quietly and to make small vocalisations.

When I took over the case following the departure of the student he was very interested in using the baritone, initiating games where he would gesture to me to make a sound into the mouthpiece and responding by vocalising or blowing a raspberry back down the bell. He would then request to alternate roles, and he would try to make a sound into the mouthpiece and I would respond with a raspberry or vocalisation back. These exchanges were silly, raucous and very playful. He became more confident about using his voice in this way, and I wondered whether he found it reassuring that his sounds were contained within the bell of the instrument as he didn't risk vocalising in this way outside of the container of the bell. It felt like the baritone provided a kind of halfway house between silence and sound – a crucial space for him to experiment with his voice in an early developmental way, and for him to re-experience, or experience for the first time, being responded to via 'affect attunement' (Stern 1985). Leon eventually started to generalise this new-found confidence around using his voice to other settings, and started to whisper and eventually talk in the classroom, and it felt that using the baritone had been an important part of this process.

Case vignette: Kareem

Kareem, a 12-year-old boy with moderate to severe learning difficulties, was referred for music therapy by his class teacher at the school for children with special educational needs that he attended owing to his challenging behaviour in the classroom, his unwillingness to comply with demands and his neediness and desire for staff attention. He sought physical proximity to female staff, wanting to hold their hand and for them to rub his back, and found managing their attempts to put boundaries in place around this very difficult. He had spent his early years moving between his grandmother, his mother and various aunts, and old school reports stated that he had found this arrangement very anxiety-provoking, which had impacted negatively on his behaviour. He had several older half-siblings in the Caribbean who he didn't know, and he had never known his father. His behaviour fluctuated between being infantile and aggressive, but after observing him in the classroom I felt strongly that there was an intelligent boy existing behind what seemed like an inarticulate facade of attention-seeking and demanding behaviour.

Kareem initially found engaging in music therapy very difficult and struggled to manage physical boundaries, asking 'Can I touch you?' and coming closer when I replied in the negative, reaching out his hand but stopping just short of my arm. He continued to explore physical boundaries in his sessions, moving gradually closer as he played until his instrument was millimetres from mine, and it felt very much that he was testing my responses to this, as well as checking what was and was not acceptable. After a few weeks he was finding it easier to respect the physical boundaries but started to find being in the room overwhelming and would make frequent requests to leave before eventually just walking out.

A boundary established in conjunction with his teacher, whereby he could leave if he found the session too difficult but would not get his choice activity in the classroom until the time the session was meant to finish, helped him to manage his time in the room a little. He began to explore the possibilities of playing in short bursts, echoing short snippets of song or phrases from films and repeating them over and over, and responding with enthusiasm when I echoed them back to him. It felt very much like he was role-playing something on a loop, and it was difficult to see a way out. When we broke up for the summer term after six sessions I continued to feel as if I had no sense of who he was at all.

After the summer holiday I took a six-week sabbatical to work abroad. On my return Kareem came to his session readily, but it quickly became clear he was furious with me, saying 'You didn't come'. I agreed that I hadn't. I acknowledged that maybe this had made him angry and he agreed, which felt very significant and the first time we had experienced something 'real'. Kareem started to become interested in the baritone, which was new to the room. He lacked the confidence to try it himself, occasionally picking it up and giving it a short blow before handing it to me and requesting that I do it. He asked that we use it continually, his preferred method being for us to exchange sounds down it, with him shouting or vocalising loud harsh sounds or phrases such as 'Shut it' and 'You liar' into the bell and me responding, either musically into the mouthpiece or by using my voice to sing through the tubing to reflect his phrases back to him.

After several weeks of exchanging vocalisations Kareem suddenly said 'Hello?' into the bell. This was the first spoken word other than insults he had used during these exchanges and it suddenly felt like his mask had lifted slightly. I responded in the same way, saying 'Hello' back, and he replied with 'Are you all right?' This again felt very significant. In another session he picked up the baritone and started to sing into it, a gentle lyrical song that sounded vaguely familiar and included a line that said 'don't leave me...stay here with me'. I began to accompany quietly on a conga drum, the first time we had improvised spontaneously together in this way and a marked contrast from the endless to-ing and fro-ing of repeated shouted, aggressive-sounding phrases that had formed the basis of our sessions up until that point.

This work is ongoing, but Kareem's use of the baritone has felt a little like a transitional object (Winnicott 1971) within our sessions, enabling him to move from a safe, repetitive way of interacting to a more expressive, freer, if slightly riskier way. He returns to it frequently, often requesting that I play it in response to his singing, but he no longer vocalises into it and will sing and speak freely instead, and our interactions with it seem to have enabled him to begin to explore, albeit tentatively, new aspects of himself.

Lower brass characteristics in music therapy practice

First-study brass players

All three contributors felt they were first-study trombone and euphonium players and, therefore, felt at ease using their instruments in their clinical practice. They did, however, mention that they also used other instruments and that in some cases they did not use their brass instruments.

The physical appeal of the instruments

The appealing shiny aspect of the instruments was mentioned and the fact that they were often novel, unfamiliar and had a very distinct sound.

The vibrations produced by the instruments

Several cases were mentioned where clients were fascinated by the vibrations they could feel through the bell of the instruments. The players consciously changed these vibrations through varying the pitches they played.

The variety of pitch

The fact that the trombone and the euphonium can function both as a bass line as well as a melody line was seen as an advantage in various therapeutic situations.

The variety of volume

The ability to play very loudly and support a client playing the drum kit or shouting in anger was mentioned as an advantage. However, the fact that both the trombone and the euphonium can play quite whispery sounds was also written about.

Making funny sounds

The playful and sometimes comical sounds a euphonium and a trombone slide can make, were mentioned as a good way of engaging people in playful and humorous dialogues.

The mobility of the players

The fact that the trombone can be used to give directions through pointing and that the right-hand movements of the player mirror the sounds produced was felt to be an advantage. One contributor also mentioned how the trombonist could effectively lead processions while playing the instrument. The euphonium player also moved around the room while playing her baritone, but found the

CHAPTER 12

The Oboe

*Contributors: Nathan Bettany, Stella Compton Dickinson
(introduction and case vignette) and Špela Loti Knoll*

Introduction

Ancient traditions of playing double-reed instruments are common
across the world. It is as a result of the traffic on the old Silk Road
across central Asia (Baines 1967) that these instruments have
developed from ancient Graeco-Egyptian designs with ongoing
cross-fertilisation between east and west. According to the *Jewish
Encyclopedia* ancient Hebrews used the *halil*, a reed instrument, to
accompany festive meals and the *ugab*, a bagpipe-type of instrument,
to express joy.

The horn pipe was used in megalithic rites in Britain, Scandinavia,
the Basque Country and the Baltic. This instrument is a double-reed
pipe to which the bell of a cow horn is attached. The Welsh version,
called the pibcorn, has an additional horn on the top, which protects
the reed, thereby keeping it comparatively dry. It is from this horn
pipe that the bagpipe developed. The reed protection system enabled
the instrument to work despite variations in temperature, humidity
and climate. However, unlike the oboist, the bagpiper has no direct
control over the enclosed reed of a bagpipe.

It is notoriously difficult to produce a sound on a horn alone,
such as the Jewish *shofar*, which is made from a ram's horn. By
attaching a reed pipe to the horn of other instruments that were
used in religious rituals, the player could then make the instrument
speak more easily. This would have been a practical solution, which

not only made the musician's life easier, but also facilitated a greater range of pitch and expressivity.

In ancient civilisations a double reed was made by flattening one end of the plant or cane that made up the whole pipe instrument; one such primitive form of reed horn called the Whit horn survives in Oxfordshire. This, according to Baines (1967), was traditionally used on Whitsuntide Monday to accompany the Spring Festival. There were similar developments of a one-note bamboo reed pipe in China called a *kuan-tze* and in Japan a similar instrument called the *hichiriki*.

The shawm is the medieval precursor to the oboe. This instrument was brought back to Europe from the Middle East by the crusaders. Shawms were used as outdoor instruments and could produce very loud and raucous sounds. They consequently had the carrying power to act as signal instruments and to intimidate invaders, as happened in the siege of York by William Wallace.

The oboe became a far more refined instrument within the court of Louis XIV, the Sun King, before which it was played mainly as a military instrument. The oboe is the highest in pitch of the orchestral woodwind reed instruments. The name oboe is derived from the French *hautbois*, which means 'high wood'.

The oboe range lies within the female vocal range:

Figure 12.1 The range of the oboe

Dictionary descriptions vary subjectively by describing the oboe's tone qualities as 'penetrating and poignant' to the more derogatory 'nasal sound'. This judgement suggests that once an oboe is heard played badly it may have a lasting effect on the listener. The online *Urban Dictionary* sums up the problem: 'A beautiful instrument, in looks as well as in sound. Beautiful when played by a good player – duck-like when played by a not-so-good player.'

Burgess (2004) quotes oboist Robert Bloom in describing the experience of producing a sound on the oboe:

> The oboe is a narrow channel through which one must push a
> flood of expression. It takes control and restraint. When I play,
> I feel all this emotion, expression, concentrated like a continual
> knife stabbing at your (my) heart – but never going into it –
> never damaging. (Burgess and Haynes 2004, p.249)

During the 19th and 20th centuries the main developments of
the modern oboe continued through innovative improvements to
keywork and bore design and through the virtuoso tradition of the
Paris Conservatoire. The French influence had an effect on the two
styles of British oboe playing (Baines 1967). Both of these styles are
worthy of consideration in deciding how to temper one's playing to
a music therapy setting.

The traditional English style uses a fairly thick reed capable
of producing a full, rich tone quality with good carrying power.
The French style is flexible, characterised by a softer reed and the
introduction of a shimmering vibrato (Goosens and Roxburgh
1977). It is this style that lends itself to the music therapy context
because the sound with a softer reed is easier to sustain and control.
This type of playing uses a wide palette of tone colours, as was
taught in the UK by Janet Craxton at the Royal Academy of Music,
and subsequently by her pupils, who include Nicholas Daniels.

The oboe and how to connect

Stella Compton Dickinson

Like all professional oboists I spend hours making reeds to suit
specific concert venues and professional engagements. There is a
profound sense of purpose and attention to detail and a unique tone
quality when making and honing one's own reeds. The commitment,
time and skill that this takes may be considered philosophically as
not dissimilar to the level of dedication of the samurai sword-maker.
In conversation with Jazz Rasool, a UK-based life coach who works
with managing the relationship between energy and inertia, we
reflected together that while the sword-maker hammers, tempers and
hones the metal blades of his weapon to lethal precision, the oboist
may apply the same levels of precision in creating and honing the
two blades of his double reed. The correct dimensions of the reed

are central to enabling the player's abilities of creative expression to shine. Every stage of this process is measured to the precision of a thousandth of an inch.

These exacting standards may not always be possible for the music therapist; however, it is worth considering that the energy of the sound-producing agent (i.e. the reed) is an energy that is brought to the session and that this energy may inform the musical communication on subtle levels. Thus, I suggest that in the degree of attention invested in making the reed, one is offering to the client within one's own form of musical expression, a skilled balance between humility and nobility. Such qualities must surely have the capacity to enhance the therapeutic experience and relationship. On a practical level, when using the oboe in music therapy it is necessary to ensure that the reed is set up to be comfortable, otherwise the player's range and versatility can be restricted.

The music therapist may need to play fairly spontaneously and without much opportunity to warm up the instrument or the reed, yet attuning to a client's mood. This involves being sufficiently in practice to know and predict one's own limits and to have an ability to play quietly and tenderly or in a strong and containing manner. Whatever the mood, the oboe can be a channel for the creative player to communicate a broad range of emotion, which may otherwise not be recognised by the client. The primitive reed instruments described earlier are not far removed from the Nordoff-Robbins reed horn, which has been developed specifically for music therapy. This instrument enables easy communication from the child client, even if they are non-verbal. The child can explore the horn with their mouth and discover how to communicate by blowing into the instrument. The music therapist can enhance and elaborate on the child's reed horn communications through developing a melodic line on the oboe, which could meet the child's perceived mood. This would then create harmony and connection within a related timbre through the double-reed principle of both instruments.

The difficulty with sharing the oboe with clients is that unlike bespoke music therapy instruments, there are right and wrong ways to play it. Generally it is too precise to work properly if it is incorrectly played, and the margin of error is minimal, thus it has the potential to sound awful. If the therapist were to hand the oboe to a client to play, but with a plastic reed to avoid risking damage, this would inevitably produce an unrewarding sound. There are also hygiene issues with sharing reeds. I have found that clients treat the instrument with a surprising reverence, curiosity and respect, and that they have generally handled it with interest and attuned to it with care and understanding. This has meant that during my 20 years as a music therapist I have always used a very good-quality instrument, rather than taking a spare second instrument, and it has never been damaged.

When working with a group improvisation, the tonality of the oboe has the ability to cut across other sounds. This is one reason it is used to tune up the orchestra. Similarly the tone quality can enable the oboe to be used to create group cohesion by interweaving the individual motifs of group members into an overall musical structure, thereby creating a containing effect by holding a simple and beautiful melodic line.

Some oboists use multiphonics, and the fact that these sounds can be fascinating, transparently beautiful or ugly gives them a place in music therapy expression. Flutter-tonguing and double-tonguing are useful in expressing and mirroring emotions such as anger and anxiety. None of these effects can speak unless the reed is sufficiently free and light. These strange noises can be useful in mirroring and expressing distress, chaos and conflict and in whole-tone as well as atonal musical improvisation techniques, ultimately with an ability to resolve into peaceful tranquillity with ethereal sounding harmonics.

Yalom (2008) states that people frequently come to therapy to address death anxiety, whether overtly or covertly. The poignant sound of the oboe, arguably one of the most expressive orchestral instruments, may facilitate these processes within the therapeutic relationship by eliciting sorrowful feelings of loss, regret and yearning, as well as joy in overcoming fear and adversity.

An example from work on an acute psychiatric ward occurred when a young man who had suffered with prolonged drug misuse was brought to the open music therapy group. He was in a 'zombied out' dissociated state and was looking pale and sallow as he leant against his nurse for support. I played three notes: the interval of a minor sixth resolving to the dominant as a motif by which to tune in to his presence. The sound of the oboe and the poignantly sad interval immediately reached this patient's mood. His face crumpled and he wept, saying 'I miss my mum'. He had re-connected with his feelings, which until then had been too unbearable to express.

J.S. Bach made use of the deeper members of the oboe family: the oboe d'amore and the cor anglais. The darker, deeper sound of the cor is profoundly expressive, and this instrument is often used to represent deathly qualities, for example towards the end of the *St. Matthew Passion* when sorrow and loss pervade the narrative and mood. Additionally in *The Swan of Tuonela* by Sibelius and the *New World Symphony* by Dvorak, the sound of the cor creates a spiritual and mournful mood which hints at the oppression of slavery and the comfort of the lullaby. From this it may be seen that in music therapy, there are endless chromatic possibilities for the music therapist who plays the oboe to use their knowledge of orchestral repertoire as a basis for improvisation.

In this way a connection can be built between something as simple as a client's one-note reed horn or their vocal utterances and the therapist's own musical voice, as expressed through the oboe, yet one can still maintain a sensitive client focus through using subtle motifs and ideas rather than eclectic orchestral quotes. Consequently the oboe may not be overwhelming and it can facilitate the development of transference within the musical therapeutic relationship and dialogue.

Some people feel that the oboe does not have the flexibility of tone of other wind instruments, such as a soprano saxophone, perhaps because of the precision of the oboe double reed as opposed to the saxophone single reed. Thus it does not naturally lend itself to the jazz medium; however, it has been successfully used in cross-over jazz-orientated music by Paul Hart (2012) and as a jazz instrument by the American player Paul McCandless, an expert jazz oboist.

The oboe timbre has been likened to that of the trumpet. This is no bad thing when epitomised by the legendary trumpeter Miles Davis in his seminal best-selling album *Kind of Blue* (1959). The many adjectives that one may use to describe the mellow beauty of Miles Davis's sound are an inspiration to any aspiring oboist who wishes to explore the jazz medium. If one is working as a music therapist with a musically skilled client in the jazz medium, the oboe and the voice can be the most powerful tools by which to match and mediate the client's own musical input.

Case vignette: John

I will describe a little of my long-term work with a man who had committed a serious offence and who was receiving treatment in a secure hospital setting. He had some musical skill and knowledge of folk music. During the assessment period neither the music therapist or the patient played on instruments in which they had special skills. This proved to be effective towards creating a balanced and collaborative therapeutic relationship, so that the patient would not feel diminished, nor grandiose or overly dominant on his main instrument. Once a rapport had developed in which emotionally related musical improvisation had developed, a far greater range of expressivity and meaning was reached following mutual agreement to introduce the specialist instruments (Compton Dickinson 2003). The reason for this decision, which was jointly made with my supervisor, was that I wanted to maintain a client-centred focus with clear therapeutic goals, rather than allowing the session to dissolve into a good-fun jamming session, which risked a loss of focus on the therapeutic content, process and eventual outcome. This decision also ensured that I did not encourage counter-therapeutic narcissistic tendencies in John. The treatment could otherwise have been unconsciously sabotaged owing to John's seductive responses, which were recognised in supervision as an erotic transference. The realisation of the relational impact of an erotic transference and the risks to the music therapist if there were a repetition of an unhealthy oedipal-relating pattern, challenged the music therapist's boundaries. These risks were considered carefully, as otherwise the client and therapist could not engage safely in the tasks of therapy (Compton Dickinson and Benn 2012; Odell-Miller 2013).

Later, as the treatment progressed towards more sophisticated improvisations, we reached a landmark session where we agreed that we required the additional expression of our first instruments. In this way John was able to engage with emotional depth in the meaning of the loss of many aspects of his life and eventually in expressing feelings about ending long-term therapy. The poignancy of the oboe sound and the flexibility and fluidity of technique that was possible, facilitated the process of mourning and ensured that the therapist could maintain a balanced musical relationship.

This model can be viewed as developmental, in that John reworked his early relating patterns with the usual music therapy instruments. These reminded him of relevant times during his earlier years, and enabled him to connect with a renewed childlike ability to play, without seeking to be admired for his later-developed musical skills, which could take him to a narcissistic place. I too had to consider how to remain supportive rather than indulgent, so that it was John's music and not mine.

To conclude, I urge oboe-playing music therapists to consider developing the use of the oboe by taking a positive view, rather than that of the old-fashioned, archetypal neurotic oboist. The oboe can be used in therapy with sincerity and fun, providing one can relax and be friends with it, and love it passionately. Then it is a very rewarding experience for all involved.

Searching for identity

Špela Loti Knoll

I heard the oboe for the first time at a concert, played as a solo instrument. and enjoyed the warm but clear and powerful sound; this provided the motivation for me to start learning the oboe. Soon enough I learnt that it was a very demanding instrument to play in order to achieve such a sound. It requires a strict and careful breathing technique and a lot of physical power. Sometimes I felt as if I was participating in a sport rather than music-making. Later on I also had to learn how to make the reeds for my oboe, and then I felt like a woodcarver. Somewhere beyond that I had to stay connected to music. In mastering the perfect oboe sound and its clarity, these different levels have to be considered at all times. Therefore, for me the oboe symbolises many levels of existence that need to be in balance in order to play music, express myself or to communicate with others through music.

In music therapy this balance has to be achieved as well; it needs to exist and coexist with the needs of the therapeutic setting. During the time that I have been practising as a music therapist, I have used the oboe only at special times and just with particular clients. The following case vignette may explain why using the oboe in music therapy is for me not an everyday practice but happens only at certain times.

Case vignette: Women and children's groups

For several years I have been working in a safe house for women and child victims of domestic violence. Sometimes the groups have been composed only of women, sometimes only of children and in some cases of whole families. Each of these settings had its own characteristics regarding the use of music, the use of verbal conversation and the balance of these two forms of communication. Even though every group had its own agenda, there were some general similarities to be found in these specific formations.

Perhaps the biggest difference was between children's and women's groups. Children's groups were loud, chaotic and energetic. It was difficult to find and maintain contact with each child in a group, even though the groups were small, comprised of three to five children. Women, on the other hand, played less music and talked more. It was again difficult to maintain contact with them, but the reason was avoidance, particularly through music-making. Furthermore, family groups had their own specific problems. I never used the oboe with children because the instrument could easily be damaged and I felt that I could best meet the children in their music through playing other instruments, particularly percussion and guitar. In family settings I rarely played the oboe as the instrument was too strongly imposing and put me in a leadership role within the group. There was a greater need for the families to find their own voices inside the family structure; therefore I took the role of a mediator. An interesting development regarding the use of instruments and also the oboe took place in the women's groups; spontaneously at first and later on it remained as a symbolic pattern that I started to use and develop. I will try to explain this phenomenon.

As mentioned before, the women avoided expressing themselves through music. They preferred conversations about insignificant everyday topics to playing, and when they did make music they used small, quiet instruments and stayed in a passive role rather than taking the initiative. The time frame of therapy was rather short, about three months, so it was difficult to change a lot of these behavioural patterns in depth. Nevertheless, there was some progress and interesting developments to be observed during this therapeutic process.

There were five women in the group I am going to describe. They were between 25 and 62 years of age and all shared a history of domestic abuse from their husbands, one also from her son. All of them had children, and the younger women stayed in the safe house with their children, while the oldest woman was there on her own.

They all lived in the same house with their own room and shared facilities. They attended a music therapy group once a week and, except for some conversations with a psychologist, they received no other therapeutic intervention.

After the first three sessions I decided to introduce some structure into our music-making, trying to provide them with a greater feeling of safety and making them feel at ease. We decided to base our next few sessions on specific topics regarding their process of coming, staying and eventually leaving the safe house. This provided them with a kind of overview of their personal experience through specific musical mirroring of each phase. This was demanding, since not all of them came to the safe house at the same time and therefore went through particular phases at different times. Nevertheless, they found this idea interesting. We decided that they would specify an emotion typical for each phase they were going through and then improvise on that theme.

During the first session the women decided on their first emotion, one that had been caused by aggression and their arrival at the safe house: fear. The music that presented this emotion was quiet and undefined; the instruments that were used were small and made bizarre sounds, without any rhythm. They each seemed to play on their own but remained inside the group. There was no communication between them or with me. The music they made could be performed with percussion instruments, which made sounds similar to the emotional state they were in and which did not expose my musical presence.

The second time, they were hesitant; it seemed that the feeling of fear from the first session was still lingering somewhere in the room. It was hard for them to take the next step. In a way this was a reflection of their reality in attempting to get away from fear and view the situation from another perspective. Eventually they agreed that the fear was followed by anger, which was not at all an easy emotion for them to express. The music was at first similar to the fear from the previous session. Gradually the women made suggestions to each other to start taking bigger, louder instruments, such as drums or sticks to play percussion, and at the end of that session they started to play louder and louder. It was the first time in the therapy that I thought I might be able to play the oboe with them, because the music started to become loud and energetic; however, at this point it was more than enough for me to play the big drum. The music of anger was a new exploration for them in making a solid statement. Nevertheless, I decided to bring the oboe with me to the next session.

The third emotion the women decided to express was sorrow. If the anger brought some outward energy and external expression, sorrow was the one that took that back. Still it felt significantly different to the portrayal of fear. It seemed that there was more direction and they began to develop greater understanding of what was being played in the music. If the music they played had not been so tentative, fragile and quiet, I might have used the oboe here, but at that time I thought they would just start to listen to 'this nice instrument' and stop focusing on themselves and their own music.

Following fear, anger and sorrow, the women decided they wished to start playing in an expressive way about love, an emotion that they had lost and wanted to find again. This was a difficult issue for them as they had lost the ability to trust others. This time the music was diverse and the women chose to play different instruments individually, expressing a variety of rhythmical and musical elements. It was a quest for them and a long search to find their true self, a remembrance of what they used to be, know and desire. I did not play much at this point at all. It was important for them to use music at last as a source of finding their own identity.

The last stage needed some discussion between the women; they appeared to be very positive and enthusiastic. They named the last stage 'hope and a new way'. They decided that now it was time to live again. There was enough confidence in their appearance and they had increased inner strength, so that it seemed the right time for me to play the oboe with them. They were able to accept my strong voice and also use their own voices on other instruments, which they found to suit them best on their journey. We all played 'our instruments', enabling each of us to take our own stand and express our individual identities. Music was playful, funky, invigorating and simple to engage with.

Later on we had some more sessions in which we reflected on the symbolic path that we had created. In those sessions there was time for each of the emotions that they had named. There were also opportunities for me to play the oboe, whenever I felt it would not have a disruptive effect, but rather would provide support and another voice for our music.

This was a very important experience for me. I could find a connection to other therapy cases where I had used the oboe in a similar way. I had often wondered why I could play the oboe with some clients and not at all with others. It did not depend on their diagnoses or whether I was working with them in a group or individually. I think it depended on their ability to be self-accepting and to have a strong sense of identity. I used the oboe only when I felt that my playing would not be overwhelming for the clients but would provide an opportunity for us to connect through music and feel a similar sense of individuality. This is possibly because when I play the oboe I also feel comfortable in my own skin and experience my strongest identity.

Doubt, persistence and prophetic pandas

Nathan Bettany

I am writing this with sore, swollen lips following a busy week of jam sessions with a range of musicians. At the moment I feel good about being an oboe player; however, this has not always been the case. At various points in my life I have abandoned the oboe in a fit of disillusionment, and temporarily decided to focus on other musical activities instead. As a teenager, I often felt like I was leading a double life. I seemed to be lurching inexorably towards becoming a classically trained musician, yet I spent all my spare time and creative energy writing and rehearsing songs with my band, or experimenting with multi-tracked sound-collages in my bedroom. I never listened to pre-20th-century classical music and rarely practised with anything like the commitment that my oboe teachers encouraged. I felt like an impostor, and it has only been in recent years that I have begun to find satisfying ways of integrating these different musical identities.

I remember one of our first tasks during my music therapy training was to write a letter to our instrument. I took the opportunity to give my oboe a thorough interrogation: 'Why are your reeds so temperamental?', 'Why does playing feel so physically restrictive?' and 'Why can't you sound more like a saxophone?'.

Despite its lack of resemblance to a saxophone, the oboe does have advantages. It can produce a unique range of tone colours from sickly sweet to gum-shreddingly harsh, alongside a vast array of multiphonics and other extended techniques. This sound palette can be twisted to sit nicely alongside electronic sounds, feedback, tape manipulations, acoustic sound-making devices and conventional instruments. This makes the oboe ideally suited for the range of music with which I am currently involved.

Of course, being able to draw upon a healthy variety of sounds and techniques can be very useful in music therapy work. However (at the risk of stereotyping) I wonder whether there may also be certain character traits that make oboists particularly well suited to becoming music therapists?

A colleague recently showed me a book called *The Right Instrument for Your Child* (Boyd and Ben-Tovim 2012). The authors state that 'the oboe is not for generous extroverts: determined, tight-lipped, stubborn children do best'. Certainly the stereotype of the oboe player is of a rather obsessive, introverted person, frequently preoccupied with reeds and technical problems. By nature, oboists have to be pretty good at tolerating frustration and sticking with things, even if progress feels painfully slow. This is essential since, for the first few years of playing, the oboe mostly sounds like a constipated duck (a sound not without its merits). Being able to tolerate frustration without acting upon it, and not giving up when things feel stuck are surely important attributes for any therapist.

There are also practical considerations to bear in mind when using the oboe in music therapy work. First, there are the reeds. These tend to be expensive, delicate and temperamental. (When explaining the intricacies of reed anxiety to a friend recently, he suggested that oboes might be 'the pandas of the instrument family'). Reeds need soaking and preferably 'crowing' before playing, making it a challenge to pick up an oboe some way into a session and begin playing cold. Having a pre-soaked, softer-than-usual reed to hand can be useful, as these tend to be easier to play quietly without warming up if the situation demands this.

Of course, sometimes these practical issues around getting started can be exploited. I have worked with a few clients who could, on occasion, present as extremely busy and anxious, filling every space and leaving very little thinking time. In these cases, taking a little longer than usual to sort out my oboe and get the reed ready has been a useful way of slowing things down whilst also creating some space to reflect together on what is happening, rather than rushing on to the next thing.

It is also worth remembering that, for many people, the oboe is a strange and unfamiliar instrument. When I use it for the first time it often provokes curiosity from clients. This can potentially be very useful in certain situations. However, it can also be distracting and even intimidating for some people, who may already be feeling anxious about seeming musically inferior. Of course, these feelings are important to pay attention to and explore, but flashing around an expensive musical instrument that takes years to learn may not be the most sensitive way to do this. I always think carefully about if, when, how and why I will introduce the oboe.

The following vignette outlines the use of the oboe during an initial music therapy session.

Case vignette: Arnold

Arnold was suffering with long-term mental health issues and had used hard drugs since his teens. He was referred for individual pre-assessment music therapy with me as part of one of my student placements. Arnold had previously attended an open music therapy group that took place on an acute ward. The music therapist had noted that Arnold could be disruptive and musically irritating during these sessions, rarely leaving space for other participants and frequently romanticising his past drug use. It was thought that individual music therapy might be a good opportunity for him to explore these aspects of himself and perhaps experience different ways of being with another person.

Arnold chose to begin our first session with a drumming duet. He began suddenly, quickly settling into repetitive patterns that were static in dynamic and tempo, and played with a sense of lazy nonchalance as if trying to look cool. Arnold's playing did not suggest much awareness of what I was doing, and the duet ended suddenly. After we had finished, Arnold began to talk about how the music reminded him of jamming at music festivals, and he reminisced at length about his own previous festival experiences. He interspersed this monologue with questions about my own knowledge of festivals and bands. After some more drumming Arnold said that he would like to try the piano and he began to jab at it in the busy and irritating manner that his previous therapist had described. I decided that now would be a good time to introduce the oboe. This would provide an opportunity to slow things down whilst I put it together and got the reed warmed up. Arnold seemed genuinely curious about the oboe, and our verbal interaction began to feel less like a one-sided monologue or interrogation.

We left a few seconds of silence before beginning, and then Arnold proceeded to become absorbed very quickly with the white notes of the piano. The music felt intense, hypnotic and still, almost as if we had moved into a kind of merged, symbiotic state. Arnold's playing gradually became more rhythmic and technically ambitious, whilst still maintaining the same hushed, static and diatonic character. His playing felt subtly responsive to my musical contributions, and it felt like he was using the piano to accompany my oboe playing in a kind of role reversal of the usual client–therapist relationship. The music continued in this fashion for around 15 minutes.

During subsequent sessions Arnold began to speak about looking after fellow drug users in the past at the expense of looking after himself. These comments resonated with his apparent keenness to look after me and be a good patient so that I could impress my supervisor. We were able to begin to reflect on this to some extent despite the brevity of our work together. With hindsight I began to think back to the role reversal, when Arnold had musically looked after me during our first session. I suspect that the specific soloist connotations of the oboe may have hastened the unconscious re-enactment of a style of interpersonal relating, which turned out to be of some significance for Arnold. I am not sure that this would have happened so quickly and so strikingly if I had been using a different instrument.

Oboe characteristics in music therapy practice

Range and quality of sounds

Several oboists mentioned the range of sounds available and the particular palette of tone colours available to respond to clients, either through mirroring or supporting. Flutter-tonguing and similar techniques can be used to meet the client musically and emotionally.

Capacity of the oboe to be strident and cut through sounds

Several oboists indicated that the oboe is a dominant type of instrument that can be easily heard in a group setting. This can be a useful tool when running groups if used in a sensitive and therapeutically appropriate manner. When the therapist used the oboe, it gave the sense of control and leadership, which could be helpful in certain situations. The dominating character of the oboe possibly makes it difficult to use with more vulnerable clients.

Capacity of the oboe to express and reflect sorrowful or anxious moods

One oboist suggested that the oboe might be a particularly useful instrument in matching clients' moods when they are feeling sad or depressed. It was also suggested that the sound of the oboe in orchestral music could be linked with death and loss, which was helpful to consider in improvisation when enabling clients to confront anxieties around these themes.

Value of therapist having their own instrument

Several oboists suggested that there could be advantages to the therapist remaining separate with their own instrument, but that this could also have an inhibiting effect on the client, as they felt that the specialist instrument was inaccessible to them. The element of curiosity could be useful in gaining the client's attention, and one oboist used the preparation of the oboe as a tool to slow down the client's responses and contributions.

The oboe as a reed instrument

Two of the oboists wrote about the difficulties of needing to plan ahead with reed preparation when using the oboe in therapy sessions, which sometimes reduced the capacity of the oboist to respond spontaneously to clients. Parallels were drawn between the meticulous attention needed to attend to the reed, and the focus that the therapist invests in the client in order to have successful therapeutic outcomes.

The oboe as solo instrument

One oboist discussed the use of the oboe as a solo instrument, which enabled the client to act as an accompanist and facilitated an exploration of a change of dynamic in the client–therapist relationship.

References

Baines, A. (1967) *Woodwind Instruments and Their History*. London, UK: Faber and Faber.

Boyd, D. and Ben-Tovim, A. (2012) *The Right Instrument for Your Child*. London, UK: Orion.

Burgess, G. (2004) 'Diversifying Streams Since World War II: The Traditional Stream.' In G. Burgess and B.D. Haynes (eds) *The Oboe*. New Haven, CT: Yale University Press.

Compton Dickinson, S.J. (2003) *Community, Culture and Conflict: The role of creativity*. London, UK: British Society of Music Therapy Publications.

Compton Dickinson, S.J. & Benn, A. (2012) 'Discovering Harmony; Music Therapy in Forensic Settings.' In A. Aiyegbusi and G. Kelly (eds) *Professional and Therapeutic Boundaries in Forensic Mental Health Practice*. London, UK: Jessica Kingsley Publishers.

Compton Dickinson, S.J., Gahir, M. (2013) 'Working with conflict: a summary of developments of a man suffering with paranoid schizophrenia, who committed manslaughter.' In S.J. Compton Dickinson, H. Odell-Miller and J. Adlam, eds. *Forensic Music Therapy: A Treatment for Men and Women in Secure Hospital Settings*. London: Jessica Kingsley Publishers.

Goosens, L. and Roxburgh, E. (1977) *Yehudi Menuhin Music Guides: Oboe*. London, UK: Macdonald Futura.

Hart, P. (2012) *Star Pieces for Oboe* (S.J. Dickinson, ed.). Forton Music.

Odell-Miller, H. (2013) 'Inside and Outside the Walls: Music Therapy Supervision in a Forensic Setting .' In S.J. Compton Dickinson, J. Adlam and H. Odell-Miller (eds) *Forensic Music Therapy: A Treatment for Men and Women in Secure Hospital Settings*. London, UK: Jessica Kingsley Publishers.

Yalom, I.D. (2008) *Staring at the Sun: Being at Peace with Your Own Mortality: Overcoming the Terror of Death*. San Francisco, CA: Jossey-Bass.

CHAPTER 13

The Saxophone

*Contributors: Luke Annesley, Susanna Crociani, Billy
Davidson (introduction and case vignette) and Anita Vaz*

Introduction

The saxophone (or sax) is a woodwind instrument dating from the
mid-19th century. Its creator, the Belgian instrument maker Adolphe
Sax, believed that a bridge was needed between the brass and the
woodwind sections of the orchestra and thus the saxophone was
born (Segell 2005). Sax wanted to create a group of instruments
each of which had the projection of a brass instrument together
with the agility of a woodwind instrument, and he patented the
saxophone in 1846. This new instrument was constructed of brass
and played with a single reed.

The saxophone family is made up of nine types: sopranissimo,
sopranino, soprano, alto, tenor, baritone, bass, contrabass and
subcontrabass. Of the nine forms, four are widely used: the soprano,
alto, tenor and baritone. All nine types of saxophone are pitched at
either Eb or Bb, although C and F versions were patented early in
the 20th century.

The saxophone became popular with marching bands and soon
moved into jazz bands, notably big bands such as those of Duke
Ellington and Fletcher Henderson. Other jazz players, such as
Sidney Bechet and Charlie Parker, helped to make the saxophone a
leading instrument in jazz, inspiring a new wave of musicians in the
1950s, including John Coltrane and Dexter Gordon. Although not
always prominent in orchestras, the saxophone has become a leading
instrument in most genres of music (Gioia 2011).

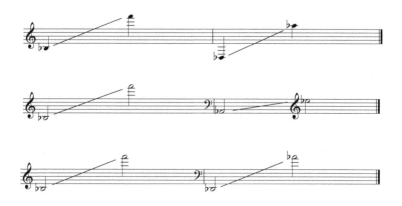

Figure 13.1 Saxophone ranges

Setting up music therapy at a day centre for the homeless

Billy Davidson

Throughout my work as a music therapist, I have been fortunate to use a range of different instruments. As a woodwind player in particular, I am able to use the flute, clarinet and various forms of saxophones. However, as the saxophone is my principal instrument, it is when playing it that I feel most comfortable, whether in improvised or structured pieces of music.

My interest in playing saxophone started when I first saw Sade and the Blow Monkeys on *Top of the Pops*. At that time, I had no real insight into the saxophone and, certainly, no knowledge of how difficult an instrument it would be to learn. I was awestruck by the beautiful sound produced from the sax and how cool the saxophonists in both bands seemed to be. I somehow cajoled my parents into helping me to buy a tenor saxophone and immediately got to work on trying to produce a sound and – perhaps somewhat ambitiously – a scale or a riff. I had little success with this, so I sought out a teacher and was fortunate to discover a saxophone teacher with a love of jazz music. He introduced me, quite early on, to improvisation, with its freedom to react to a mood or an emotion. As my technical ability and confidence grew, I found myself playing for a local ska-reggae band, whose emphasis was on improvisation within song structures. With this band I toured Britain, Ireland and mainland Europe. Since joining my first band, 25 years ago, I have played and toured with a variety of instrumentalists, which has enabled me to become competent and confident enough to improvise in any setting, whether in a concert hall or in a music therapy setting.

In my recent clinical work I was able to apply my skills as a saxophonist to help create and shape a model for helping homeless people to engage within a music therapy group.

The music therapy department at Anglia Ruskin University was invited by Cambridge City Council to bid for funds from its homelessness grant, Kick Start. The successful bid was a collaboration between a charity for homeless people, Wintercomfort, and the music therapy team, based at the university. I was employed as the music therapist for this project and my aim was to establish music therapy at a day centre for the homeless run by the charity and to link this to the music therapy clinic at the university. This exciting collaboration between a charity for the homeless and the university was the first of its kind in the UK. The nine-month innovative project engaged over 60 homeless people in weekly musical performance and improvisation groups and offered a new service to the community, which assisted in effecting a positive change in lifestyles and outlook, as well as helping to foster an interest in music and provide meaningful activity for the participants.

The setting at Overstream House is a drop-in centre for homeless people. Those that use the centre are people sleeping rough; some are staying at one of the local hostels or night shelters, and others have their own tenancies but are struggling with what may be for them a new situation. All have a history of homelessness; many have mental health issues, drug and alcohol problems or learning difficulties and sometimes a combination of these issues. In addition, many are poorly educated and have few social skills. Generally, a lack of self-esteem and confidence exists among the service users and this centre is a place where they can feel safe, and where they are recognised and respected.

Many of the homeless readily identify with music, whether that is from an active perspective or from the enjoyment of listening to music. With this in mind, I started from the positive standpoint that participants' motivation was closely linked to their personal experience of music and its meaning for them. The groups provided encouragement and were a way of connecting people through the music-making, whether the music was improvised and experimental or involved structured pieces of music. Through coming together and participating within the music sessions, the homeless community at the centre was able to receive support and, in turn, provide support for others. This ultimately led to greater motivation on the part of the participants, which, in turn, fuelled confidence – qualities that are often lacking amongst the service users. In addition, participation in the music therapy group appeared to motivate and inspire participants to become involved in other activities, such as creative writing and art groups. The therapeutic space seemed to have helped service users, through heightened motivation and confidence, to extend their world beyond daily attendance at day centres and night shelters.

The Performance Space

Initially, I spent time getting to know the staff and the members, chatting with them as they sat around the main meeting space. I then put on an informal performance using the soprano saxophone to introduce myself musically, timed to take place just before lunch in the main room of the centre when most members were present. I learned from the members that the saxophone had an interesting appeal, as it was an instrument that was not uncommon, but one that a lot of regulars had not heard live before. There were some people there who readily identified with jazz music, and as the saxophone is a prominent instrument in this genre, it encouraged their participation. There was then a knock-on effect as their participation seemed to encourage that of others.

It could be argued that the saxophone's appeal is no different to that of other instruments. However, for me, there is a unique 'coolness' that surrounds the sax. This coolness appeals to performers and observers alike and is indeed what originally drew me to the saxophone.

The portability of the instrument was particularly useful when moving between members/performers (often they would sit independently of one another). This helped, not only with encouraging participation but with reciprocal interchanges as well. The tonal quality of the saxophone, especially against another instrument, seemed to help create a sense of a conversation in a similar way to everyday verbal conversations, where individual accents and nuances within our speech differ. Here lies a true reflection of conversing with one another. The saxophone is a versatile instrument, where trills, flutter tonguing, vamping as well as squeaking can be created to add colour to the musical interaction.

I continued to lead the performance on the saxophone, changing the style of music from week to week, often with requests given to me the week before and always encouraging openness, with opportunities for anyone to join in.

Members began to spontaneously join in with the performance, discussing the music and making suggestions. I then brought out some musical instruments, including tuned and untuned percussion, and members started using them to play along with the music. This evolved into the Performance Space and became a regular feature of the work. Although it was not planned as such, it developed a particular purpose and life of its own and provided:

- a way of sparking people's interest and confidence in using music
- a chance for members to take part in music-making without any commitment
- an introduction to the music therapy group later in the day
- a chance for people to offer suggestions of song choices or musical genres and to be received positively by others within the Performance Space
- a way of connecting new members to the centre with existing members
- a chance for key workers to assess their clients' interaction within a group environment.

This Performance Space became a regular feature at the centre. Occasionally, the Performance Space received peripheral negative responses from the other service users in the room. By venturing around the room after the performance, usually with untuned percussion instruments, I could address this negativity with those peripheral members. Actually, there were occasions when some of these people went on to attend the music therapy group as a result of this. Some members used this opportunity to perform music themselves, and this became an important experience for them.

It was also at times a difficult space; some members heckled when the music was being played and made derogatory comments about the others and the sounds produced. It was important to withstand these attacks and to understand them as perhaps being a defensive response to something positive and creative, which had to be rubbished, in much the same way as homeless people often feel rubbished by others. It was interesting to discover how individuals within the Performance Space became supportive of one another and how the music was performed in a more defiant way.

Case vignette: Nick rediscovers his blues banjo music

Working with the homeless community, and certainly within the music therapy setting, helped me to discover a range of talents that many of the clients had either kept hidden away or guarded through fear of rejection; this I learned later through open discussions within the group.

I discovered that one such individual, Nick, was a talented musician who initially did not want to rediscover and showcase his talent. The Performance Space helped to trigger and reignite this over a period of time. I later learned that Nick had felt embroiled in the street musician culture, which he did not enjoy. He was an accomplished musician, a skilled banjo player, who had a particular passion for blues music. Nick said that after hearing me and others playing in the Performance Space, particularly the sound of the saxophone, that he was drawn towards the group and he eventually became involved in our playing. Nick's role, over a period of time, became invaluable to the group, not just because of his large and diverse repertoire of songs but also because of his great affinity with all those who attended.

As time passed Nick's role within the group increased. Eventually we were able to take the performance group outside of the homeless charity's day centre to a local coffee bar, where the group began to perform music to people enjoying a coffee. Those who took part were all from the homeless community; both musicians and non-musicians. Again, Nick's role was important in that he positively supported all of those who attended.

Nick spoke often about the trigger that he had recognised as refuelling his desire to start playing music again. He talked about hearing the saxophone, particularly in a setting where he would not have imagined finding it. Nick concluded that it was the saxophone and the style of music that I was playing that had helped to motivate him to become more involved in participating in the activities at the centre.

To summarise, there were both positive and negative aspects to using the saxophone in this setting. I found that because the saxophone was viewed with high regard, I was able to gain the respect of the members of the Performance Space, the groups, and the individuals. There were, however, some disadvantages to playing the saxophone; specifically the issue of hygiene, as well as the expense and the fragility of the instrument. I felt it was important to address these issues with the members and found that nearly all who attended respected this and, in some cases, became quite protective towards me and my instrument.

Thoughts about the saxophone and music therapy
Luke Annesley

I remember going for an audition for a music therapy course and using the saxophone. There was a clear suspicion that the instrument might be too loud and unwieldy for clinical work, and surprise was expressed that I was able to play it quietly. Conversely, it was my interest in improvisation as a jazz saxophone player that led me to wonder about the possibility of music therapy as a career in the first place. Here was a profession, I thought, where my experience as an improviser might be a transferable skill.

The saxophone has been at the centre of many of the important developments in jazz – the tenor styles of Coleman Hawkins and Lester Young, bebop developed by Charlie Parker, the harmonic and sonic explorations of John Coltrane, the extended techniques incorporated into the saxophone's palette in free jazz. In music therapy sessions there are a lot of musical possibilities made available when you have control of a saxophone.

However, music therapists are often wary of using their first instrument, if it's not the piano, because of the negative feelings that can be stirred up – envy, idealisation of the therapist, a feeling of inadequacy in a client with fragile self-esteem – and the saxophone is particularly prone to many of these. It is impressively big and shiny and has lots of complicated-looking key-work. Of course feelings of envy can equally be stirred up by the therapist's technical expertise on any instrument, but from a purely clinical/musical point of view the saxophone has much to offer:

- You can play it quietly or very loudly, often needed when matching a client who is playing a drum kit at a high volume.

- As someone who doesn't have a strong singing voice, for me the saxophone can become *my* voice. It can be used lyrically, to express poignant, contemplative qualities, but can also express anger or aggression through the use of growls, multiphonics or honking low Bbs.

- I also find it useful to pare my music down to a single line at times, to get away from the harmonic approach of the piano and find a simpler way of being in the music.

Case vignette: Steven and the tenor sax

I worked with a young man called Steven in a mainstream secondary school for about 18 months before he changed schools, bringing therapy to a somewhat abrupt end. Steven found verbal communication difficult and was academically far behind his peers, though he continued to attend mainstream lessons. He appeared to be isolated and required a lot of support. In music therapy he found something useful. Right from the first session, he was able to express a more vibrant side to his personality, to display a creativity and spontaneity in his music that was way beyond how he appeared in other aspects of his life. For the therapist, this can be an exhilarating revelation, and I found myself feeling excited about the music-making in these sessions. At that time I was in a phase of not using the saxophone, and in his sessions most of my music was being played at the keyboard. If I did use a wind instrument, it tended to be the clarinet, partly for reasons of portability.

Steven used various other instruments, such as bass guitar and electric guitar, and very occasionally a fragile singing voice would emerge, but the drums were his safe base. After a few sessions, a pattern began to appear where I would spend a large part of the session at the keyboard trying to match his energy. Steven's pulse would be unsteady at first but more solid as the session progressed, perhaps helped by my grounding music. I was working hard to create a firm tonal and rhythmic base to support his playing. Sometimes I found that I was working so hard that my arms would get tired. Matching his intensity level at the keyboard was not always easy. My supervisor listened to some of this music with me and made the observation that I was trying very hard to *make sense*. There was an energy coming from him that was being frustrated by my efforts to find a focus and to guide the music towards greater organisation. My supervisor suggested I try the saxophone. This made immediate intuitive sense and (as can often happen in supervision) I was impatient to try this in the next session.

The results were instantaneous. I found that by playing the tenor saxophone I could respond more intuitively to Steven's playing, using a single line to 'get into the cracks' of his drumming. I could also match his volume and, using certain sonic effects on the instrument, match the feeling of controlled chaos. His music sounded less constricted, and I realised that I had been trying too hard to mould it. What he was responding to at this time was musical empathy, rather than musical grounding or support, so he readily entered into a dialogue. After this, the saxophone became a consistent feature of our sessions. I did not totally abandon the keyboard, but found that the availability of this new element added more dimensions to the music, allowing us to move forward in our developing musical relationship. Steven and my supervisor had helped me to learn an important lesson, and since that time, in that setting, I have always had a saxophone available.

There are still situations where I will avoid using the saxophone. In one particular school, where I work with students who have emotional and behavioural difficulties, I find that envy and rivalry are such pervasive aspects of the work that I am still wary of introducing it. However, it may be that I am being over-cautious. Sometimes, I find that certain clients are delighted with the sound of the sax, and where I had been concerned about the danger of overwhelming them, they are actually energised by it. I continue to try to keep an open mind.

Finding peace through the saxophone

Susanna Crociani

One autumn evening I had my first encounter with the saxophone. I was 11 years old and, since the school said I was musically gifted, my parents had sent me to take free music lessons offered by the town's band, which included the loan of an instrument.

The band room was in an old Italian farmhouse where there was a fire burning in the fireplace. There were other children there like me, to learn from our teacher, who was an older musician, a carpenter by trade but a passionate band director in his spare time. We were introduced to music theory and musical notation first, and I quickly became fond of those strange balls called notes. Between one theory lesson and another, there was plenty of time to play with the other children. Probably because of this, music has always been associated with play and friendships for me. The day finally arrived when the instruments were distributed. I would, like my best friend, have preferred a trumpet, but I was given an ancient alto clarinet instead, so as soon as my parents offered to buy me an instrument, I jumped at the chance and chose the saxophone.

I had many excellent teachers who not only taught me to play but also encouraged me to feel the emotion that a musical phrase expresses. I learnt to be in harmony with my instrument. During the difficulties of adolescence, the sax was my way to be with others and find my own expressive space. There is a certain feeling that comes when playing together that is much more than simply playing the right notes in tune. I learnt to have faith in the music and to entrust myself to its sounds, which could express emotions that I couldn't put into words.

I feel that if I had never encountered music and never played it, I would be very different. The sax has helped me on many occasions, since playing it activates the body (posture, fingers and mouth) and increases breathing; therefore, it is physically energising. At a psychological level, its rich sound full of harmonics, broad range of timbres and dynamics captures the attention and can provoke a change in mood. Because playing the sax had such a strong effect on me, I felt that its music could help other people.

While I was attending the music conservatoire, I found that the notes had lost their emotional meaning because the training was mainly based on technique, with no space for creativity. I had begun working as a street cleaner, and my soul did not sing any more. I would have probably stopped playing as soon as I had done my last exam if I hadn't been to a festival of street musicians with a sax quartet. Through this experience I rediscovered that sense of freedom, lightness and passion that comes from being at one with the sound, the other musicians and the audience.

With time, an idea formed in my mind: if music could make me feel better, maybe I could use music to make others feel better. So I enrolled in a four-year course of music therapy in Assisi, Italy, and found my home. Those four wonderful yet difficult years were full of creativity, sounds and magic. While the course taught me many things, music therapy has, more than anything, enabled me to learn about myself, because every client mirrors aspects of me, as I do for them. This results in a continuous process of discovery of who I am, both as a person and as a musician. During my training I continued to play my sax in the piazzas and streets of Assisi, experiencing new sounds, dances and voices whenever I could.

Music therapy has allowed me to learn many things – new information on how to play new instruments, different music therapy models and techniques – but most importantly it has guided me in knowing myself, recognising my talents, my limitations and light and darkness within myself. It is work that never finishes because every person we meet shows their own light and darkness, which allows theirs to encounter ours in a mirror image. It is a continual development of knowledge and a way to define ourselves as people and musicians.

My way of playing the sax has changed a lot over the years as I have explored new styles in timbres, dynamics and melody in my use of improvisation with my clients and musical groups. This has taught me to immerse myself in the flow of the music, to accept myself without judging, and to live in the here and now. It has also encouraged me to experiment and to become increasingly in tune with my own musicality and the potential of my instrument.

I like playing the soprano sax best because it is the easiest of the saxophones to handle. It can be played while sitting on the ground and can be quickly put together and taken apart. I feel that the timbre of the soprano sax is very versatile, allowing me to experiment using different styles: classical, jazz and ethnic. Since it is this sax that enables me to express emotion and nuances most easily, it is the instrument that I use when improvising with other music therapists and musicians. However, a few years ago, a large boy with autism picked up my concert sax, which I had left on a table. He was very rough and had a reputation for breaking things. I couldn't breathe while I watched him miraculously play it properly and then put it gently back. The next day I bought a good-quality student sax to use in my music therapy work.

When I first started working as a music therapist, I didn't use the sax. I limited myself to using the same instruments I had observed during my music therapy course at Assisi (keyboard, percussion, guitar and recorders). Then I had a chance to work with the elderly in a rest home. Using the repertoire of songs from the 1930s to the 1960s that I knew and had seen colleagues use, I starting using my sax. The result was incredible for both me and my clients. I brought a piece of myself to therapy. I could make music in a way I never could have done with another instrument. Now I use the sax intensively in all my work. During every session, the sax breathes along, supports, guides, leads and follows. I continue to use all the other instruments, but my sax is always present, even if only in its case in a corner of the room.

Figure 13.2 Making a connection

I use the sax in the following music therapy contexts:

- **In rest homes and centres for the elderly.** I play songs the clients know on the sax (dances, songs, music from operas and hymns), accompanied by percussion instruments. We improvise a lot. A person might start a rhythm, which another follows, and then I join in with the sax, the sound of which I feel is similar to the human voice. Because of the clear sound of the sax I am able to guide the group, pick up a rhythm from one member, play it, and enable others to imitate it. Since it can move from a sweet pure sound like that of a flute to a powerful one like a trumpet, working with the sax is like having many instruments in one. I can also experiment with changes in rhythm and with stopping. This creates structure, which creates an ensemble and challenges at the same time.

- **With children or adults who are physically disabled and/or have psychiatric problems.** The sax allows me to play from *pianissimo* to *fortissimo*. Since its vibration can be felt through touch, it allows me to enter into contact even with the very seriously disabled. Being able to play both melodies and rhythms, I can accompany, guide, challenge and move between different timbres.

- **In psychiatric prisons.** I worked jointly with one or two other music therapy colleagues and we focused on more traditional types of music-making. The sessions usually began with chaotic improvisations, which we gradually structured into musical pieces. In one situation we were able to create a band in which I contributed by playing saxophone. An important part of this work was that we gave concerts with the band and recorded two CDs.

Music therapy and Neuro-Linguistic Programming techniques with the saxophone

Seven years ago in a Neuro-Linguistic Programming (NLP) meeting I was teaching a group of students, using musical mirroring techniques to match people's movements. NLP is an approach to communication, personal development and psychotherapy created in the 1970s by Richard Bandler and John Grinder in the USA (Bandler and Grinder 1989). They filmed and analysed hundreds of therapy sessions run by Erickson, Satir and Perls, discovering that, despite their different approaches, their use of language, body, voice and breathing was similar and effective in mirroring their clients' inner world.

In Italy the psychotherapist and music therapist, Mauro Scardovelli (1999) has applied NLP to music therapy, creating what he calls 'sound dialogues'. While matching the other person, he applies the three different phases described by Bandler and Grinder (1989): matching, pacing (going at the same pace) and leading. During the course I was using these ideas. I had my sax, and an older, heavy, participant presented himself saying that he had a horrible relationship with his body. I suggested that he move freely while I played the sax. After his initial embarrassment, his body began to move, and I found myself involved in his dance, and he, involved in my sound. It was beautiful, as it seems every time I match a person's movements with my saxophone playing. Some years later, I met that same man on another course. He recognised me, and thanked me, saying that since that experience he had taken possession of his body again and had signed up for a dance class.

Case vignette: Maria

Maria is eight years old. She is blind, has some autistic traits, and still goes to pre-school. She is very interested in the world of sounds and uses her voice sometimes, but not when she is asked, both for speaking and singing. We have worked a lot with the piano and with her voice. Maria alternates between moments of great co-operation and involvement to moments of total closure. I let Maria live her moments of closure and withdrawal from relationships by maintaining a bond through music. While I play for her, she gives small signs that she is listening: her foot beats to the rhythm, she makes little sounds until a finger moves, and then she begins to play again and engage in our relationship. During one session, her closure was so persistent and complete that I stopped playing and felt utterly powerless. But from the corner of the room my sax 'called' to me – my anchor of salvation. I did not know if it was the right thing for Maria at that moment, but it was for me. I got my sax and put it near Maria's hands to present it first as an object, then I began to breathe into the sax with the same rhythm as the little girl's breathing. I slowly began producing long and delicate sounds. The effect was extraordinary: a flower blossomed. From closure, we moved to a slow opening that progressed to dance and then to a rhythm on the drum. We started improvising together, and for the first time I heard Maria laugh.

Case vignette: Flavia

Flavia was an elderly concert musician and piano teacher. She had continued to play until she was 79 years old, but after a stroke she had been put in a rest home. She was not close to anyone, did not participate in any activity, and was cross with the whole world. Her children had put her baby grand piano in the rest home's chapel, but she wanted neither to see nor hear it. When I entered into her building to organise a group singing activity, she yelled curses at me from her wheelchair and said: 'This music is horrible.' However, I noticed that when I played the sax she calmed down. I began to perform pieces that were more complex and seemingly more enjoyable for a musician like her. She began to make requests and to participate in the group. Finally, one day, she accepted the idea of going to the little chapel and asked me to play her piano. I felt very inadequate and I said so, but she encouraged me and so I played the melody from *Ave Maria* by Franz Schubert while using chords in the root position for the bass. We were both musicians and both of us felt inadequate, but the music held us together. Flavia told me: 'Finally, I have heard the sound of my piano again.' Gradually, Flavia began to play her instrument again with only one hand in order to accompany me while I played the sax. She was at peace again with her own instrument, which perhaps enabled her to be a little more at peace with the world.

Thoughts about using the saxophone in music therapy

Anita Vaz

My music therapy work is in special needs schools and a children's hospice. I have a background of working with children and young people with special needs, and have always been interested in the very individual responses to music. My first instrument is flute; this is the instrument that I studied at university and used throughout my music therapy training. I also learnt the piano and the viola. I enjoy many different styles of music but my training was mainly classical. About two years before beginning my training as a music therapist, I bought a tenor saxophone after trying someone else's instrument and realising the potential for different styles of playing and opportunities it could bring. Although the technique for blowing is different to that of the flute, the fingering is very similar, meaning that it was not too difficult for me to learn.

A year after qualifying as a music therapist, I decided to use my tenor saxophone in sessions. I had previously thought about doing this, but several factors had prevented me from acting on it. First, I was doing a lot of private and freelance work in my first year and I feared that the size and weight of the tenor saxophone would make it extremely difficult to juggle among all the many boxes and bags that I carried (I am sure most music therapists can relate to this juggling on a daily basis.) Second, I did not feel the need to use my saxophone when I was finding the flute such a very useful and well-received instrument in music therapy.

When I did begin to use my tenor saxophone with some of the young people I work with, I saw almost a fascination with the instrument. There was a mystery to the saxophone; the size, the shape, the texture and the sound are, I believe, all factors that contribute to this fascination. The size of the keys and buttons themselves are big circles, which make a 'pat-pat' sound as they are pressed. It can be a very sensory instrument with this sound – its breathy-sounding timbre and the vibrations that it makes, especially in the lower register. It is big, bright and reflective – there is enough space to see your face near the bottom of the instrument. The bell of the instrument is a large hole, big enough to peer into and put your hand down, yet not big enough to climb into. All of this is very appealing and mysterious. Some of my clients seem to become completely still and listen to the instrument when I begin playing it.

Case vignettes: Lucy and John

I had been working with a girl of 12 years old for around 19 sessions. Lucy, who has an attachment disorder, possible autistic spectrum disorder and pathological demand avoidance syndrome, and an extremely high level of anxiety, enjoys playing the piano and is very focused on playing chord sequences, over and over again. I often felt very stuck when improvising with her. One day I asked her if she would like me to bring in a saxophone (showing her a picture of a saxophone as I said this). She said she would, so the following week I brought my tenor sax to the school. Lucy laughed a lot when I first blew the instrument, saying that it sounded like hip-hop. At that session, her improvisation became much less stuck, as she began to use a different chord pattern, At one point, Lucy came out of this pattern to tell me that it sounded 'funky'. It was following this session that I wondered about whether other clients might find this beneficial.

I then decided to use the saxophone with John, a 12-year-old pupil at the same school. John has a diagnosis of autistic spectrum disorder and is extremely musical, with perfect pitch. John presents as a very bright and intelligent young man who simply finds it very difficult to relate to people in everyday life, and I had seen his behaviour around school, which could be quite challenging and defiant. The head teacher informed me that when she had been singing in assembly one afternoon, John had approached her and put his arms up to her saying 'sing'. He was referred for music therapy by his class teacher, with the aim of offering him a non-verbal means of communication that he could relate to and a space where he could express himself freely. John engaged with music therapy from the very first session and I found it interesting to work with him. He was not very attracted to the flute, preferring it when I played the piano or joined him on percussion instruments.

The week that I brought my saxophone to school for the first time, he immediately stopped what he was doing, looked at me and laughed. He began to play along with the saxophone, touching it and trying to blow it. This was when I realised the fragility of the instrument; the reed was broken when he grabbed at it and it was difficult to manoeuvre the instrument away, owing to its size. John then decided to put small percussion instruments in the bell of the saxophone – beaters, velcro bells and egg shakers all found their way into the saxophone, and John tried inserting several other instruments to discover whether their size would allow them to fit. In doing this, he was making eye contact and communicating when he wanted me to play, seemingly to test whether it would still make a noise.

As the weeks went on, John continued to be fascinated by the tenor saxophone and its size, shape and sound. John and I engaged in interactions where he had a reed horn and I had my saxophone, taking it in turn to play. He enjoyed my responses to the music he played and remained interested in the shape and size of the instrument. I wonder whether he found it a mystery what is inside the big hole he sees on the end of the saxophone, and where the sound comes from. In later weeks, he also took to tapping the side of it with a stick, in the spacious gaps on the instrument where there are no keys. Although he only did this gently, I could see where it would be a problem, should a client hit the instrument very hard with a drumstick or indeed any other object.

Despite the many advantages to using the tenor sax in music therapy, I have also discovered several disadvantages. One, mentioned above, is the fragility of the reed and how easy it is to break. The reed of a woodwind instrument also needs to be moistened before use – most woodwind players will do this by sucking the reed in their mouth. However, if the therapist wanted to play the saxophone later into a session, the reed might need to be re-moistened, which could perhaps break up the flow of the session.

Owing to the size of the instrument, it is difficult to move quickly; it is joined by the neck strap or body brace, and is a heavy and long instrument. Therefore, if the therapist needs to leave the room quickly, or needs to take the instrument out of sight for any reason, it would be difficult to do this. Again owing to its size, the therapist may have difficulty in sitting on the floor playing with a client. Playing the tenor sax means that the therapist needs to be more static, rather than moving around with a client in the same way as perhaps one can with a flute. As mentioned above, the bell of the saxophone is almost ergonomic, with something for the client to grab onto if they wanted to – and I sometimes feel that it almost invites grabbing.

I feel that the tenor saxophone is an extremely sensory instrument, and this makes it potentially very useful to use with any client with autistic spectrum disorder or other learning disabilities where there is a high sensory response. I am interested in looking closely into the saxophone's effectiveness due to its sensory nature, as I believe it is one of the more sensory instruments when compared with other woodwind and string instruments. My saxophone has only just begun its journey as a therapeutic instrument, and I look forward to discovering the ways that it might be received by clients.

Saxophone characteristics in music therapy practice

The 'coolness' of the saxophone

The aspect of 'coolness' was mentioned by all therapists as important for both the players and the observers. In music therapy work with the homeless, the sax was perceived as a cool street instrument, which was important for the group therapy process. In another setting, one young music therapy client said the sax music sounded like hip-hop, and its links with jazz music and particularly pop music meant that it was generally respected and well-received.

Issues around envy and rivalry

Although these could be applied to a therapist's expertise on any musical instrument, it was felt that the saxophone in particular had the potential to evoke these emotions, which for certain clients could become overwhelming.

Portability

All of the therapists mentioned the importance of movement with the sax, although one therapist found the tenor sax less portable (especially when compared to her flute). The soprano sax was generally considered easier to handle and to move with in sessions.

Tonal quality

The saxophonist's ability to create a sense of conversation, similar to our everyday conversations, and to move from pure, sweet sounds to powerful rasping (imitating the nuances of our voices) was considered a useful tool in therapy sessions. The sax can also provide a strong lyrical voice, similar to the human singing voice.

The use of the sax in jazz music, particularly free jazz improvisation

This was mentioned by all therapists as an important aspect. For some of the therapists, this was a motivating factor that had initially inspired them to play the saxophone. This useful improvisation skill was considered to be readily transferable to, and beneficial in, music therapy improvisation.

The versatility of sounds created

The use of trills, flutter tonguing, vamping and squeaking, the use of growls or honking low notes that can express different qualities; poignancy, as well as anger and aggression.

The ability to vary the volume from fortissimo to pianissimo

This ability enables the therapist to match a client's loud drumming, for example, or to play extremely gently and poignantly.

Useful as a simple, single-line instrument

One therapist explained that sometimes a strong single-line melody was more beneficial in his sessions than, for example, the full harmonic support of the piano.

Vibrations from the instrument

These could be perceived on the skin of clients, and for one therapist allowed positive connection with very disabled patients.

The sensory nature of the sax

Its shape and size, the bright reflective surfaces, the bell at the end, the pit-pat sound of the keys being pressed and the breathy-sounding timbre.

The vulnerability and fragility of both the reed and the instrument itself

In certain settings, such as when working with young people with challenging behaviour, this meant that the saxophone was not considered suitable to use in sessions.

The need to wet the reed before playing

This can affect spontaneity and impede playing, sometimes diminishing the therapist's ability to be ready to respond promptly in sessions.

Hygiene issues

These were also noted (as with all mouth-blown instruments).

The mystery or fascination of the sax

Two of the therapists talked about its ability to make listeners stop in their tracks and just listen.

References

Bandler, R. and Grinder, J. (1989) *The Structure of Magic: A Book About Language and Therapy.* Palo Alto, CA: Science and Behavior Books.

Gioia, T. (2011) *The History of Jazz.* Oxford, UK: Oxford University Press.

Scardovelli, M. (1999) *Musica e Trasformazione.* Rome, Italy: Edizioni Borla.

Segell, M. (2005) *The Devil's Horn: The Story of the Saxophone, from Noisy Novelty to King of Cool.* New York, NY: Farrar, Straus and Giroux.

CHAPTER 14

The Bass (the Double Bass
and the Bass Guitar)

Contributors: Joseph Piccinnini (bass guitar case vignette),
Paolo Pizziolo (double bass introduction and case vignettes)
and John Preston (double bass and bass guitar case vignettes)

Introduction: Double bass

> The double bass is far and away the most important instrument in the
> whole orchestra ... the orchestra [may exist] without a conductor
> any time but not without a double-bass. ... The orchestra starts
> to exist when the double bass is there... Metaphorically speaking,
> the bass is the cornerstone on which the whole magnificent edifice
> [of the orchestra] rises. (Süskind 1987, pp.6–7)

Although this may be a slight exaggeration, there is no doubt that
the natural environment for the double bass was originally the
orchestra, where it provided 'power, weight and the basic rhythmic
foundation' (Slatford and Shipton n.d.)
    The double bass has a violin or viola shape.

> Of the smallest basses (bassetti and chamber basses) some are
> little bigger than a cello, while some of the larger (full-size)
> instruments can have a body of anything up to about 140 cm
> in length. The normal (three-quarter) size found in orchestras
> is about 115 cm. One of the largest is 4·8 metres high and was
> built by Paul de Wit for the Cincinnati music festival of 1889
> (Slatford and Shipton n.d.).

The double bass can be played either using a bow, typical of classical music, or by plucking which is more common in jazz. Its four strings are usually tuned to E-A-D-G and it has a range exceeding three octaves, excluding harmonics.

Figure 14.1 Double bass range (as heard – not as written, as bass parts are written an octave higher to avoid ledger lines)

Although the first reference to the double bass appears in Agricola's *Musica instrumentalis deudsch* (1529), it is not until 1690 that there is any music specifically written for the instrument and only after the mid-18th century does it become a regular component of the orchestra. Major composers who have written for the double bass include Haydn, Mozart, Beethoven, Schubert, Mahler, Stravinsky, Prokofiev, Rossini and Britten (Slatford and Shipton n.d.) In the past half-century, interest in the double bass as a solo instrument has increased with major contemporary composers such as Philip Glass and Nino Rota writing solo works for it. There has also been great interest in experimenting with its sonority, including a particular way of playing called 'speech sounds', where the instrument mirrors the sound of speech.

Unique among the orchestral bow instruments, the double bass has also gained an important role in jazz formations, replacing the tuba in the 1920s because of its greater range and percussive sound. Bass players, such as Jimmy Blanton, explored the soloist potential of the instrument, developing many different phrasings and improvisations for the various different jazz styles. In addition, the double bass is a characteristic feature of many types of popular and folk music, from the tango and polka to the ethnic music of the Roma people, rockabilly and American country music.

Considering its great versatility and its vast number of soundscapes, the double bass is particularly useful for music therapy, as it is capable of providing a wide range of channels for connecting with clients. However, its size can be a problem for transportation and may constitute a physical barrier between the therapist and the client. The double bass player may not be able to move freely or quickly around the room, which could be a difficulty when working with children or clients with disruptive behaviours.

There are only a few references in the literature to the use of the double bass in music therapy. However, Ian McTier (2012) described the use of the double bass with five patients with autistic spectrum disorder in a school in Scotland, highlighting the many psychodynamic qualities of its low-frequency sounds.

Introduction: Bass guitar

Most double bass players also play the bass guitar, which has the same four strings (E, A, D and G) and sounds similar in pitch. Some music therapists find it easier to transport the bass guitar than the double bass, although of course they will need an additional amplifier and a lead, which in some cases could be a disadvantage. The bass guitar is less fragile than the double bass but amplifiers and lead connections may be temperamental and it can be frustrating when they fail to function. However, having an amplifier means that interesting special electronic effects can be used. For many clients the bass guitar will be associated with popular music and playing in a band, which could be a distinct advantage.

Like the double bass, the bass guitar can provide a wide range of bass lines and establish reassuring harmonic grounding.

Connecting to dementia patients

Paolo Pizziolo

Figure 14.2 The double bass provides a significant presence in the room

I became interested in the double bass when I was 16, after having played electric bass in a few bands at high school. The double bass allowed me to play in many different musical contexts, and as I had very eclectic musical tastes, ranging from symphony orchestra and chamber music to jazz trios, Mediterranean ethnic traditions, pop music and punk rock, I could integrate all these musical styles as well as staying linked to the electric bass. Consequently, I decided to attend a double bass class at the Cherubini Conservatory in Florence.

The bass frequencies peculiar to the instrument fascinate me. They give me a sense of solidity and grounding, as well as contributing energy and power to the music I play with other people. These low frequencies are natural supports for singing. Even at the beginning of my studies, while I practised long notes to improve my sound quality with a bow, I enjoyed singing along with improvised modal Gregorian melodies using the long notes as an organ pedal or *cantus firmus* (i.e. long notes used as a base on which to build a vocal counter-melody). At that time the energy of the bass lines in Beethoven and Schubert symphonies greatly appealed to me, and some years later, when I had the opportunity to play that music in an orchestra, it was very musically fulfilling for me.

The physical shape of the instrument and its sound are also alluring elements; this is an instrument that needs to be practically hugged when it is played and produces a deep embracing sound, yet despite its imposing size, it is actually quite delicate. Symbolically, it could also be seen to have a double personality: feminine and masculine. As Ian McTier describes, in its feminine role it 'promotes several of the more maternally-based underpinnings of psychotherapy' (McTier 2012, p.153). In music therapy the double bass, with its versatility of sustained pedal notes and combination of rhythm and bass when gently played pizzicato, is an ideal 'container' (Bion 1967) in the way that it can frame a client's music.

McTier also highlights that the double bass can take on the role of the 'good enough mother' (Winnicott 1990) by providing a nurturing backdrop of sustained sound and supporting the development of ego strength, through allowing clients to risk exploring their creativity. Both the physical dimensions of the instrument and its sound can provide a stimulus for play.

In its male role, McTier mentions its imposing dimensions and its rhythmic intensity and insistence as elements that 'create a rugged, authoritarian framework' (McTier 2012, p.154) and that can draw the client towards independence. This is well illustrated in Beethoven's orchestral bass lines. Moreover, McTier likens the low frequencies and the rhythmic stability typical of the double bass to the regular rhythm and low-frequency notes perceived by the foetus in the mother's womb and that are therefore apprehended as safe and comforting.

The double bass is a very demanding instrument, where playing in tune and the effective use of the bow require regular practice. However, playing and improvising on it has provided me with great comfort during difficult moments in my life. In the words of Nachmanovitch, 'in improvisation, the time of inspiration, the time of technically structuring and realizing the music, the time of playing it and the time of communicating with the audience are all one' (Nachmanovitch 1990, p.18). I can do this best with the double bass.

The double bass in music therapy with elderly dementia clients

Introducing the double bass is important in music therapy. At the beginning of the session, I leave it lying down unused in a position not too close to the clients, while starting the session with singing activities or with the introduction of the other musical instruments available, typically xylophones, a variety of small percussion instruments, guitar or piano. After the clients have explored the use of the instruments and we have already improvised some music or sung a couple of songs, the double bass can be introduced, possibly after a little break from playing or after discussion, which can mark the start of a new direction in the session and perhaps move towards a greater level of interaction and involvement of the clients.

As the bass is as tall and wide as a person, and even larger than some of my more elderly patients, it is like introducing a new participant. I feel it is necessary to introduce it first with words, by asking them for permission to use 'that big instrument over there' or by simply announcing that I am going to use it. Asking for permission maintains the clients' involvement during the transition to a new situation. The first few times, the mere presence of the double bass makes the clients more alert and interested in what is happening musically. It stimulates the clients to explore something new, making it an effective trigger for participating in the improvisation by playing an instrument or singing. For example, I have been surprised by clients who normally only sit and listen to the others play or improvise, who suddenly pick up a stick and start banging it on the closest object to hand, such as a table or the arms of their chair.

The next step is to introduce the sound, which is usually not difficult because the clients themselves often ask to hear the double bass, once it has been introduced. At other times I myself might decide to use it, starting off with notes followed by long pauses to focus attention and stimulate participation. At this time, it is important to play notes that are in the same tonality as the other instruments available to the clients. This is so that if they start playing, what they produce is immediately in tune and the bass will support them in their music-making.

If the clients stick to playing the instruments rather than singing, I might play long notes or short staccato notes to match individual client's specific rhythmic styles, or an emerging group pulse, while trying to maintain a continuity of sound.

This process is illustrated in the Figure 14.3, from the initial long notes and pauses without pulse in the first four bars, to the introduction of a pulse (bars 5–7) that mirrors that of the client, which may gradually be enriched with the internal *louré* (*portato*) subdivisions of two or four (bars 7–10)

Figure 14.3 Steps in enhancing client pulse using two different bow strokes

Once the clients have started participating, the sound of the group tends to follow one of several directions, and the double bass is flexible enough to be able to match the clients' sounds. This is the way I have most frequently used the double bass. With elderly people, the group may sing old songs or opera arias accompanied by sounds from their instruments, and in this case the double bass can support their singing by providing a very strong bass line that reinforces the harmonic progressions. In addition clients sometimes comment that they feel they are being accompanied by an entire orchestra, particularly if I play arpeggios or two-note chords, which will stimulate people to sing.

When people are playing xylophones, on the other hand, I might need to reduce the power of the bow sound by switching to the pizzicato timbre so as not to overwhelm the client's often very weak sounds. This maintains the power of the bass frequencies, but the fast decay (note rapidly fading away) allows the client to concentrate on what they are playing. Good acoustics in the music therapy room makes it possible to work effectively with very quiet or loud sounds.

Initially, in 2002, when I started working as a music therapist, I used the double bass in sessions only occasionally, but in 2012 I decided to use it more regularly because I began working three days a week in a day centre for people with dementia. In this centre I worked in a very well-equipped, sound-proofed room and had a wide range of musical instruments available to me.

Case vignette: Active music therapy group with clients showing moderate behavioural and psychological symptoms of dementia (BPSD)

Twice a week I work with five female patients with BPSD, in an Italian NHS Dementia Day Care Centre in Florence. The group therapy is aimed at reducing these symptoms and increasing social interaction despite the participants' differing levels of cognitive impairment and behavioural symptoms. After working for six to seven weeks using only xylophones and small percussion, I introduce the double bass. The session is structured as follows.

I introduce the clients to each other, and to the instruments and how they work. To signal the start of making music together, I begin by singing one or two old songs or, more rarely, a hello song, which may stimulate the clients to use the instruments to accompany the song. I may use either the xylophone or the guitar. We gradually switch from singing to improvising with the instruments. Without the double bass, I often had to interact individually with each person in order to keep the clients' attention and enable them to continue playing or listening. They did not generally interact with each other. When I introduced the double bass, however, they immediately paid more attention to the music I provided, which was therefore more effective in supporting and enhancing their fragmented playing. As the individual musical contributions became more frequent, the clients occasionally interacted with each other and I could provide a simple ostinato (a simple musical phase that is constantly repeated) to support group interactions, instead of having to provide different musical prompts for each individual's sounds. In these moments of sharing in the group, the atmosphere was relaxed and joyful in a similar way to when musicians at a rehearsal or concert play a particularly heartfelt piece that makes them feel close to each other.

When using the Agitation Behavior Mapping Instrument (ABMI) (Cohen-Mansfield and Libin 2004) assessment tool, I have observed that behavioural symptoms diminish during music therapy sessions to nearly zero with the introduction of the double bass. I would like to further investigate these initial findings in the future.

Case vignette: Anna

Anna is a patient with front temporal dementia and a very low score in the Mini Mental State Examination (Folstein, Folstein and McHugh 1975) test. She was referred to music therapy as musical relationships seem to be one of the few means of lowering her aggressive contact with others, and like other dementia patients of this type, she demonstrates a set of repetitive obsessive–compulsive behaviours. It was decided to involve her in individual sessions as she would play every instrument she came into contact with very loudly and other participants would quickly become annoyed. She is also very egocentric and attention-seeking, which may be why she plays so loudly.

Anna would come into the music therapy room around mid-morning, feeling angry after her scheduled bathroom visit. Her language had diminished to repeated brief phrases or single words. When she entered, her recurring phrase was often 'you're disgusting', alternating with 'patience, patience' as she relaxed, becoming just 'patience' and then changing to 'bien, bien, bien' (good, good, good) by the end of the session. Previous to these five sessions, I had had some success in interrupting her obsessive behaviours by accompanying her on the piano. As her illness progressed, however, this no longer worked and so I tried the double bass. With the double bass she would interact for 15 to 20 minutes, quite a long time for her, and after the session, she was calmer.

To free her from the spell of compulsive behaviour (which probably functioned as a means of reassurance), I tried to play together with her, rather than in contrast to her, interrupting her or taking turns.

From a detailed review of videos of the sessions, I have selected the elements that preceded her change in mood:

Her compulsive 'mechanical' xylophone playing was intensified if I played along with the same instrument. However, if I played long notes or pedals with the double bass and then rhythmic patterns to enhance and highlight her pattern, thereby providing a sound-frame, this provoked a change either in the rhythm or the note sequence of her playing, which became less stereotypical (see Figure 14.4). My impression is that the differences in timbre, size and mode of execution of the double bass plays an important role in the interaction. It could be that the deep register of the double bass, very different from that of the Orff xylophones, enhances the perception of the two parts, which are using sound to have a dialogue.

Figure 14.4 Providing a way of 'framing' phrases on the double bass

When she stopped to swear, I would not answer verbally but responded by playing short phrases that emulated speech, using small intervals and glissando between pitches, which the double bass can do particularly effectively. The physical distance available on the neck of the double bass enables the player to produce glissandi even between very close pitches. Since her swearing was pulsed, the first two times I responded after her, but then I was able to mimic her rhythm and phrasing simultaneously. My impression is that being in unison with her made her feel accepted and contributed to making her calmer. See Figure 14.5.

Figure 14.5 Emulating speech

With Anna, the double bass offers me a series of polar opposites with which I can immediately respond to her extreme and sudden changes in mood: differences in timbre (pizzicato versus bowed), in register (C2–C3 played in the second position sounds very different from C3–C4), in style (accompaniment like ostinato or bass lines as opposed to playing a melody; classical versus pop/jazz; instrumental versus speech imitation).

My modulated response to her spontaneous alternating of moods and behaviours using the versatile characteristics of the double bass was aimed at making her feel that I was with her while she changed. At the same time I tried to offer a stimulus to break the spell of repetitive behaviour. Improvising with Anna was very tiring for me because her anger seemed to stem from her frustration regarding her ongoing degenerative process, and made me feel sad and frustrated on her behalf. At the end of the last two sessions, when she was saying 'bien, bien, bien' and sitting back in her chair with her legs stretched out, her playing had slowed and I improvised a relaxing lullaby-like melody in the lower register of the instrument. This closed the session and created a safe and comforting atmosphere that made an impression on me at the same time as being a very enjoyable moment that reinforced my relationship with the instrument as a powerful containment tool.

The disadvantages of the double bass are mainly linked to its size, which makes it difficult to move from one workplace to another and means calculating extra time for transport and preparing the setting. It can also be difficult to get physically close to your clients and to move around freely. It is a delicate instrument and there is a real risk of it being damaged by physically agitated clients. However, its large body gives it a strong symbolic value and great potential as a means of resonating.

Bass-centred music therapy

Joseph Piccinnini

I have been using the electric bass guitar in clinical music therapy sessions since 1977. I am personally drawn to the sound of the bass for many reasons. It gives support to the music and provides balance for a wide range of sounds. In my professional experience as a drummer, I collaborate with the bass player in subtle ways to underpin the musical structure. The result of this collaboration is the 'groove', the basic feeling of the music. In creating the groove, the bass player can assume the primary role of time-keeping. This allows the drummer to move from beat to beat and participate in aspects of the music in addition to simply keeping the beat going. I feel this is when music sounds best. I look to the bass for the creation of the essential 'one' in the music – the first beat of the bar. The second beat is where the drummer's snare usually comes in. Thus the bass players 'one' is the foundation for the creation of the drummer's 'two'. The other instruments assume their respective parts on the basis of the activity of the bass and drum. Each measure is an interpersonal exchange between all group members.

I am personally influenced by bass players from the Los Angeles-based band Wrecking Crew and Motown songs. These groove-based songs feature the bass working interactively with the drums and other instruments.

I first suggested the use of the bass guitar and other instruments (drum set, electric guitar) in music therapy groups in the New York University Music Therapy Program. Up until that time, groups that made music together and processed musical interactions had used small pitched and unpitched percussion instruments almost exclusively. From that time forward, the bass guitar has been incorporated as an option in musical ensembles in the graduate programme. Shortly after its introduction in the NYU graduate programme, the bass guitar was incorporated into courses of therapy at the Nordoff-Robbins Center for Music Therapy at NYU. Years of clinical experience have shown it to be effective in courses of therapy with standard music therapy goals, including improving physical, cognitive, social, emotional and spiritual functioning (Aigen 2002). Other music therapy programmes are now using the bass guitar as well.

Case vignette: Dustin

Figure 14.6 Playing as a band

Dustin was diagnosed at birth with Down's syndrome. He faced numerous medical complications at birth and, as a result, was hospitalised for 16 days before discharge. He was diagnosed with hypothyroidism as a one-year-old and has been on medication ever since. Dustin started wearing prescription glasses at that time as well. Dustin currently receives speech therapy, occupational therapy and physiotherapy within his school.

Dustin began music therapy with me at Richmond Music Center in Staten Island, New York, in August 2011. He continues to attend weekly 45-minute individual sessions. He is now almost 14 years old. Dustin's attendance at music therapy sessions had been perfect and his parents are very supportive and trusting of the process.

The structure of the bass-centred music therapy is important. There is a clear beginning, middle, and end to the 45-minute session. Thus each session began with a hello or greeting song and concluded with a goodbye song. Between these, there were opportunities for improvisation as well as periods when familiar music could be brought into the session. Therefore there is a degree of predictability that is comfortable in the session, and there are parts that are less familiar that can be less comfortable but extend Dustin's tolerance for new things and push him in alternative directions. In general, sessions conformed to the model suggested by the Nordoff-Robbins approach to music therapy (Nordoff and Robbins 2007). Using the bass guitar with Dustin provides an atmosphere of deep grounding, giving a supportive foundation to the music. The vibrations of the bass resonate throughout the body, leading to better-grounded communication and a positive sense of self.

Dustin usually plays drums as I play bass guitar. We use an improvisational style. A microphone is set up for Dustin to use. At times he may move from the drums and start moving and dancing in a happy and playful way. We engage in a call-and-response type of music. I often leave space in the music for him to play his part. Sometimes he sings; sometimes he does a drum solo; sometimes he laughs or makes gestures. He is fully engaged in the moment and clearly becomes more present and lively during his solos. He sometimes chants music he creates on his own with support from the bass guitar.

Dustin's playing varies in tempo and speed. He ranges from steady to chaotic. The bass steers the music from tension to release. Dustin's unsteadiness is guided towards more consistent beating. He has a good physical relationship to whatever instrument he is playing and moves quite easily and fluidly. He often carries two drumsticks in his hands throughout sessions. This appears to give him a sense of comfort and helps keep him calm. Its effectiveness is such that he now carries the sticks even when he is not in music therapy. Perhaps this enables him to remain connected to the possibilities that music presents for him.

Dustin played drums while I played bass at a Richmond Music Center recital in 2012. As in our sessions, the music we played was improvised. There were 350 people in attendance. As Dustin walked into the recital room he appeared expressionless, with flat affect, almost as if he were in a catatonic state. I greeted him earlier for our dress rehearsal. He reluctantly sat behind the drums and I began playing bass. Dustin just sat, motionless and speechless. We had a microphone set up for him so he could sing an improvised song. I initiated the music and played for about two minutes, and then Dustin enthusiastically joined in, playing drums and singing along to the bass. I breathed a sigh of relief. After playing for about three minutes he stood up, raised his arms triumphantly, drumsticks in hands, with a big smile on his face. He had done remarkably well, and had enjoyed himself tremendously.

Overall, Dustin is doing very well in music therapy. His intense engagement in the musical process and his determination to express himself are key factors in his progress. Dustin is creative and spontaneous; these are wonderful traits to employ in clinical music therapy improvisation. His creativity, self-expression, speech, communication skills, motor skills and interpersonal skills improve weekly. Dustin has become more accepting of changes in the music and this has generalised to him being increasingly able to accept transitions in life. In terms of life skills, Dustin has shown significant improvement in his ability to speak clearly and in complete sentences. When he began music therapy he spoke in incoherent, not quite understandable phrases. Now he is able to hold a conversation in a pleasant manner. Dustin sings his own song, in his own way, and is comfortable doing his own musical thing. Music therapy has given him an opportunity to realise his full potential.

What the family thought

Here are some of the things Dustin's mother said about the family's perception of music therapy for Dustin:

> When my husband and I first decided to provide music therapy for Dustin, we recognised that as in any form of therapy, results would not be immediate. We needed to be willing to be patient with the process. We decided to invest in one year of music therapy and then assess whether it was worth continuing. Almost three years later, Dustin is still in music therapy because we are seeing positive progress. Dustin enjoys attending music therapy because it is so much fun for him. He gets undivided attention from another person while experimenting with various instruments. What is there not to like?
>
> It is difficult to quantify the progress we observe in Dustin as it is difficult to isolate the various factors that may contribute to his development. But our gut feeling is that something is working. I do not understand the musical theory behind music therapy but I know that it is helping him somehow. The first change we noticed about Dustin after a few months of music therapy was that he appeared to be calmer. He became more vocal and expressive, although his speech was still not clear at that time. He became more aware of his surroundings and more interactive socially. His speech continues to improve, not only in the length of his utterances, but also the clarity as well. Most recently, I am finally having conversations with him, a moment I have awaited for many years.

Providing grounding and stability to unleash creativity

John Preston

I started playing the electric bass guitar when I was 17 years old in a band with two mates who were guitarists and they needed a bass player. My stepfather had a short-scale electric bass (rather like a kid's bass), so this was what I started on. We were inspired by punk music: a seminal fanzine (fan magazine) of the time published a chart showing three guitar chords, with the incitement 'now go and form a band'. This idea demystified music for me; we felt that anyone could pick up an instrument and create music with others. Simple structures and riffs was how a group of semi-educated teenagers transformed rudimentary skills and inchoate ideas into forms and structure. Our limited musical knowledge meant we found jamming together to create songs easier than trying to copy other people's songs. Although I had no idea then that being a music therapist would be my future, this way of working has stood me in good stead.

Playing the bass was a pragmatic decision, but it also made more sense to me than the guitar. I did not start playing the double bass until my 30s when a friend left his double bass in my house while he was away for a few months. Of course, it looked and sounded cool and my encounter with it in my early 30s reinvigorated my enthusiasm for music. I was able to learn on the job in the Norfolk folk scene and took lessons for the first time in my life. My first teacher, who is now a dear musical friend, had to put up with some miserable bow work initially as I took steps towards more formal study. The deep resonant warmth of the double bass offers a rich sound-world that can simply accompany solo voice or piano, or hold its own in larger ensembles. The double bass immediately has an impact because of its size. The fact is, it is subtle and has a more nuanced voice than the bass guitar. There is an ensemble saying that when the band is playing you can't hear the bass but you can hear if it stops.

I have used both the electric bass and the double bass throughout my music therapy practice in a psychiatric hospital. In post-punk musical culture there were a lot of bass-heavy ostinato riffs and grooves (e.g. as used by the bands Public Image Limited and Joy

Division), so, in a similar way, when improvising in a music therapy group I can provide grounding for disparate elements in the group. This reminds me of Miles Davis's *Bitches Brew* (1970) and *Live-Evil* (1971) with shards of sound and progressions merging but with a steady bass throb throughout. The bass line is very simple, but there are lots of complicated guitar and trumpet interventions above.

In addition to underpinning sometimes disorganised melodic improvisations, the bass can provide an accompaniment for piano and guitar playing in rock/pop idioms. It can also facilitate those without any musical experience. When accompanying an individual client on the piano, for example, the double bass can come into its own providing a warm, solid background for tentative melodic experiments.

Unfortunately it is also a delicate and fragile instrument. On one occasion my double bass was standing in a corner of the music therapy room and during a group improvisation it fell over and smashed. I did not see any reason to stop the group playing as the damage was already done. Of course there was concern and perhaps shock, but the improvisation continued and concluded. At the end of the piece, I went to pick it up and realised the damage was substantial. I was lucky to find someone willing to repair it but did not get any help from my employers for this, so the bass came home.

The electric bass will often be associated with bands and popular music and may therefore carry cultural fantasies for some clients. Obvious slow and simple pop clichés can be demonstrated and learned. I was able to teach an untrained but very musical patient to play T. Rex's 'Get It On' (1971) in five minutes, and we eventually performed it as part of a larger ensemble on a secure ward.

The bass guitar can also provide pulse and cues to support patients who are interested in the drum-kit. This allows patients to feel secure and confident and immediately have a musical identity. For example, a rhythm such as dotted crotchet–quaver–minim offers a familiar rhythmic pattern to lock onto. The bass guitar and the double bass also both lend themselves easily to offering cues through gesture or body movements. This is something I have learned in my band work, where often I find myself cueing the ensemble as the piece progresses.

Also, within a group context, if the client is playing the drum kit and just doing their own thing rather than attempting to connect with others, the bass can still hold the piece for the rest of the ensemble, while giving the drummer free rein, or allowing them to find their way in if this is possible. The bass can help provide the necessary coherence and integration to enable clients to feel reassured and to stay in the room, as chaotic elements settle.

Because you can amplify the electric bass, its lower frequencies sit nicely below the guitar and piano. This enables the electric bass to be rhythmically and harmonically 'holding', offering a strong pulse.

Case vignette: Group on an acute psychiatric ward

In one particular group offered to the acute psychiatric wards, the group was playing in fits and starts and the music was not going anywhere. I was playing the double bass and it was hard to find a groove. I slipped into a two-chord trick based on the opening riff of Eddie Cochran's 'Summertime Blues' (1958). A member of the group started improvising a song: 'I've got the Fulbourn Blues' (Fulbourn was the name of the village near the hospital). The chorus developed into: 'Help, help, I've got the Fulbourn Blues, which everyone joined in with, vocally and instrumentally. She went on to ad-lib words in the verses incorporating medication, psychiatry and her present situation. The group was able to come together with some humour regarding the common experience of being together as psychiatric patients on an acute ward. The bass line held the frame so the music could have a volition of its own.

Another musical highlight from this group was when playing a 12-bar blues and one gentleman played a solo on the flexitone (a most improbable instrument for such a feat) with the double bass walking a jazz blues. It had a surreal humour as well as astounding inventiveness.

Case vignette: Lorna

I worked individually with Lorna, an accomplished visual artist, on a weekly basis for two-and-a-half years. She suffered from acute anxiety and depression. After attending the 'Open Acute group' she was referred for individual work as an out-patient. Her artwork was methodical, deeply thought out and researched, and exquisite. We explored control and how managing everything was a way for her to keep depression at bay and yet pushing her to exhaustion. We used musical improvisation with her playing the piano, which she had learnt in the past, while I accompanied her on the double bass. For her, this was an arena to explore and accept uncertainty and imperfection. The double bass was grounding and reassuring; it could hold dissonance and allow her to move between the abstract and melodic. The improvisations were not predictable as she did not have the musical skill to control this, and she was keen to explore this opportunity.

When things were difficult our bass and piano improvisations were often murky and dissonant with piano clusters in the lower third of the keyboard. I was able to match this dark confusion with simple double bass pulses and tones, which the piano could ride with, enabling phrases to come together and be concluded. Gradually patterns emerged and sequences began to form. Although talking was a strong feature of this therapy, the move between the verbal thinking, the feeling realm and the more intimate musical exchange offered contact with the immediacy of a relationship (musical in this case) that could not be managed or controlled.

Stability, self-awareness, flexibility and happiness became accessible to Lorna. On my desk sits an exquisite picture she gave me of a double bass player. The picture is beautiful and betrays a loving attention to detail and technique, yet, for her, growth was made possible by exploring art 'outside of her comfort zone' as she used to say, where the relationship was more negotiable and thus more reciprocal.

Many years later I contacted Lorna and asked her whether she would allow me to write this case vignette and print a copy of the picture she drew and gave me. She agreed to both these requests and wrote the following paragraph to add to the case:

> I think of all the instruments that accompanied my piano playing in the music therapy session, I most preferred the double bass. Its resonance and the undercurrents of the bass notes underpinned my own chattering fingers which skated so much on the surface, just like my anxiety and constant filling of my life with stuff so one doesn't have to think or feel. It felt supportive but resonated at a deeper level of consciousness that I could not analyse or control, so much my usual modus operandi of choice. I can feel it now, even years later, when I remember, its sound resonating in the heart, soft deep thudding notes sounding in an interior cave. Warm, calm, all embracing, quite primeval.

Figure 14.7 Double bass drawing by Lorna

Double bass and bass guitar characteristics in music therapy

Low notes

All the contributors felt that the fact that the bass played low notes was crucial. This enables both the double bass and the bass guitar to provide reassuring solidity and grounding.

Ideal accompanying instrument

The depth and possible simplicity of bass lines were given as reasons by all three contributors as to why the double bass and the bass guitar can be effectively used to improvise an accompanying part for individual or group music therapy work.

The vibrations produced by low instruments

Instances where clients were drawn to the music played by the bass instruments because of the vibrations they perceived were mentioned by all three contributors.

Bass instruments are 'cool'

The important role that the bass guitar and the double bass play in popular music was highlighted as having an impact on the motivation of clients to become engaged with music played on these instruments, as well as allowing the therapists the flexibility of playing in a wide range of different styles.

Size of the instrument

Both double bass contributors mentioned that the size of the instrument was significant and, as a result, difficult to carry around. It was likened to having another person present in the room, and its size made it important and powerful.

Fragility of the double bass

The fact that such a large instrument is so vulnerable and fragile was mentioned as important and had an impact on the work of the double bass contributors.

Gender associations with the bass

Both male and female characteristics of the double bass were written about in relation to clinical casework as well as to existing literature.

A way of emulating speech

Two of the contributors suggested that the bass was particularly useful for having non-verbal conversations with clients, partly because of the possibility of shifting pitches and imitating vocal sounds.

References

Agricola, M. (1529) *Musica instrumentalis deudsch* (Wittenberg, 1529/R, enlarged 5/1545); Eng. trans. by W. Hettrick (Cambridge, 1994).

Aigen, K. (2002) *Playin' in the Band: A Qualitative Study of Popular Music Styles as Clinical Improvization*. New York, NY: Nordoff-Robbins Center for Music Therapy.

Bion, W.R. (1967) 'Attacks on Linking.' In *Second Thoughts: Selected Papers on Psychoanalysis*. London, UK: Maresfield.

Cohen-Mansfield, J. and Libin, A. (2004) 'Assessment of agitation in elderly patients with dementia: Correlations between informant rating and direct observation.' *International Journal of Geriatric Psychiatry 19*, 9, 881–891.

Folstein, M.F., Folstein, S.E. and McHugh, P.R. (1975) '"Mini-mental state": A practical method for grading the cognitive state of patients for the clinician.' *Journal of Psychiatric Research 12*, 3 189–198.

McTier, I. (2012) 'Music Therapy in a Special School for Children with Autistic Spectrum Disorders, Focusing Particularly on the Use of the Double Bass.' In J. Tomlinson, P. Derrington and A. Oldfield (eds) *Music Therapy in Schools: Working with Children of all Ages in Mainstream and Special Education*. London, UK: Jessica Kingsley Publishers.

Nachmanovitch, S. (1990) *Free Play: Improvisation in Life and Art*. New York, NY: G.P. Putnam's Sons.

Nordoff, P. and Robbins, C. (2007) *Creative Music Therapy* (2nd edn). Gilsum, NH: Barcelona Publishers.

Slatford, R. & Shipton, A. (n.d.) *Double bass*. Retrieved 20 April 2014 from www.oxfordmusiconline.com:80/subscriber/article/grove/music/46437.

Süskind, P. (1987) *The Double Bass*. London, UK: Hamish Hamilton.

Winnicott, D.W. (1990) *The Maturational Processes and the Facilitating Environment: Studies in the Theory of Emotional Development*. London, UK: Karnac Books.

Reflections

Amelia Oldfield

Several common themes seem to emerge from the 14 instrumental chapters in this book. In many cases it would appear that music therapists using the same instruments have come to similar conclusions; accordionists, for example, all mentioning their use of the bellows to mirror breathing patterns, and several violinists commenting on the interest created by the physical movement of the bow on the strings. In their practice, music therapists have come to the same conclusions, but this has not previously been documented.

Overall, mobility and the fact that the smaller instruments allow the music therapist to move around and be close to patients appears invariably to be considered a particular advantage. With the larger instruments, such as the double bass and the harp, the physical presence of a large important object in the room is mentioned as being significant.

Interestingly, in nearly all the chapters, authors mention that they feel their instrument is similar to the human voice. I have always been convinced that the clarinet was very like the human voice, but it was surprising to find that most other instrumentalists also believe this about their own instrument. The specific tone colour of the instruments is frequently cited as being influential, and the particular associations that may be made with instruments, which are often linked to styles of music peculiar to a particular era, were shown to be significant.

It is often mentioned that clients feel connected to the therapist because the therapist has made the effort to bring their own instrument to the session. This point is linked to what appears to be the most crucial consideration: the fact that the therapist's own instrument is the one they feel closest to and the one they will be able to be most expressive on. The strong emotional tie that links the therapist to their instrument is sometimes a disadvantage, and for some therapists such as Harrison (viola) this will be one of the reasons why they will chose not to play their instrument in music therapy sessions. Several authors mention fearing for the safety of their instrument, and at times this will also mean that instruments are not used. However, overall, it is the strength of the emotional connection the therapist feels to their instrument that is the very thing that makes it possible to connect emotionally with clients, allowing therapists additional freedom of expression and access to greater creativity.

Both the chapters and the biographies show that nearly all of the music therapists continue to play their instruments and develop their musical skills outside music therapy sessions. For myself I know that I need to nurture and treasure my passion for playing and for music in general, not only to maintain the standard of my playing but also in order to feel fulfilled and to remain creative in my music therapy practice.

When teaching students to use their first instrument in clinical practice, it is important to explore the relationship they have with their instrument. Most musicians who train to become music therapists will have spent huge amounts of time playing and practising their instrument, often more time doing this than anything else, and often more time with their instrument than with anyone else. Playing our instruments can be both the most wonderful, exciting and fulfilling experience, but also sometimes frustrating, disappointing and at times destructive. For us as music therapists, it is essential to be aware of our feelings towards our instruments and our playing, and to be able to harness the healthy and positive aspects of these relationships so we can connect effectively through our playing with our clients.

Thus my first task when working with music therapy students is to help them to pinpoint why they love and treasure their instrument and in some cases help them to rediscover their joy in playing their instruments. They need to celebrate those aspects of playing they feel good about before identifying specific areas they can improve on. Early on in the course I suggest to students that they write a letter to their instrument and read it to a few of their fellow students. The following letter was written by Caroline Swinburne, who qualified in 2013. She attended the course as a mature student, having decided to train after having a family.

Dear Horn

So you finally got me back, after all these years – well whoever would have thought it! But things are different now, they have to be, we both know that. We are both much older, and surely at least a little bit wiser?

We were the classic teenage sweethearts, you and I. You were my first love, and I simply adored everything about you. I loved the way that when you spoke everyone else seemed to go quiet, as if no one else could possibly be as important, as charming and as beautiful as you. I was so proud to be seen out with you, and for us to be making such beautiful music together.

Well OK – that was on a good day! On the other hand, don't think I've forgotten just how bad things could be, just how two-faced, deceitful, and downright humiliating you could be when you wanted to. Don't think I've forgotten – don't think I could *ever* forget – the Mahler 1 episode in Nottingham (that was meant to be my big break – what a joke!). Or the Schubert Octet in the church in Clapham. Or the horn quartet when we played on the river boat on the Thames – you know the time I mean…

And why? Never have I understood why you turn on me in public like that. Never, never have I been able to predict your mood swings. You can be so lovely, so gentle, so compliant when we are alone together, then you can turn in a flash, and humiliate me in front of everyone.

Of course I shouldn't have cared so much, at least I should have pretended not to mind. But no, young and foolish as I was, I minded too much – loved too much. Things got worse, much worse, and eventually I learnt to put a name to it. Abuse. Emotional – sometimes even physical. There, I've said it. But you were just so demanding, so controlling. Every day you

insisted we met, never mind how busy I was, never mind what
else was going on, if I missed a date – even for a day – you
let me know about it. And if I didn't see you for two or three
days – well goodness me, then you would get your own back
as only you could.

Meanwhile, all my friends seemed to be in relationships
which were just so much more healthy. Those string players,
those pianists, the singers – they knew when to be there for
each other, but they also knew when to give each other space.

So eventually I rebelled. No one thought I'd have the guts
to do it but I took myself off to the other side of the world
for a whole six months – without you! For once in my life
I just wanted that little bit of independence. But you could
never cope with that, your pride was hurt big time. When I
came home it was downhill all the way. If we'd had our bad
times before – well that was as nothing, compared to now.
Humiliation. There was no other word for it. And after all the
new things I'd seen, there was just no way I was going to stand
for that any more. I'd grown up.

So I did it, I actually did it, I told you it was all over!

For all that time after we split – I told myself – well no, I
think I really believed it most of the time – that I'd just wasted
all those years. After all I wasn't exactly twiddling my thumbs,
there were many other suitors, many other opportunities, I
didn't hang about.

I'm not pretending that I never gave you a thought – I'd hear
a Brahms symphony, or some Strauss or Wagner on the radio
and yes it would bring a lump to my throat – momentarily. But
then I'd pull myself together. Remind myself that you might
be beautiful, charming, charismatic – but that simply wasn't
enough. So we were apart, for all those years. You know how
long it was, I don't have to put a number to it, it makes me
feel old.

But then somehow, against all my better judgement, just a
few years ago we bumped into each other again. You probably
never realised just how nervous I was, that day in the music
rental shop. I can't deny I was excited to see you. And yes, I did
agree to meet again. But it was only ever meant to be as friends

this time. I thought I made that very clear, just the odd lunch now and then for old time's sake.

And for a while – for a year or so anyway – we managed to keep things more or less under control. But somehow, despite everything I just couldn't help it, I still found myself spending more and more time with you. And like in the old days, the more I was with you, the better your mood – always the same old story.

And I've loved getting to know your new friends. You've always been a sociable bunch, you horns. All those late evenings in the pub or the curry house, far more than is sensible for a middle-aged woman with a family to look after (yes let's not ignore 'all that' as you call it – but then you never could cope with commitment).

But all the same it is different now though isn't it? Of course I still think you're gorgeous – you know that don't you, you vain bastard. And despite everything you can still do the dirty on me when you want to. Yes, I am thinking of that top B – or lack of! – in Shostakovich 5 just the other week. How *dare* you??? Of course now I'm so mature I almost laughed it off. Almost. Well OK maybe not quite.

But I have changed. Yes, really I have. You certainly don't terrify me quite as much as you used to. Of course even now I do still get a bit nervous sometimes when I'm with you, the odd flutter of the heart, that's only natural, surely. But I'm really not the sweating trembling blushing wreck I used to be. I am definitely calmer, more balanced, more mature. And you've changed too, grown up a bit, mellowed with the years. Now you're a 'Paxman' not an Alexander you are definitely at least a little more predictable, kinder, at least a tad less controlling.

So maybe now that we are both so very much older, we can grow to trust each other a bit more, to be friends as well as lovers? I guess I have resigned myself to the fact that we are fated to be together, to grow old together even. So let's try and do it at least a little bit gracefully, shall we? Please…

With all my love for ever,

Caroline

This letter highlights Caroline's relationship with her horn in a very humorous and poignant way, showing how the relationship has changed and mellowed over time. Through these reflections and explorations music therapy students gain confidence in their ability to play more freely and confidently. We also look at more traditional ways of developing improvisational skills, such as playing in different modes or keys, using short repetitive phrases, alternating with vocal singing, combining playing with movements or adapting some of the keyboard techniques explored by Wigram (2004).

It isn't easy to teach improvisation skills to students who play a wide range of instruments and have very different experience ranging from years of professional orchestral playing to jazz improvisation or playing in pop groups. One helpful teaching technique has been asking our second-year students to run workshops for first-year students on how they have used their instrument on clinical placements. This means that first-year trombonists, for example, may get specialised insights from second-year trombonists, providing expertise that the course tutors may not have. In the end each student learns to adapt their own skills to the clinical situation, developing self-insight into their own strengths and difficulties and learning both from the course tutors, their clinical placement supervisors and the other students.

This book will hopefully be helpful to students who are developing confidence in using their instruments in clinical work. It may also encourage experienced music therapists to use their own instrument or additional instruments in new ways. This is a first attempt at gathering information that will hopefully encourage others to write more in this field. The three editors very much hope that this book will lead to more publications and an increase in interest in music therapists' use of a wide range of instruments in their clinical work.

To conclude the book I am including another letter written in the form of a poem by Shannon Perkins Carr, who also qualified as a music therapist in 2013. This is a thoughtful and emotional poem highlighting the special relationship and links between a music therapy student and her instrument.

Dear guitar

The world is held in every vibration of string and
wood
Memories etched in your body
We have no need for words
My slightest movement is read with ease
To sound to feeling to truth
You are the point where I start to be myself
Some wrong notes make sense
Given time
We improvised through endings
Seeking out glory
Toured a continent
Of broken hearts
Lost and found again
I was in pieces but you were whole
We've crossed oceans and unravelled
A few knots tied on the ends of your strings
To slowly unbind my heart
And what did it all mean to you?
To end up there and find our way here
Perhaps you knew all along
Where we were meant to belong

References

Wigram, T. (2004) *Improvisation: Methods and Techniques for Music Therapy Clinicians, Educators and Students.* London, UK: Jessica Kingsley Publishers.

Authors' Biographies

Dr. Trygve Aasgaard received his doctorate in music therapy from Aalborg University in Denmark (2002) and is currently Professor in Music and Health at Oslo and Akershus University College of Applied Sciences and the Norwegian Academy of Music. His main areas in music therapy research and practice are related to paediatric oncology, hospice care, and mental health, with a special interest in songwriting, community music therapy, and the role(s) of professional musicians in health institutions. He has also worked many years as a performing artist on (baroque) trombone and as a composer/arranger/accompanist in various genres.

Caroline Anderson completed her music therapy training at Anglia Ruskin University in 2009 and is currently doing a PhD in intercultural music therapy. Since qualifying as a music therapist, she has worked with adults and children with learning disabilities and autistic spectrum disorders, in a young oncology unit, and as a volunteer in an overseas music therapy skill sharing project. Before training as a music therapist, Caroline worked for a county music service as a flute teacher and conductor, and still performs regularly in a wind band and chamber groups.

Luke Annesley has worked as a freelance saxophone player and teacher since 1992. He has played in various jazz, big band and orchestral settings, such as his own quartet (with the guitarist Dave Cliff), the ensemble Saxtet, the John Wilson Orchestra, and the BBC Concert Orchestra. He qualified as a music therapist in 2008 and now works for Oxleas Music Therapy Service (NHS), continuing his performing career alongside this. He works in schools and core service and in partnership with CAMHS and Housing for Women with children exposed to domestic violence.

Veronica Austin qualified from the Roehampton music therapy training course in 1985 and completed an MA in music therapy in 1999. She has worked extensively as a music therapist with children, young people and, more recently, infants and families, predominantly in the education sector. She regularly uses the flute in her music therapy work and also teaches flute and performs in small ensembles. Veronica is currently researching her own method of evaluating the impact of music therapy, running her own private supervision practice and working for Key Changes Music Therapy Charity in Hampshire, and at Chelsea and Westminster Hospital in London.

Katy Bell qualified as a music therapist from Anglia Ruskin University in 2008, having spent her earlier career in roles including proof-reader, parent, student adviser and Braille teacher. She currently works as part of the therapies team in a special school where she has helped to establish a permanent music therapy post. In addition, she works at a residential centre for young adults with life-limiting conditions and complex learning difficulties, and also in private practice. Katy meets weekly with her own string quartet, which is coached by visiting chamber musicians, and is a member of a local symphony orchestra.

Nathan Bettany qualified as a music therapist from Anglia Ruskin University in 2009. Since then most of his work has been with Nottinghamshire Healthcare NHS Trust. Initially he was based in the adult learning disability department, covering a range of community and in-patient services across the county. Recently Nathan has been employed by Rampton Hospital, specifically to develop a number of new external contracts. This included embedding music therapy within two new prison-based democratic therapeutic communities for offenders with low IQs, as well as running music therapy pilot projects in a low-secure forensic mental health unit and in a community mental health service.

Penelope Birnstingl graduated from the Guildhall School of Music and Drama and worked as a freelance bassoonist and early music specialist in London and the West Country before becoming a music therapist. Always curious to try different instruments, she took up the flute during the Bristol course, but totally failed to master the guitar; more than one person has been known to say 'If you can blow it, she can play it!'. Now retired, she maintains her keen interest in music therapy by participating as a member of the Music as Therapy International Advisory Panel, based in London.

Joanna Burley is an experienced freelance musician and music therapist whose career has included working with young people in schools, accompanying choirs, teaching woodwind and coaching youth bands and wind ensembles in the North. She has performed regularly as an orchestral bassoonist and as a piano accompanist for choir tours in the UK and abroad. Joanna qualified as a Music Therapist at Guildhall School of Music and Drama and now works in private practice at her studio in West London. Alongside her work with young people on the Autistic Spectrum, she is also passionate about the needs of older adults, especially those with dementia.

Stella Compton Dickinson is an HCPC Registered Music Therapist, Accredited Cognitive Analytic Therapist and Supervisor with 20 years of clinical experience as Head of Arts Therapies and Clinical Research Lead. She is a professional oboist and teacher with an illustrious career in which she recorded and performed solo, chamber and orchestral music for BBC Radio and TV and collaborated with composer Paul Hart to create the highly acclaimed CD *Love's Lore*: original arrangements of British folksongs for oboe, harp and strings. She has edited and published original works written for her, now available on the ABRSM 2014 syllabus for oboe called *Star Pieces*.

Emily Corke completed her music therapy training at Anglia Ruskin University in 2012. Emily currently works with children with profound and multiple learning disabilities at several schools in the Cambridgeshire area. Emily also works privately at Anglia Ruskin University's Music Therapy Centre with children and adults with profound and multiple learning disabilities as well as in palliative care. As part of Emily's private work she runs music therapy sessions for St. Edmund's Trust and Arthur Rank Hospice in Cambridge.

Susanna Crociani is a music therapist, art counsellor and master in NLP (Neuro-Linguistic Programming). Since 1997 she has worked with disabled children and from 2000 with elderly people, especially those with dementia. She also works in a psychiatric centre. Susanna is an enthusiastic saxophonist who performs regularly in various music groups, particularly jazz and ethnic bands. She has played with the female saxophone jazz quintet Girl Talk at Italian and European festivals and is the wind player in Italian ethnic group Bizantina (toured in Italy, Portugal, Spain, France, Cabo Verde). Susanna has performed on all four of Bizantina's CDs.

Billy Davidson was 17 when he began playing the saxophone and became involved with bands in Leicester, touring throughout Europe. In 2001, he started a music composition degree and then studied for his music therapy MA at Anglia Ruskin University. As a music therapist, he was employed to establish a new model of music therapy with the homeless community. In 2008 this project gained the ARU's Vice Principal's Award for work within the community. During this time he also worked with children with complex needs at a special school in Northampton. Billy currently lives in the Forest of Dean.

Dr. Philippa Derrington is currently leader of the MSc Music Therapy programme at Queen Margaret University, Edinburgh. She previously worked in Cambridge as a music therapist for 12 years in a variety of settings with adults and children. She established a full-time music therapy post in a secondary school there and carried out a research investigation into the effectiveness of music therapy for young people at risk of underachievement or exclusion. She has published her work, was co-editor of *Music Therapy in Schools* (2012, Jessica Kingsley Publishers) and has presented at various conferences nationally and internationally. She is a keen clarinettist and saxophonist.

Henry Dunn has worked in an arts therapies service with Devon Partnership Trust since 2002, having qualified from Roehampton shortly before. The team addresses the mental health needs of adults of all abilities through art, drama and music therapies. He has played the clarinet since he was about nine, having heard it played and fallen in love with its sound. He plays jazz when he can and loves using it in his therapy work. He lives in Exeter with his wife and three children, one of whom is also learning the clarinet.

Mary-Clare Fearn qualified as a music therapist from Roehampton in 1990. Since then she has worked extensively with children and adults with a range of learning disabilities, leading the music therapy department at the Chelsea and Westminster Hospital for ten years with Rebecca O'Connor. In addition to her clinical work, she is a visiting lecturer and workshop leader for Roehampton University, has presented papers at conferences, works with the British Association for Music Therapy on the Supervision and CPD subcommittee and has a private supervision practice in Dorset. She continues an active musical life with her voice, the piano and flute.

Mike Gilroy qualified as a music therapist in 2005 at Anglia Ruskin University. Since then he has practised as a music therapist at Martin House Hospice, as well as also currently working in numerous SEN schools. He has particular interest in the use of music technology in music therapy, and has also gained experience working in the fields of adult mental health and dementia. In addition, he is often involved in a variety of contemporary ensembles and is an accomplished musical director in numerous theatre venues in the North of England.

Rivka Gottlieb is a harpist and music therapist. She graduated from the Juilliard School, where she studied harp, in 1994 and completed her music therapy training at Guildhall School of Music and Drama in 2004. Rivka currently works as a music therapist in a specialist provision for children on the autistic spectrum in a mainstream secondary school. Previously she worked for Ealing Music Therapy at a school for children with severe and complex learning disabilities, in the NHS within Ealing Community Team for People with Learning Disabilities specialising in challenging behaviour, in forensic psychiatry and at a children's hospice. Rivka performs as a solo and chamber harpist.

Susan Greenhalgh began learning piano at the age of three and later studied music professionally in Liverpool and Oxford, gaining a place at the Guildhall School of Music. In 1995 Susan studied music therapy at the Anglia Ruskin University, Cambridge, and since then she has worked as a music therapist in psychiatric, residential and educational settings, as well as teaching GCSE music. Susan's experience as a classical pianist includes solos, ensembles, workshops for the London Ballet and Ballet Rambert, incidental music and composition for shows. She also has experience singing in and leading choirs, and playing rhythm guitar, violin and piano accordion.

Nicky Haire is a violinist, violin teacher and music therapist. She has worked in a variety of settings with a broad range of client groups, including children with special needs and elderly clients with dementia. She has a special interest in intercultural work and creative improvisation. Nicky is part of Music as Therapy International's Project Rwanda team and is a member of their Advisory Panel. She currently works as a freelance music therapist and violinist in Edinburgh.

Angela Harrison joined the North Yorkshire Music Therapy Centre as an assistant in 1993, whilst still playing viola with the Hallé Orchestra. She qualified in Cambridge two years later and progressed to managing the charity in Yorkshire. Angela works in special schools and in the community with children, adults and older people. She lectures, writes and presents her work internationally. Formerly Chair of the British Association for Music Therapy, she is a Governor of the Music Therapy Charity and a council member of the World Federation of Music Therapy. Angela plays chamber and orchestral music and is currently exploring multi-arts improvisation.

Shlomi Hason trained as a music therapist at Roehampton University and has worked in various settings including the Wolfson

Neurorehabilitation Centre and Whitefield Schools and Centre for children with special needs. In recent years Shlomi has done pioneering work with orthodox Jewish families from Stamford Hill, North London. He is currently setting up a music therapy post at Side By Side School in this community. Shlomi continues to see clients from difficult backgrounds in his private practice, Inner Echo Music Therapy, in Hackney, East London. Shlomi is also a singer-songwriter. His debut album *Abandoned State* was released in December 2014.

Philip Hughes qualified as a music therapist in 2000 from Anglia Ruskin University. He has worked with children in a special school, but recently has focused more on adults with learning disabilities, and adults with mental health difficulties. He worked for three years at Rampton high-secure hospital and currently works in a low-secure unit in Hertfordshire. He has presented eight papers at music therapy conferences, been involved in several arts therapies research projects and published a book chapter. He plays several different instruments in music therapy sessions, but his first instrument is the violin and for relaxation he enjoys playing Irish traditional music.

Oonagh Jones has worked as a music therapist with children and adults since qualifying in 2004. She trained at Nordoff-Robbins in London and her MMT dissertation explored the instruments therapists use in sessions, particularly focusing on whether therapists chose to use their first-study instrument. Oonagh currently works at the Nordoff-Robbins London Centre with children and adults and for Oxleas NHS Foundation Trust with children and young people. Prior to her music therapy training Oonagh worked as a freelance violist based in London and taught violin and viola to children and adults.

Špela Loti Knoll is an academic musician, oboist, oboe teacher (Music Academy, Ljubljana 2000) and MA music therapist (ARU Cambridge 2008) from Slovenia. She played cor anglais for several years with the Slovenian Radio Symphony Orchestra and is a member of several music and dance groups. She works as music teacher and music therapist in private practice. She was manager of six international music and arts therapy projects in Bosnia and Herzegovina. Since 2014 she has been the director and head of the first music therapy training programme at Knoll Institute for music therapy and supervision in Kranj, Slovenia.

Anna Lockett studied the harp at Colchester School of Music, where she gained her degree. Later, she studied with Imogen Barford, Professor of Harp at Trinity School of Music, and obtained her harp teacher licentiate. She is now a freelance harpist. She has worked with orchestras in Oxford and across the Midlands, including the Oxford Symphony Orchestra, as well as being a harp teacher/coach for the Oxfordshire County Youth Orchestra. Anna also works as a music therapist at the Fitzwarren School, Wantage, Oxfordshire.

Caroline Long has recently qualified as a music therapist. During her training at Anglia Ruskin University, she developed an interest in sounding bowls and their potential to promote health and well-being, particularly with older adults and in end-of-life care. She is a mezzo-soprano and has, for many years, sung with various professional choirs, as well as performing as a soloist. Caroline continues to enjoy singing and exploring the infinite possibilities of the human voice.

Dawn Loombe is a piano accordionist, accordion teacher and music therapist. She completed her music therapy training at Anglia Ruskin University in 2005 and her MA dissertation explored the use of the piano accordion in music therapy in a variety of settings. Dawn currently works as a music therapist at the Child Development Centre, Addenbrooke's Hospital, Cambridge, and also in private practice with adults with profound and multiple learning disability. She has also worked in schools, children's centres and in residential care homes. Dawn performs as both a solo accordionist and with a variety of musicians and vocalists.

Steven Lyons earned his undergraduate degree in English and Music from Plymouth University Faculty of Arts and Humanities. He later, in 2006, completed his music therapy training at Anglia Ruskin University. Steven currently works with a team of art and music therapists at the London-based organisation Resources for Autism. He continues to use the guitar in clinical work and at home he can also be found practising the banjo. In 2013 Steven completed a part-time MSc in Music, Mind and Brain at Goldsmiths, University of London.

Lisa Margetts has been a music therapist for 20 years. Currently, she is Head Music Therapist for Norwood, managing a team of five therapists working with children and adults with learning disabilities. Lisa is also Senior Lecturer in music therapy at the University of Roehampton, now on research leave while undertaking a PhD research project at a special school in Minsk, Belarus. She has written for refereed journals, and has presented her work widely at conferences in the UK and abroad. Lisa studied bassoon and piano at the Royal Northern College of Music. She continues to perform regularly in a chamber orchestra and chamber ensemble.

Holly Mentzer completed her music therapy training at New York University in 2009, where she is currently pursuing a PhD degree. She is a music therapist and internship supervisor at Memorial Sloan Cancer Center, and has presented her work at interdisciplinary conferences and music therapy conferences. Holly studied flute at the Juilliard School and is a versatile performer on early winds, strings and harp in the New York City area. She was formerly Editor for Serious Music at the publishing firm of Boosey & Hawkes, and is a section leader at St. John's Episcopal Church in Larchmont, NY.

Esther Mitchell qualified as a music therapist from Anglia Ruskin University in 1997 and has worked predominantly with children and adults with learning disabilities and with families over the past 17 years. She is currently practising privately in two special schools and works as Lead Music Therapist for Thomas's Fund, a registered charity providing music therapy in the home for children and young people with life-limiting conditions and/or disabilities, who are too unwell to be in school.

Trisha Montague has worked as a music therapist in a variety of settings since qualifying in 2003. These have included adult and child mental health, learning disabilities and palliative care. She has been employed as a music therapist by the North London Forensic Service for the past ten years. Since completing an MA in Psychodynamic Counselling in 2010, she has also been offering individual psychotherapy sessions in the NLFS and in a London-based community mental health charity. Trisha has played the 'fiddle' in a traditional band, in local orchestras and in a regular string quartet since 1986

Helen Mottram qualified as a music therapist five years ago. She currently works in London, employed in two large special schools for children and young people with severe learning disabilities and with the children's charity Coram, which offers music therapy as a means of post-adoption support to children who have been adopted and their families. She has previously worked abroad as a music therapist in Ontario, Canada, and more recently as co-tutor on the Music Therapy PG Diploma training programme in New Delhi, India. She is an active euphonium player, performing regularly with a London-based brass band.

George Murray completed his music therapy training at Guildhall School of Music and Drama in 2003. Since graduating George has mainly worked with children and adults with learning disabilities, people with dementia, and carers and patients in palliative care settings. George is currently based in Yorkshire and works in Wakefield Hospice and at a large school for children with special educational needs and disabilities. George is particularly interested in improvised music, both in music therapy and in performance. He plays the trombone and is regularly invited to perform, compose and record with other musicians, usually in jazz/improvisation contexts.

Dr. Amelia Oldfield has worked as a music therapist with children and families for over 34 years. She currently practises as a clinician in child and family psychiatry in Cambridge and lectures as a music therapy professor at Anglia Ruskin University where she co-initiated the MA Music Therapy course in 1994. She has completed four music therapy research investigations and published six books and many articles in refereed journals. She has presented papers and run workshops at conferences and universities all over the world. She is an enthusiastic clarinettist who performs regularly in various chamber music ensembles around Cambridge.

Shannon Perkins Carr qualified as a music therapist in 2013 with an MA from Anglia Ruskin University. Originally from Canada, she studied composition and classical guitar at the University of British Columbia, obtaining her Bachelor of Music in 2005. Prior to training as a music therapist, Shannon worked as a guitar instructor and rock/pop musician. Currently employed as a music therapist with Richmond Music Trust, she works with a range of clients, including children with ASD, and is also the administrator at Music as Therapy International.

Joseph Piccinnini received undergraduate and graduate training at New York University. He is certified professionally by the American Music Therapy Association (CMT), and licensed by the State of New York (LCAT). Joseph founded the Richmond Music Center in Staten Island, New York, in 1989. This award-winning community-based programme brings the benefits of musical involvement to all. It offers music therapy, instruction on standard and adapted instruments, and varied performance opportunities. Joseph is a consultant to clinical settings, training programmes, and individual music therapists. He is a vital resource, a 'go-to guy', for local practitioners while presenting and conducting workshops nationwide.

Catrin Piears-Banton completed her music therapy training at Anglia Ruskin University (2003). Catrin works for Surrey and Borders NHS Trust in adult mental health, and for Norwood with adults with learning disabilities (Ravenswood). Previous roles have included working with children with developmental disabilities and a locum position at the Royal Hospital for Neurodisability. Catrin's master's dissertation explored the possibilities of self-referral to music therapy. This has resulted in the running of a weekly drop-in Open Music Therapy Group at Ravenswood. Catrin plays clarinet with Four All Seasons wind quartet and sings with the contemporary a capella group Academix.

Paolo Pizziolo is a double bass player and music therapist. He obtained a Diploma in Music Therapy from the University of Bristol in 2001 and a MA in Music Therapy from the University of the West of England in 2014. He has worked as a music therapist with people with dementia in Florence, Italy, since 2002. He currently also works in adult psychiatry and with adolescents with eating disorders, combining independent music therapy work with work for national health institutions. Paolo is the double bass player of the Italian traditional folk music group Bizantina and performs with a variety of other groups (chamber music, various orchestras, jazz trios).

Dr. Jonathan Poole has worked as a music therapist with children and young people with learning disabilities for six years. He has worked with people with acquired brain injury for five years and currently practises as a researcher-clinician at The Children's Trust in Tadworth. He trained as a music therapist at Anglia Ruskin University, where he gained his MA Music Therapy, followed by his PhD for research in music therapy for acquired brain injury. He has presented papers and posters at international conferences. He is an enthusiastic guitarist and enjoys mixing styles such as blues, flamenco, classical, jazz and rock.

Harriet Powell (Nordoff-Robbins) graduated from the Royal Academy of Music (piano and organ) and then, in the 1970s, learnt to play accordion whilst working with all ages for community arts organisation Inter-Action. This culminated in a book of children's songs (*A and C Black*). Musical work then included touring theatre and directing music/drama performance projects. For 15 years she has continued to develop the use of the accordion in music therapy, specialising in services for older people and those with dementia. Harriet has a collection of accordions, some now too heavy to lift after playing for 45 years!

John Preston was born in 1960, the son of a jazz trombonist and a beatnik lapsed Catholic. He started playing music aged 17, inspired by the punk scene in and around London. John began learning the notes, playing with Norfolk folkies and dance groups before embarking on an Anglia Ruskin University music degree in 1996 as a mature student. He has worked at Fulbourn Hospital (adult psychiatry) for 12 years as a music therapist. Alongside this John has been building a straw-bale house with his wife, music therapist Carol Hunter, as well as putting together a Zen/art Punk band – The John Preston Tribute Band.

Sarah Rodgers is a composer and conductor. Her antecedents include John Broadwood the English piano-maker and the composer Henry Purcell. After graduating from Nottingham University, and a two-year stint in Sierra Leone with VSO, Sarah returned to the UK to develop her career. While her focus is composing and conducting, she is a well-known advocate for contemporary British music, serving as Chairman of the Composers' Guild of Great Britain and of the British Academy of Composers and Songwriters, as well as representing composers on the boards of the UK collecting societies. In 2003, she founded the British Composer Awards.

Colette Salkeld is a clarinettist, clarinet teacher and music therapist. Prior to training as a music therapist at Anglia Ruskin University she worked as a professional clarinettist with Bournemouth Symphony Orchestra. Colette has a special interest in working with families and in 2007 completed her MA looking at the role of music therapy in developing secure attachment in adopted children. Colette is currently senior music therapist at The Portland Hospital for Women and Children and the adoption lead for Chroma Therapies. Colette continues to perform regularly as an orchestral clarinettist.

Bert Santilly is a performing accordionist and retired teacher, Bert has always taught music in a therapeutic manner, although not formally trained as a music therapist. He worked as a school teacher and head in mainstream primary and secondary schools in London in the 1960s and '70s and then in special education around Cambridgeshire, using his accordion with children with special needs. Bert performs regularly as a solo accordionist and with several multi-instrumental groups. He regularly runs accordion jazz workshops, as well as other music workshops involving disabled and able-bodied musicians working together.

Alex Street trained at the Guildhall School of Music and Drama, completing in 2004. Since then he has increasingly specialised in the use of neurologic music therapy and psychodynamic techniques, together with music technology to treat the effects of neurological disease and injury with adults and children. Alex is also researching a technique for upper limb rehabilitation with stroke patients as part of a PhD. He is passionate about improvising with other musicians on acoustic guitar and exploring ways in which to adapt the instrument in order to make it a widely accessible and effective tool within clinical settings.

Prodromos Stylianou has worked as a music therapist in Cyprus for the past four years. He has a private music therapy practice as part of the Ministry of Health in Cyprus. He also collaborates with several other organisations. Prodromos has taken part in a number of television and radio shows introducing music therapy to the people of Cyprus, and for the same reason he has written articles for newspapers and magazines. In addition, he performs traditional Cypriot music in festivals both in Cyprus and in Europe.

Caroline Swinburne qualified as a music therapist in 2013 and now works for Coram, with adopted children; she also teaches piano. Caroline originally studied music at Nottingham and London Universities, working briefly in music broadcasting before making a sideways move into radio feature production, and spending many years as a broadcaster and producer, travelling widely especially in Africa. Eventually – after what she now regards as a two decade long 'gap year' – Caroline rediscovered her first love the French horn, and is much enjoying playing with local orchestras and chamber groups; she is also a keen pianist.

Dr. Concetta Tomaino is the Executive Director and co-founder of the Institute for Music and Neurologic Function, and Senior Vice President for Music Therapy at CenterLight Health System, where she has worked since 1980. She is internationally known for her research and lectures on the clinical applications of music and neurologic rehabilitation. Her work has been featured in the media, documentaries and in books on health and healing. Oliver Sacks's book *Musicophilia* is dedicated to her. Dr. Tomaino is Past-President of the American Association for Music Therapy and faculty of the Albert Einstein College of Medicine, and Lehman College, City University of New York.

Jo Tomlinson (née Storey) has worked in schools since 1995 and was Head Music Therapist for Cambridgeshire Music from 2002 to 2006. In 2013 Jo carried out a research project working alongside teaching assistants looking into the development of vocal skills in children with special needs, and started a PhD at Anglia Ruskin University in October 2014. She co-edited the book *Music Therapy in Schools* (2011, Jessica Kingsley Publishers) and has also presented papers at numerous conferences. Jo is a performing musician on both flute and piano, although more recently has focused on accompanying for singers and instrumentalists and exploring solo piano repertoire.

Annie Tyhurst is a senior music therapist working for the charity MusicSpace in Bristol. She has a background in psychiatric nursing and mainstream/special needs teaching. Her current work is with children who have been recently diagnosed with ASD and their families. Annie was the first tutor of the India Music Therapy Trust's Diploma in Music Therapy and is the assistant trainer for a new course in Guided Imagery and Music. She currently performs as a cellist/singer with the band Rivers of England.

Anita Vaz is a music therapist working with children with special needs and life-limiting conditions, both in schools and in a children's hospice. She began using the saxophone in music therapy work to see whether certain clients may benefit from particular qualities of the instrument. Anita enjoys playing the tenor saxophone in big bands, as well as playing informally, and she continues to develop her interest in jazz music.

Michael Ward-Bergeman lives in New Orleans, Louisiana. Michael graduated from Berklee College of Music, Boston. He performs worldwide as an accordionist. His compositions have been commissioned and performed at Carnegie Hall and he has worked on several movie soundtracks. Although he has not undertaken any formal music therapy training, he has many years of experience working therapeutically with music and expressive arts therapists; in the USA as a musician in hospitals and nursing homes, with children and adults with brain trauma at St. Charles Rehabilitation Center in Long Island New York, and in the UK at the Royal Hospital for Neuro Disability in London.

Dr. Catherine Warner worked as a freelance cellist (as Cathy Durham) before training as a music therapist at the Guildhall School of Music and Drama. She is currently Programme Leader of the MA Music Therapy training course at the University of the West of England and regularly uses her cello in clinical work, improvising groups and chamber music in Bristol. Her research interests include participatory action research and the use of musical improvisation as a participatory technique for data collection.

Sharon Warnes is a violinist, violin teacher and music therapist. She completed her music therapy training at Anglia Ruskin University in 2005 and initially worked with children with special needs in Warwickshire schools, before moving to Oxfordshire in 2007. Sharon is a music therapist for Headway Thames Valley, for adults with acquired brain injury, and Guideposts Music Therapy service for adults with dementia, working in residential homes and day care centres. Sharon performs regularly as a solo violinist, a chamber musician and an orchestral player; she also plays electric violin in an acoustic rock band, Kubris.

Tessa Watson is a music therapist and trainer with over 20 years' experience in various clinical settings. Currently Convenor of the MA Music Therapy at the University of Roehampton, Tessa also has a clinical post in an NHS/social services community team for people with learning disabilities. She holds several roles within the British Association for Music Therapy, is one of the *British Journal of Music Therapy* editorial team, and is a Health and Care Professions Council partner working on the CPD scheme. Tessa has written and presented widely both in the UK and internationally. Tessa maintains an active musical life, playing cello and singing with local amateur ensembles.

Grace Watts has worked as a music therapist with children and young people within special educational needs settings since completing her music therapy training at Roehampton University in 2011. She has also worked in a hospital for adults with acute or severe mental illness. Grace currently works as a music therapist at the Cheyne Child Development Service at Chelsea and Westminster Hospital. In her other role, Grace works for the British Association for Music Therapy, leading on PR and communications, and co-ordinating national Music Therapy Week. Grace performs as a bassoonist and contrabassoonist with a range of chamber and symphony orchestras.

Subject Index

Author Index

344

FLUTE, ACCORDION OR CLARINET?

Laney, M. 179
Lee, C.A. 138
Lewis, C.R. 196
Libin, A. 295
Lim, H. 88
Lo, F.S.Y. 14
Loombe, D. 14–5, 45

Machover, T. 97
McHugh, P.R. 295
McTier, I. 15, 184, 289, 291
Meadows, T. 15
Menuhin, Y. 95
Monks, G. 111

Nachmanovitch, S. 291–2
Nordoff, P. 16, 96, 300

Odell-Miller, H. 253
Oldfield, A. 15, 16, 22–3, 37–8, 169

Patey, H. 16
Paull, E. 238
Pavlicevic, M. 63, 75
Pedersen, I.N. 103
Perkins, L. 136
Powell, H. 15, 48–51, 63
Priestley, M. 107

Rensch, R. 177–8
Robbins, C. 16, 96, 300
Roe, N. 14
Rogers, C. 30, 240
Rostropovich, M. 98
Roxburgh, E. 249
Ruud, E. 63

Salkeld, C. 15, 22, 37
Sand-Jecklin, K. 196
Santilly, B. 47, 54, 57–9, 63–6
Scardovelli, M. 278
Schroeder-Sheker, T. 179–80, 185, 196
Segell, M. 265
Service, T. 166
Shipton, A. 287–8
Slatford, R. 287–8
Sobey, K. 74–5
Stern, D.N. 32, 89, 174, 239, 241
Stowell, R. 95
Süskind, P. 287
Sweeney-Brown, C. 72

Talbot, J. 98
Thompson, W. 43
Tomlinson, J. 16, 72, 89

Torrance, K. 15
Tsui, L. 14

Van den Broek, M.D. 128

Waddell, M. 130
Wade-Matthews, M. 43
Walker, K. 135
Ward-Bergeman, M. 47, 54, 58–9
Warwick, A. 53
Watson, T. 98
Wigram, T. 103, 314
Wilkinson, D. 72
Wilson, R. 70
Winnicott, D.W. 76, 98, 152, 235, 240, 243, 291
Winston Morris, R. 238
Woodcock, J. 74–5

Yalom, I.D. 236, 251

CPSIA information can be obtained
at www.ICGtesting.com
Printed in the USA
LVHW042111151220
674262LV00011B/883

9 781849 053983